Historicism

Historicism

A Travelling Concept

Edited by
Herman Paul and Adriaan van Veldhuizen

BLOOMSBURY ACADEMIC
LONDON • NEW YORK • OXFORD • NEW DELHI • SYDNEY

BLOOMSBURY ACADEMIC
Bloomsbury Publishing Plc
50 Bedford Square, London, WC1B 3DP, UK
1385 Broadway, New York, NY 10018, USA
29 Earlsfort Terrace, Dublin 2, Ireland

BLOOMSBURY, BLOOMSBURY ACADEMIC and the Diana logo
are trademarks of Bloomsbury Publishing Plc

First published in Great Britain 2021
This paperback edition published in 2022

Copyright © Herman Paul, Adriaan van Veldhuizen and contributors, 2021

Herman Paul, Adriaan van Veldhuizen and contributors have asserted their right under
the Copyright, Designs and Patents Act, 1988, to be identified as Author of this work.

For legal purposes the Acknowledgements on p. vi constitute
an extension of this copyright page.

Cover image © Andrew Merry/Getty

All rights reserved. No part of this publication may be reproduced or transmitted in
any form or by any means, electronic or mechanical, including photocopying,
recording, or any information storage or retrieval system, without prior
permission in writing from the publishers.

Bloomsbury Publishing Plc does not have any control over, or responsibility for,
any third-party websites referred to or in this book. All internet addresses given
in this book were correct at the time of going to press. The author and publisher
regret any inconvenience caused if addresses have changed or sites have
ceased to exist, but can accept no responsibility for any such changes.

A catalogue record for this book is available from the British Library.

Library of Congress Cataloging-in-Publication Data
Names: Paul, Herman, editor. | Veldhuizen, Adriaan van, editor.
Title: Historicism: a travelling concept / Herman Paul,
and Adriaan van Veldhuizen.
Description: London ; New York : Bloomsbury Academic, [2020] | Includes
bibliographical references and index.
Identifiers: LCCN 2020025150 (print) | LCCN 2020025151 (ebook) | ISBN
9781350121959 (hardback) | ISBN 9781350121966 (ebook) | ISBN
9781350121973 (epub)
Subjects: LCSH: Historicism–History.
Classification: LCC D16.9. H5327 2020 (print) | LCC D16.9 (ebook) | DDC 901–dc23
LC record available at https://lccn.loc.gov/2020025150
LC ebook record available at https://lccn.loc.gov/2020025151

ISBN:	HB:	978-1-3501-2195-9
	PB:	978-1-3502-1618-1
	ePDF:	978-1-3501-3876-6
	eBook:	978-1-3501-3877-3

Typeset by Integra Software Services Pvt. Ltd.

To find out more about our authors and books visit www.bloomsbury.com
and sign up for our newsletters.

Contents

Acknowledgements	vi
Biographical Notes	viii

Introduction: Historicism as a travelling concept
Herman Paul and Adriaan van Veldhuizen — 1

Part 1   Travels through time
1   Historicism through the lens of anti-historicism:
    The case of modern Jewish history *David N. Myers* — 15
2   Historicism as a modern theological problem *Gary Dorrien* — 35

Part 2   Travels through space
3   Historicism and positivism in sociology: From Weimar Germany to
    the contemporary United States *George Steinmetz* — 57
4   Historicism's arrival in the United States: Two routes
    from Germany *Adriaan van Veldhuizen* — 97

Part 3   Travel companions
5   The spectre of historicism: A discourse of fear *Herman Paul* — 121
6   Thinking in uncertain times: Raymond Aron and the politics of
    historicism *Sophie Marcotte-Chenard* — 141

Part 4   Travels beyond historicism
7   Friedrich Meinecke's *Historism* or the defeat of German
    historicism *Audrey Borowski* — 165
8   Karl Löwith's historicization of historicism *Bruno Godefroy* — 187

Index — 204

Acknowledgements

For three years in a row, we have been fortunate enough to spend the last days of August in Amsterdam, in the stimulating company of colleagues interested in the entangled history of the humanities and social sciences. In all three cases, the entanglements on which we focused our attention consisted of historical concepts or historical modes of reasoning employed by scholars across the social sciences and humanities. No matter how diverse these fields may be in terms of research topics, methodologies, intellectual orientations and working habits, sociologists, political scientists, historians and literary scholars have at least one thing in common: they all relate to their disciplinary past, inscribe themselves in historical narratives, dissociate themselves from 'conservatism' or 'backward mentalities' and warn their students against 'unhistorical' or 'overly historical' approaches. Our workshops therefore focused on how scholars in the nineteenth- and twentieth-century humanities and social sciences quarreled over historical modes of thinking – on arguments they shared or borrowed from each other, on concepts that travelled across disciplinary divides, on historical sensibilities that got lost in translation and on philosophies of history that clashed because they were rooted in irreconcilable 'regimes of historicity'.

This volume emerges out of the second of these workshops, held on the top floor of the Amsterdam Public Library, where magnificent views over the city competed with intellectual vistas opened up by papers that traced the fortunes of 'historicism' through a variety of disciplines and intellectual traditions. (A volume based on our first workshop, which seeks to offer a comparative history of 'post concepts' like post-bourgeois, post-Christian and postmodern, will soon appear, too.)

It is a privilege to acknowledge that all three workshops were made possible by a generous grant from the Statesman Thorbecke Fund (Royal Netherlands Academy of Arts and Sciences) – a fund that originates in a bequest by Willem Thorbecke (1920–2014) and is named after Willem's great-grandfather, Johan Rudolph Thorbecke (1798–1872). Although the latter is best known as the Dutch prime minister whose liberal constitution of 1848 laid the foundation for parliamentary democracy in the Netherlands, Thorbecke was also a historian and philosopher, arguably even a philosopher of history, whose 1824 book *Ueber das Wesen und den organischen Character der Geschichte* (On the Nature and the Organic Character of History) demonstrates his intellectual affinity with German Romantic figures like Johann Gottfried Herder. We are pleased that our project 'The Demands of Our Time', led by Herman Paul and coordinated by Adriaan van Veldhuizen, was among the first that the Statesman Thorbecke Fund deemed worthy of financial support.

We would like to thank the Amsterdam Public Library staff for their hospitality in August 2018 and Martine Koot from the Royal Netherlands Academy of Arts and Sciences for invaluable assistance in organizing the workshop. We gratefully mention Manon van den Brekel's many hours of meticulous editing and Selin Kuşçu's sharp eye and careful reading of the manuscript. At Bloomsbury, we would like to thank Emily Drewe, Dan Hutchins, Abigail Lane and Kumeraysen Vaidhyanadhaswamy. It has been a great pleasure to work with you.

Biographical Notes

Audrey Borowski is completing her doctorate at the University of Oxford. She has held various fellowships including at the Lichtenberg-Kolleg – the Göttingen Institute of Advanced Study, the Max Planck Institute for History of Science (departments I and II) and Leibniz-Zentrum für Literatur- und Kulturforschung in Berlin, the IZEA (Interdisziplinäres Zentrum für die Erforschung der Europäischen Aufklärung) in Halle, the Ecole Normale Superieure in Paris and the Cohn Institute for the History and Philosophy of Science and Ideas at Tel Aviv University. She is the editor of a volume on Leibniz's reception and legacy in the Humanities, and the co-editor, with Nicholas Halmi, of a special issue of *Intellectual History Review* on 'Universal Histories'.

Gary Dorrien teaches social ethics, theology and philosophy of religion as the Reinhold Niebuhr Professor of Social Ethics at Union Theological Seminary and Professor of Religion at Columbia University. He was previously the Parfet Distinguished Professor at Kalamazoo College, where he taught for eighteen years and also served as Dean of Stetson Chapel and Director of the Liberal Arts Colloquium.

Bruno Godefroy is Lecturer at the Department of Law, University Paris II Panthéon-Assas. He received his PhD in philosophy from the University Jean Moulin – Lyon III and the Friedrich-Alexander University Erlangen-Nuremberg. His last publications include articles on Eric Voegelin, Karl Löwith and Reinhart Koselleck.

Sophie Marcotte-Chénard is Assistant Professor in Political Philosophy at Carleton University. Her research focuses on theory and philosophy of history, German and French political thought and contemporary political philosophy. She has published on those themes in the *Review of Politics*, the *Journal of the Philosophy of History*, *Politique & Sociétés* and *Methodos*. She is also the author of a forthcoming book entitled *History in Crisis: Political Philosophy and Historicism in the Interwar Period* (Presses de l'Université de Montréal).

David N. Myers holds the Sady and Ludwig Kahn Chair in Jewish History at UCLA, where he also serves as the director of the UCLA Luskin Center for History and Policy. His books include *Resisting History: The Crisis of Historicism in German-Jewish Thought* (Princeton University Press, 2003) and *The Stakes of Jewish History: On the Use and Abuse of Jewish History for Life* (Yale University Press, 2018). He is the co-editor of the *Jewish Quarterly Review*.

Herman Paul is Professor of the History of the Humanities at Leiden University, where he directs a research project entitled 'Scholarly Vices: A Longue Durée History'. He is the author of *Key Issues in Historical Theory* (2015) and *Hayden White: The Historical Imagination* (2011) and editor, most recently, of *How to Be a Historian: Scholarly Personae in Historical Studies, 1800–2000* (2019). In addition, he is on the editorial board of the *Journal of the Philosophy of History* and associate editor of *History of Humanities*.

George Steinmetz is the Charles Tilly Professor of Sociology at the University of Michigan, and has also been a tenured professor at the University of Chicago and The New School and a Visiting Professor at the Institute for Advanced Study in Princeton. He has held fellowships from the National Endowment for the Humanities and the Guggenheim Foundation. In 2020 he is a Fellow at the American Academy in Berlin and was awarded the Siegfried Landshut Prize by the Hamburg Institute for Social Research. His research interests include the sociology of empires, states and cities, social theory, and the history and philosophy of the social sciences.

Adriaan van Veldhuizen is a scientific researcher for the Dutch government, and is on the editorial board of literary journal *De Gids*. He has a one day a week appointment as an assistant professor in philosophy of history at Leiden University. He published a book, articles and essays on history, philosophy and literature.

Introduction: Historicism as a travelling concept

Herman Paul and Adriaan van Veldhuizen

Abstract

Starting with the fictional figure of Mme. Historicist as invoked by Joan Copjec, an American psychoanalytic critic of historicism, this introduction sets the stages for the volume by arguing that historicism can productively be interpreted as a 'travelling concept'. Historicism is not only a technical term for nineteenth-century modes of thinking; it is also a term of abuse, a word of warning and a derogatory concept invoked by humanities and social science scholars throughout the twentieth century. Precisely as such, the term has travelled across disciplinary divides as well as through time and space. It has aligned itself to other concepts, such as relativism ('travel companions'), and been charged with emotional meaning ('luggage'). After specifying the historiographical advantages of studying historicism as a travelling concept, the introduction explains the structure of the volume and briefly introduces the chapters that follow.

Mme. Historicist

What is wrong with Michel Foucault? For Joan Copjec, a Lacanian psychoanalytic theorist who teaches at Brown University, the problem with Foucault is not that he consistently analyses society in terms of knowledge-power relations. The problem is that Foucault's analytical apparatus leaves little space for anything but competing relations of knowledge and power. Whatever the theme at hand, the bottom line is always that regimes of power determine what counts as knowledge. Copjec therefore dubs Foucault a 'historicist', that is, someone guilty of a 'reduction of society to its indwelling network of relations of power and knowledge'.[1]

Copjec's choice for historicism as a polemical term may surprise at first sight. Is history – historicism's root word – as conceptualized by Foucault the focus of her critique? Or is it his totalizing conception of power? If readers consult the index to find more relevant occurrences of the term 'historicism', some more surprises await them. Not only is Copjec's book one of very few that have an index entry on 'historicism and breast-feeding anxiety', the author also turns out to personify historicism into a pedantic young woman, Mme. Historicist, who demonstrates her inability to see anything else than barren facts of history by exclaiming in the midst of an emotional conversation over fear of suffocation: 'In the old days, three or four people were needed to pull on the laces of a corset to tighten it.'[2] Like Foucault, Mme. Historicist seems to miss the point, that is, a psychoanalytically relevant point that cannot be captured in terms of historical facts.

Perhaps the most helpful clue as to the meaning and origin of 'historicism' in Copjec's book is a passage that invokes Lacanian psychanalysis as a 'challenge to the historicism that pervades much of the thinking of our time' – immediately followed by the claim that psychoanalysis and historicism as represented by Lacan and Foucault, respectively, are among the most powerful discourses in modern intellectual life.[3] This draws on a longer tradition of representing the relation between psychoanalysis and historical study in antagonistic terms (a tradition that goes back at least to Erich Fromm in the early 1930s).[4] More specifically, in contrasting Foucauldian historicism with Lacanian psychoanalysis, Copjec repeats the received idea that Foucault has little positive to say about psychoanalytic theory.[5] Also, she varies on the trope of 'Foucauldian historicism' that circulated among American humanities scholars in the 1980s and 1990s.[6] Copjec's charge of historicism, therefore, draws on older polemical discourses. Perhaps one might even say: it was meaningful precisely because it was not original.

Indeed, throughout the twentieth century, intellectuals in a wide variety of disciplines have been accused of historicist habits of thought. For instance, in the 1970s, the American philosophers of science Thomas S. Kuhn and Paul Feyerabend were frequently labelled as historicists because of their claim that assumptions guiding scientific enquiry can change over time (even though Kuhn believed paradigm changes to be much rarer events than critics worried about incompatible modes of scientific rationality suggested).[7] Musicologists in the 1960s complained about a 'doctrinal historicism' dominating at Princeton's Music Department ('They admire a limited body of old music, mostly Mozart and the three B's'),[8] while already in the 1930s historians had demonstrated how to use the term with polemical force in a controversy elicited by Carl Becker's presidential address to the American Historical Association, 'Everyman His Own Historian'.[9] And so one could go on, with linguists, literary theorists or theologians worried about a historicist mode of enquiry that 'kills the soul and retains the corpse' (by dissolving the Bible into an incoherent collection of historically unreliable fragments).[10] Easily recognizable as a threat to be averted, historicism was a convenient polemical devise, which could be employed against a broad variety of thinking styles that were perceived as giving too much weight to historical arguments, facts or contexts. As a Union Theological Seminary professor succinctly put it in 1946: 'Historicism is a bad philosophy resulting from a hypertrophical growth of the historical view.'[11]

Existing scholarship

When, how and why did this originally German word, *Historismus*, travel to the United States? As Annette Wittkau and others have shown, *Historismus* emerged in mid-nineteenth-century Germany as a pejorative term for modes of historical thinking that were found wanting – though on different grounds. For instance, in 1857, the philosopher and publicist Rudolf Haym censured G. W. F. Hegel's philosophy of history for being insufficiently based on empirical historical research. Nine years later, the philosopher and economist Eugen Dühring made an almost opposite argument by scoffing at the *Historismus* of scholars who devoted all their energy to increasing their knowledge of the past, without caring for a moment about the use or value of this knowledge to their readers. Characteristically, then, both authors associated historicism with a lack of 'proper' historical thinking or with a one-sidedness that was in need of correction.[12] From the late nineteenth century onwards, similar uses of the term can be found elsewhere in Europe, especially in countries with an intellectual orientation towards Germany.[13]

Despite the widespread of historicism as a polemical term, there are surprisingly few studies that trace how historicism has travelled between disciplines, nations or confessions. While, for instance, 'rationalism', 'psychologism' and 'nihilism' as intellectual terms of abuse have been subjected to extensive research, such studies do not exist for historicism.[14] Although various authors admit that historicism was first and foremost a *Kampfbegriff*, the dominant trend in historical studies has been to take the term either as denoting a nineteenth-century ('Rankean') paradigm of historical scholarship or as shorthand for the problem of 'historical relativism' that was central to the early twentieth-century 'crisis of historicism'.

Although a range of factors contributed to historicism becoming a proper name instead of a derogatory term, the interpretation that equates historicism with nineteenth-century historical scholarship in the tradition of Leopold von Ranke has been developed most forcefully by the German historical theorist Jörn Rüsen and his students in the 1980s and 1990s. Emphasizing the methodological innovations ('source criticism') propagated by Ranke and his pupils, Rüsen argued that *Historismus* is best understood as the name of a paradigm in a Kuhnian sense of the word.[15] Historicism, for him, refers to a historicizing gaze that sought to understand ideas or practices in their historical particularity, paired with a commitment to doing this as 'scientifically' as possible (*das Prinzip der Wissenschaftlichkeit*).[16] In this reading, it was the historicist commitments of nineteenth-century German historians that made it possible for their discipline to 'professionalize' and to earn a worldwide reputation for being at the forefront of science. English-language studies following this interpretive strand include Frederick C. Beiser's *The German Historicist Tradition*. Although this book focuses on a period that saw the rise of historicism as a polemical device, it understands the term in a quasi-Rüsean manner as denoting a 'single, coherent and continuous intellectual tradition' in Wilhelmine Germany that was, most characteristically, committed to 'justifying the scientific stature of history'.[17]

Rather different has been a second strand of thinking, according to which historicism is not a Kuhnian paradigm, but a relativist stance that posed, and still poses, major challenges to normatively oriented fields like theology, ethics and philosophy. Otto Gerhard Oexle, most notably, has argued that historians should not focus their attention on the *term* – after all, what some called historicism, others preferred to label as relativism – but on the existential *problem* of historicism ('the all-encompassing historicization of the world, the human being and all aspects of his culture') that threatens to undermine universal standards in philosophy, theology and ethics.[18] In English-language scholarship, this perspective has been adopted by Thomas A. Howard[19] and Allan Megill, who in response to Howard suggests that a 'crisis of historicism,' usually associated with intellectual life in the Weimar Republic, manifested itself already in the 1830s, with the publication of David Friedrich Strauss's provocative piece of Biblical criticism, *Das Leben Jesu*.[20]

Both lines of research have turned out to be productive: both have generated fresh insight into the importance and contested nature of historical thinking in nineteenth- and early twentieth-century Germany. However, precisely to the extent that these approaches have come to dominate the field, they have marginalized the question how the pejorative term that historicism was for most of its users prior to Rüsen and Oexle managed to travel from Berlin to New York, or from the pages of Protestant theology journals to the world of Lacanian psychoanalytic theory.

Travelling concept

It might be fruitful, therefore, to study historicism as a 'travelling concept' – a phrase that refers to its travels across disciplines, countries and confessional divides (from a largely Protestant intellectual milieu into, for instance, Catholic philosophy textbooks).[21] According to cultural theorist Mieke Bal, who coined the term 'travelling concepts' in her 1999 Green College Lectures, concepts like historicism can hardly ever be pinpointed to specific cultural locations. They tend to travel 'between disciplines, between individual scholars, between historical periods and between geographically dispersed academic communities'.[22] However, in doing so, some concepts earn more air miles than others. Some manage to reach far-away places, heavily loaded with luggage, while others travel lightly or stay relatively close to home. Some travel alone; others do so in groups. Applied to the case of historicism, this implies that historians cannot content themselves to tracing historicism's itineraries or to unravelling the manifold meanings associated with this essentially contested concept. It is just as important for them to study historicism's travel companions, be it other concepts, such as relativism and nihilism, or emotions like anxiety for what the German theologian Ernst Troeltsch fearfully called a stream of history 'without beginning, end and shore'.[23]

Studying historicism as a travelling concept is, of course, not an end in itself. We would like to think that such a project may serve at least two intellectual agendas. First, a rhetorical analysis of historicism as a *Kampfbegriff* (referring to what users of the term perceived as *dangerous* modes of relating to the past) may shed light on underlying philosophies of history (what these same users of the term believed a *beneficial* relation to the past to look like). Not unlike John Edward Toews and Mark Bevir, who have detected developmental modes of historical thinking in fields as diverse as architecture, law, philology and history,[24] a study of historicism as invoked by psychoanalytic theorists, philosophers of science, musicologists, historians and theologians may unearth 'regimes of historicity' shared or disputed in a broad variety of contexts.[25] Historicism, in other words, is a suitable prism for an intellectual history of how people related to their pasts.[26]

Secondly, travelling concepts like historicism can make visible how fields that were institutionally independent and methodologically sometimes very different from each other nonetheless exchanged ideas, concepts or attitudes. A study of historicism's travels across disciplinary divides might therefore contribute to what Rens Bod and others call a 'postdisciplinary history of knowledge', characterized by a search for connections, transfers or 'flows' between fields of enquiry that are often studied in relative isolation from each other.[27] More specifically, by zooming in on fields like sociology and theology, which are conventionally classified under the social sciences and humanities, respectively, such a project may also illustrate how a rapprochement between the history of the humanities and the history of the social sciences such as proposed by Wolf Feuerhahn might look like.[28]

Accordingly, if this collection of essays approaches historicism as a travelling concept, it organizes this enquiry around a couple of closely related questions. When, how and why did historicism travel from one discipline to another, or from Europe to North America? Why was the term passed down from generation to generation, for instance in the field of Jewish studies? Who were historicism's travel companions and what kind of conceptual or emotional baggage was associated with this pejorative term?

Outline of the volume

In the spirit of Mieke Bal, this volume addresses these questions in a deliberately exploratory way. It does not offer a systematic survey of historicism's travels across time and space. Neither does the volume aim for comprehensive coverage of disciplines, countries, languages or confessions. Instead, it presents a set of original papers that, each in their own way, touch on aspects of the travel metaphor. While all the chapters deal with transmission of historicism across time and space, some of them focus on diachronic transmission within single intellectual traditions. Others zoom in on influential thinkers to enquire how, especially around mid-century, historicism acquired meanings and connotations that later generations kept associating with it. Still other contributions examine historicism's travel companions – emotions of anxiety, for instance, that contributed to rather aggressive styles of debate. Last but not least, there are chapters that seek to answer the question posed above: How did twentieth-century Americans come to appropriate German notions of *Historismus*? For the reader's convenience, we have arranged the chapters into four clusters, focusing respectively on historicism's travels through time (I), travels through space (II), and travel companions (III), with a final cluster exploring how mid-twentieth-century intellectuals, especially in Europe, tried to travel 'beyond historicism' (IV).

The two chapters that make up cluster I resemble each other insofar as they trace long-term transmissions of historicism within a single tradition. Focusing on Jewish studies, David N. Myers discusses three generations of scholars who responded rather critically to historicism. Through the case studies of Hermann Cohen, Franz Rosenzweig and Yosef Hayim Yerushalmi, Myers identifies three moments of 'crisis', each of which reflected a larger state of intellectual and political perplexity and touched on epistemological, theological as well as ideological questions. In his chapter on liberal Protestant theologians in the nineteenth and twentieth centuries, Gary Dorrien shows that historicism has been central to liberal theological concerns since the days of Friedrich Schleiermacher – even though the term itself emerged only later. Historicism touched upon all the major issues on the liberal agenda: biblical criticism, historical development (evolution), the relation between science and religion and the threat of historical relativism. By analysing the role of historicism in these debates, Dorrien shows that the concept was able to take on new meanings in new contexts, while at the same time deriving part of its authority from a long tradition of liberal theologizing.

Cluster II presents two examples of what we call 'travel through space', or intellectual transfer between Europe (Germany) and North America (United States). Focusing on the field of sociology, George Steinmetz's chapter traces how both 'historicism' and 'positivism' travelled from Wilhelmine and Weimar Germany to twentieth-century America. Often, though not always, the terms travelled together: they shaped each other's meanings in dialogues that took place across the Atlantic. Chapter 4, by Adriaan van Veldhuizen, shows that different notions of historicism caused quite a bit of confusion among American historians in the 1930s. According to Van Veldhuizen, there were at least two routes along which historicism found its way into American historians' vocabulary, each with distinct features. If anything, this suggests that analysing historicism's travels can help explain why people kept associating historicism with different threats.

Cluster III zooms in on travel companions. Focusing on the rhetorical use of historicism as an emotionally charged term, Herman Paul argues that historicism was often imbued with fear. Drawing on the case of Dutch intellectuals between the 1870s and the 1970s, he examines how these authors used historicism to frame perceived dangers, appeal to anxieties broadly shared among their audiences and depict the intellectual landscape as a battlefield with dangerous worldviews roaming around. In her chapter on Raymond Aron, Sophie Marcotte-Chenard adds that historicism was a *Schlagwort* often associated with 'relativism'. If the famous 'crisis of historicism' in interwar Europe shows anything, it is that relativism had become one of historicism's most inseparable travel companions. Interestingly, this did not imply the end of historicism: for Aron, the 'crisis of historicism' rather served as a catalyst for a renewed reflection on reason and judgement in history.

However, as the fourth and final cluster demonstrates, this was not true for all of Aron's contemporaries. Because of historicism's travel companions – be it relativism or quietism in the face of political disaster – quite a few mid-twentieth-century intellectuals began to distance themselves from it, arguing instead for a mode of scholarship 'beyond historicism' (*jenseits des Historismus*). In a chapter on Friedrich Meinecke, one of the most influential authors on the subject, Audrey Borowski argues that the German historian actively (though unintentionally) contributed to the decline of the historicist tradition in twentieth-century Europe. He did so by making visible internal tensions within historicist thinking and by demonstrating a profound inability to relate the idealism of Johann Wolfgang von Goethe and Leopold von Ranke to the mundane realities of actual historical research. Instead of reinvigorating historicism, then, Meinecke illustrated the dead ends that historicism had reached by the mid-twentieth century. In a different vein, another influential author, Karl Löwith, also illustrated the inability of mid-twentieth-century intellectuals to identify with historicism. Yet as Bruno Godefroy shows in the final chapter of this volume, Löwith was not a critic of historicism in the way that, for instance, Leo Strauss and Eric Voegelin were. Instead, Löwith sought to 'historicize historicism' – a phrase that nicely captures Löwith's programme of moving beyond historicism without relegating it to the dustbin of history.

A more voluminous collection of essays might have included chapters on different itineraries (especially outside of Europe and North America), on 'roads not taken', on other 'isms' with which historicism was frequently associated, or perhaps on travel writing. Fortunately, the ambition of this volume is not to be comprehensive. It rather seeks to convince readers that historicism can profitably be studied as a *Kampfbegriff* – in addition, rather than in opposition to more traditional lines of research – that this pejorative term found its way into a broad variety of fields, in different geographical areas, and that historicism can therefore productively be studied as a travelling concept. Readers are invited to join the journey, by reading the chapters that follow and by continuing along the path that we have embarked on.

Notes

1 Joan Copjec, *Read My Desire: Lacan against the Historicists* (Cambridge, MA: MIT Press, 1994), 6.
2 Ibid., 126.
3 Ibid., 13.
4 Dylan Evans, 'Historicism and Lacanian Theory', *Radical Philosophy* 79 (1996): 35.
5 P. Steven Sangren, 'Psychoanalysis and Its Resistances in Michel Foucault's *The History of Sexuality*: Lessons for Anthropology', *Ethos* 32, no. 1 (2004): 110–22.
6 Roddey Reid, 'Foucault in America: Biography, "Culture War," and the New Consensus', *Cultural Critique* 35 (1996–1997): 188; Christopher E. Forth, 'Cultural History and New Cultural History', in *Encyclopedia of European Social History from 1350 to 2000*, ed. Peter N. Stearns, vol. 1 (New York: Charles Scribner's Sons, 2001), 88–9.
7 Ernan Mcmullin, 'History and Philosophy of Science: A Marriage of Convenience?', in *PSA 1974: Proceedings of the 1974 Biennial Meeting Philosophy of Science Association*, ed. R. S. Cohen et al. (Dordrecht: Springer, 1976), 587. More examples are provided in John H. Zammito, *A Nice Derangement of Epistemes: Post-Positivism in the Study of Science from Quine to Latour* (Chicago: University of Chicago Press, 2004), 91–5.
8 Joseph Kerman, '"The Proper Study of Music": A Reply', *Perspectives of New Music* 2, no. 1 (1963): 152. The three B's are, of course, Bach, Beethoven and Brahms.
9 As documented by Adriaan van Veldhuizen in his contribution to this volume.
10 Richard Kroner, 'History and Historicism', *Journal of Bible and Religion* 14, no. 3 (1946): 132.
11 Ibid., 131.
12 Annette Wittkau, *Historismus: Zur Geschichte des Begriffs und des Problems*, 2nd ed. (Göttingen: Vandenhoeck & Ruprecht, 1994), 34, 40.
13 Herman Paul, *Het moeras van de geschiedenis: Nederlandse debatten over historisme* (Amsterdam: Bert Bakker, 2012).
14 Joshua Bennett, 'A History of "Rationalism" in Victorian Britain', *Modern Intellectual History* 15, no. 1 (2018): 63–91; Martin Kusch, *Psychologism: A Case*

Study in the Sociology of Philosophical Knowledge (London: Routledge, 1995), esp. 95–121; Arie M. Dubnov, '"Those New Men of the Sixties": Nihilism in the Liberal Imagination', *Rethinking History* 19, no. 1 (2015): 18–40; James Chappel, 'Nihilism and the Cold War: The Catholic Reception of Nihilism between Nietzsche and Adenauer', *Rethinking History* 19, no. 1 (2015): 95–110.

15 Jörn Rüsen, *Konfigurationen des Historismus: Studien zur deutschen Wissenschaftskultur* (Frankfurt am Main: Suhrkamp, 1993), 36–7.

16 Friedrich Jaeger and Jörn Rüsen, *Geschichte des Historismus: Eine Einführung* (Munich: C. H. Beck, 1992), 8.

17 Frederick C. Beiser, *The German Historicist Tradition* (Oxford: Oxford University Press, 2011), 6, 7.

18 Otto Gerhard Oexle, 'Krise des Historismus, Krise der Wirklichkeit: Eine Problemgeschichte der Moderne', in *Krise des Historismus, Krise der Wirklichkeit: Wissenschaft, Kunst und Literatur 1880–1932*, ed. Otto Gerhard Oexle (Göttingen: Vandenhoeck & Ruprecht, 2007), 26. See also Otto Gerhard Oexle, *Geschichtswissenschaft im Zeichen des Historismus: Studien zu Problemgeschichten der Moderne* (Göttingen: Vandenhoeck & Ruprecht, 1996).

19 Thomas Albert Howard, *Religion and the Rise of Historicism: W. M. L. de Wette, Jacob Burckhardt, and the Theological Origins of Nineteenth-Century Historical Consciousness* (Cambridge: Cambridge University Press, 2000). Howard acknowledges, however, that apart from 'crisis historicism' as defined by Oexle something like 'classical historicism' in Rüsen's sense of the word existed (13).

20 Allan Megill, 'Why Was There a Crisis of Historicism?' *History and Theory* 36, no. 3 (1997): 420–1. For a different view, see Herman Paul, 'Who Suffered from the Crisis of Historicism? A Dutch Example', *History and Theory* 49, no. 2 (2010): 169–93.

21 Examples of the latter are discussed in Herman Paul, 'Religion and the Crisis of Historicism: Protestant and Catholic Perspectives', *Journal of the Philosophy of History* 4, no. 2 (2010): 172–94.

22 Mieke Bal, *Travelling Concepts in the Humanities: A Rough Guide* (Toronto: University of Toronto Press, 2002), 24.

23 Ernst Troeltsch, *Der Historismus und seine Probleme*, vol. 1 (Tübingen: J. C. B. Mohr, 1922), 573.

24 John Edward Toews, *Becoming Historical: Cultural Reformation and Public Memory in Early Nineteenth-Century Berlin* (Cambridge: Cambridge University Press, 2004); *Historicism and the Human Sciences in Victorian Britain*, ed. Mark Bevir (Cambridge: Cambridge University Press, 2017). See also Joshua Bennett, *God and Progress: Religion and History in British Intellectual Culture, 1845–1914* (Oxford: Oxford University Press, 2019).

25 We borrow this phrase from François Hartog, *Regimes of Historicity: Presentism and Experiences of Time*, trans. Saskia Brown (New York, NY: Columbia University Press, 2015).

26 As advocated in Herman Paul, 'Relations to the Past: A Research Agenda for Historical Theorists', *Rethinking History* 19, no. 3 (2015): 450–8.
27 Rens Bod et al., 'The Flow of Cognitive Goods: A Historiographical Framework for the Study of Epistemic Transfer', *Isis* 110, no. 3 (2019): 483–96.
28 Wolf Feuerhahn, 'Les sciences humaines et sociales: des disciplines du contexte?', *Revue d'histoire des sciences humaines* 30 (2017): 7–29.

Bibliography

Bal, Mieke. *Travelling Concepts in the Humanities: A Rough Guide*. Toronto: University of Toronto Press, 2002.

Beiser, Frederick C. *The German Historicist Tradition*. Oxford: Oxford University Press, 2011.

Bennett, Joshua. 'A History of "Rationalism" in Victorian Britain'. *Modern Intellectual History* 15, no. 1 (2018): 63–91.

Bennett, Joshua. *God and Progress: Religion and History in British Intellectual Culture, 1845–1914*. Oxford: Oxford University Press, 2019.

Bevir, Mark, ed. *Historicism and the Human Sciences in Victorian Britain*. Cambridge: Cambridge University Press, 2017.

Bod, Rens, Jeroen van Dongen, Sjang L. ten Hagen, Bart Karstens and Emma Mojet. 'The Flow of Cognitive Goods: A Historiographical Framework for the Study of Epistemic Transfer'. *Isis* 110, no. 3 (2019): 483–96.

Chappel, James. 'Nihilism and the Cold War: The Catholic Reception of Nihilism between Nietzsche and Adenauer'. *Rethinking History* 19, no. 1 (2015): 95–110.

Copjec, Joan. *Read My Desire: Lacan against the Historicists*. Cambridge, MA: MIT Press, 1994.

Dubnov, Arie M. '"Those New Men of the Sixties": Nihilism in the Liberal Imagination'. *Rethinking History* 19, no. 1 (2015): 18–40.

Evans, Dylan. 'Historicism and Lacanian Theory'. *Radical Philosophy* 79 (1996): 35–40.

Feuerhahn, Wolf. 'Les sciences humaines et sociales: des disciplines du contexte?' *Revue d'histoire des sciences humaines* 30 (2017): 7–29.

Forth, Christopher E. 'Cultural History and New Cultural History'. In *Encyclopedia of European Social History from 1350 to 2000*, edited by Peter N. Stearns, vol. 1, 83–94. New York, NY: Charles Scribner's Sons, 2001.

Hartog, François. *Regimes of Historicity: Presentism and Experiences of Time*. Translated by Saskia Brown. New York, NY: Columbia University Press, 2015.

Howard, Thomas Albert. *Religion and the Rise of Historicism: W. M. L. de Wette, Jacob Burckhardt, and the Theological Origins of Nineteenth-Century Historical Consciousness*. Cambridge: Cambridge University Press, 2000.

Jaeger, Friedrich, and Jörn Rüsen. *Geschichte des Historismus: Eine Einführung*. Munich: C. H. Beck, 1992.

Kerman, Joseph. '"The Proper Study of Music": A Reply'. *Perspectives of New Music* 2, no. 1 (1963): 151–9.

Kroner, Richard. 'History and Historicism'. *Journal of Bible and Religion* 14, no. 3 (1946): 131–4.

Kusch, Martin. *Psychologism: A Case Study in the Sociology of Philosophical Knowledge*. London: Routledge, 1995.

McMullin, Ernan. 'History and Philosophy of Science: A Marriage of Convenience?' In *PSA 1974: Proceedings of the 1974 Biennial Meeting Philosophy of Science Association*, edited by R. S. Cohen, C. A. Hooker, A. C. Michalos and J. W. Van Evra, 585–601. Dordrecht: Springer, 1976.

Megill, Allan. 'Why Was There a Crisis of Historicism?' *History and Theory* 36, no. 3 (1997): 416–29.

Oexle, Otto Gerhard. *Geschichtswissenschaft im Zeichen des Historismus: Studien zu Problemgeschichten der Moderne*. Göttingen: Vandenhoeck & Ruprecht, 1996.

Oexle, Otto Gerhard. 'Krise des Historismus, Krise der Wirklichkeit: Eine Problemgeschichte der Moderne'. In *Krise des Historismus, Krise der Wirklichkeit: Wissenschaft, Kunst und Literatur 1880–1932*, edited by Otto Gerhard Oexle, 11–116. Göttingen: Vandenhoeck & Ruprecht, 2007.

Paul, Herman. 'Who Suffered from the Crisis of Historicism? A Dutch Example'. *History and Theory* 49, no. 2 (2010): 169–93.

Paul, Herman. 'Religion and the Crisis of Historicism: Protestant and Catholic Perspectives'. *Journal of the Philosophy of History* 4, no. 2 (2010): 172–94.

Paul, Herman. *Het moeras van de geschiedenis: Nederlandse debatten over historisme*. Amsterdam: Bert Bakker, 2012.

Paul, Herman. 'Relations to the Past: A Research Agenda for Historical Theorists'. *Rethinking History* 19, no. 3 (2015): 450–8.

Reid, Roddey. 'Foucault in America: Biography, "Culture War," and the New Consensus'. *Cultural Critique* 35 (1996–1997): 179–211.

Rüsen, Jörn. *Konfigurationen des Historismus: Studien zur deutschen Wissenschaftskultur*. Frankfurt am Main: Suhrkamp, 1993.

Sangren, P. Steven. 'Psychoanalysis and Its Resistances in Michel Foucault's *The History of Sexuality*: Lessons for Anthropology'. *Ethos* 32, no. 1 (2004): 110–22.

Toews, John Edward. *Becoming Historical: Cultural Reformation and Public Memory in Early Nineteenth-Century Berlin*. Cambridge: Cambridge University Press, 2004.

Troeltsch, Ernst. *Der Historismus und seine Probleme*, vol. 1. Tübingen: J. C. B. Mohr, 1922.

Wittkau, Annette. *Historismus: Zur Geschichte des Begriffs und des Problems*. 2nd ed. Göttingen: Vandenhoeck & Ruprecht, 1994.

Zammito, John H. *A Nice Derangement of Epistemes: Post-Positivism in the Study of Science from Quine to Latour*. Chicago, IL: University of Chicago Press, 2004.

Part One

Travels through time

1

Historicism through the lens of anti-historicism: The case of modern Jewish history

David N. Myers

Abstract

Crises of historicism, as instigated by philosophers and theologians, expose the underside of a methodological practice not often given to introspection. They also signal and emerge out of a larger historical moment marked by disruption and upheaval. This chapter explores three such moments from the late nineteenth to the late twentieth centuries, all of which are related to the enterprise of Jewish history. The first featured the renowned German-Jewish neo-Kantian philosopher Hermann Cohen (1842–1918), who turned his attention to the approach of his one-time teacher, the historian Heinrich Graetz. The second involved Franz Rosenzweig (1886–1929), a former student of history who would become one of the most influential Jewish thinkers in Weimar Germany and who renounced his erstwhile scholarly practice. The third was inspired by an historian himself, Yosef Hayim Yerushalmi (1932–2009), whose 1982 book *Zakhor* introduced a new degree of self-reflection into the field of Jewish studies.

Introduction

Over the past century and a half, historicism has played an important role, directly or indirectly, in some of the most interesting and consequential methodological debates in the human sciences. Indeed, it has travelled, even flitted promiscuously, across disciplines, entering the guarded precincts of, among other fields, history, philosophy, theology and economics.

A key to its ability to travel so widely has been its multivalence. Historicism, as many have noted, has had many different, even contradictory, meanings to different people – for example, to Ernst Troeltsch, Friedrich Meinecke and Karl Popper, three major theoreticians of the term in the twentieth century, each of whom operated with distinct understandings of what historicism offered or threatened.[1]

In this regard, we notice another prominent feature of historicism over the course of its career – that it has journeyed back and forth between its status as a conceptual platform for constructive or even essential scholarly labour and its status as an intellectual bogeyman used as a term of opprobrium to denounce or castigate those at whom it is flung. Historicism, in the eyes of its critics, can be methodological primitivism, scepticism, relativism or some combination of all three. Its appearance can unsettle commonplace assumptions or guiding principles, prompting wider intellectual malaise or disorientation.

It is this spectre that brings us to the heart of the matter in this chapter: the opportunity to explore crises of historicism that periodically surfaced in the late nineteenth and twentieth centuries. They arose with the aim of combating the methodological or existential threat that historicism itself was perceived to represent.

At the outset, it is important to bear in mind two points. First, crises of historicism are not cries in the wilderness reflecting the panic or outrage of a few isolated critics; they emerge out of historical moments rife with change and disruption, marked by a high degree of intellectual upheaval. The critique of historicism, in this sense, is but one arrow in the quiver of those who fear that the existing order is being undermined in a deeply threatening way.

And a related second observation: the alarm over a 'crisis of historicism' is usually sounded not by historians, but by non-historians fearful of its consequences. For example, philosophers have seen fit to decry historicism's methodological imperiousness and flaccidity, often regarding the historical discipline as a second-order scholarly pursuit. So too have theologians. One scholar of the phenomenon, Thomas Howard, has aptly noted that the 'crisis of historicism stemmed from and found its centre of gravity in explicitly theological problems'.[2] Indeed, theologians were chief among historicism's critics, bemoaning its tendency to reduce inspired figures or texts to a narrow and decidedly mundane context – and thereby convert the sacred into the profane. But theologians such as D. F. Strauss and Albert Schweitzer were also among historicism's most avid promoters – in the sense that historicism mandated an understanding of the evolution of an historical individuum in context. Indeed, one of the great modern battles among theologians was the 'Historical Jesus' controversy, which revolved around the question of whether Jesus could be understood in the context of first-century Palestine or only as the transcendent Christ of faith. In some cases, for example, Ernst Troeltsch, the battle waged within the same theologian, at once drawn to the contextualizing impulses of historicism yet repelled by its seeming relativizing impulses.

In this chapter, I would like to elaborate on and, in one case, complicate these two propositions. In doing so, I will identify three moments of crisis of historicism, each of which reflects a larger state of intellectual and political perplexity. These moments are drawn from the history of one of the most instructive barometers of change in modern European history, the Jews. By virtue of their liminal status – as 'cognitive insiders' and 'social outsiders' in Paul Mendes-Flohr's well-known phrase – Jews both participated robustly in cultural and intellectual life in their host societies and encountered clear limits to their integration.[3] This liminal status, as Mendes-Flohr and others have observed, inclined Jews towards artistic and scientific innovation – and conversely, rendered them susceptible to forces of reaction. And it is that status, at the front line between forces of innovation and reaction, that made them important actors in the battles over historicism from the last quarter of the nineteenth century up to the present.

Heinrich Graetz

The first case at hand pitted two of the most important figures in German-Jewish intellectual history of the nineteenth and early twentieth centuries, the historian Heinrich Graetz (1817–1891) and the philosopher Hermann Cohen (1842–1918). At its most basic level, this first crisis of historicism arose as a critique by a former student, Cohen, of a teacher, Graetz, as the student came to achieve intellectual maturity. At another level, it was a re-staging of the modern competition among the *Geisteswissenschaften*, pitting history against philosophy for the title of what the ancients called 'the queen of the sciences'.[4] Throughout the nineteenth century, there were intense efforts by advocates of the 'human sciences' to develop a proper scientific protocol independent of and on a par with that of the natural sciences. But there was also an intense debate *within* the various fields of the human sciences, with different disciplinary groups promoting the benefits of their respective discipline, and often insisting on their superiority over others. The result was not merely a popularity contest, but, by the end of the century, a sharpening of the methodological, hermeneutical and epistemological premises of the fields.⁵ Neo-Kantianism, particularly of the Southwest School in Germany, played a key role in pushing forward this conversation, proposing itself as an inclusive and holistic platform for defining the methodological protocol of the *Geisteswissenschaften*. And yet, as the famous debate between Wilhelm Windelband, a Southwest School representative, and Wilhelm Dilthey revealed, the project made for 'a fragile, combustible union'. The Neo-Kantians, as Frederick Beiser has observed, wanted to aid history in fortifying its precarious foundations, but they also regarded it as a threat because of its relativizing and hegemonic impulses.⁶

For all of their belief in the prospect of achieving methodological clarity in the name of *Wissenschaft*, the broader cultural ambience in which Dilthey and Windelband dwelt was rife with tension, despair and pessimism. Indeed, the last quarter of the century was known *tout court* as the age of *Kulturpessimissmus*.⁷ The sequence of events in the early 1870s makes clear why. The victory in the Franco-Prussian war followed by German unification in 1871 produced a sense of intoxicating glory, only to be followed by precipitous economic collapse in Austria and Germany in 1873. The dizzying rise and fall of fortunes not only damaged German national honour, but lent a powerful sense that the forward march of history had been retarded.

Among those who captured the sense of 'pessimism' of the day was Wilhelm Marr (1819–1904), the German journalist who invented the term 'antisemitism'. In describing what he saw as 'the triumph of Jewishness over Germanness' in an age of 'cultural-historical bankruptcy', Marr spoke of the dark shadow of 'pessimism' hovering over Germany.⁸ Of more direct relevance for this chapter is a far more notable cultural pessimist of the time, Friedrich Nietzsche, whose 'pessimism' was far more nuanced and purposive than Marr's. Indeed, Nietzsche's 'Dionysian pessimism' was not merely a reflection on the stagnant and decrepit state of the world, but a realistic sense of 'the constant processes of transformation and destruction that mark out the human condition'.⁹

The recurrent tension in Nietzsche between unsparing critique of the present – hence, pessimism – and the possibility of regeneration in the future (albeit through a dialectical process of destruction) animates his view of history. This is especially present in his well-known short essay, *Vom Nutzen und Nachteil der Historie für das Leben* from 1874. With his inimitable acuity, Nietzsche criticized the over-abundance of historical data generated in his day, which led to an unfortunate condition: people knowing more and more about less and less. This was a disappointing abdication of history's responsibility and potential:

'What if, rather than remaining the life-promoting activity of a historical being, history is turned into the objective uncovering of mere facts by the disinterested scholar – facts to be left as they are found, to be contemplated without being assimilated into present being?'[10] That was the state of affairs about which Nietzsche vented his irritation and pessimism. History harvested the chaff, but did not extract the wheat of the past. And yet, all was not lost. Nietzsche, with his conditional pessimism, held out the prospect, slim as it may be, that history – or more specifically, historical education – could be deployed to 'serve life', as the words of his sub-title suggest.

It is in this milieu – a pessimistic era marked by intense debates about the utility of history – that a young neo-Kantian philosopher named Hermann Cohen launched a volley at the well-known Jewish historian, Heinrich Graetz. Their exchange was an important and raw encapsulation of the disciplinary and temperamental differences between historians and philosophers in this period.

Graetz was a renowned scholar who, in 1854, had begun to publish what would become a monumental, eleven-volume history of the Jews, *Geschichte der Juden*. By the time that Cohen issued his first critique in 1880, Graetz had become the most famous and controversial Jewish historian of his day, a pioneer in terms of both the method and scale of his research, and a man whose passions and prejudices were rarely concealed. Graetz also happened to be Hermann Cohen's teacher at the Jüdisch-Theologisches Seminar in Breslau, where Cohen went to study for the rabbinate in 1857 before leaving to embark on a career as a philosopher. During his time at Breslau, Cohen remembered, there 'was stirring in me in those young years a kind of historical consciousness'. Graetz was apparently a major influence. Cohen recalled his teacher's 'interesting and lively presentation of the great men of our literature'. Moreover, he recalled that Graetz 'elevated us to our spiritual heights'.[11]

The passage of time obviously led to a change of heart. After leaving behind the rabbinical seminary, Cohen commenced studies in philosophy at the University of Breslau in 1861 before moving to the University of Berlin and then submitting his dissertation at Halle. In 1873, he was appointed as a *Privatdozent* at the University of Marburg, where he would spend the entirety of his academic career.[12] By 1880, he had a chair at Marburg and a reputation as a prominent Neo-Kantian philosopher of his day. In that year, Graetz came under attack from two sharply disparate sources: his former student, Cohen, on one hand, and the leading Prussian nationalist historian, Heinrich von Treitschke, on the other.

It was the most unusual pairing. Treitschke's nationalism had taken a noxious turn in a tumultuous 1870s, expressing itself in increasingly xenophobic terms, with a particular focus on Jews. Cohen, for his part, was a proud and engaged Jew who readily fought against the scourge that was now known by Marr's neologism, 'antisemitism'. One of the catalysts for Treitschke's descent into overt bigotry was his reading of the eleventh volume of Graetz's *Geschichte der Juden*. Graetz's passionate and sympathetic rendering of Jews (especially those whom he favoured) stood in contrast to what Treitschke saw as his anti-Christian bias and inadequate expression of German loyalty. Not only was Graetz guilty, but Jews at large, he lamented, held onto their insularity and exclusivity. In making this claim, Treitschke was hardly oblivious to the rising tide of anti-Jewish sentiment in German society. Rather than challenge it, he articulated great sympathy for those who stoked it. Jews were outliers who did not fit into the emergent German nation. Escalating the rhetorical temperature even further, he memorably declared, 'the Jews are our misfortune'.[13]

Treitschke's words in 1879–1880 triggered what came to be known as the Berlin *Antisemitismusstreit*, a wide-ranging public debate about the suitability of Jews in Germany. Hermann Cohen, as one of the most notable German-Jewish intellectuals of the day, jumped into the fray with an essay in 1880, 'Ein Bekenntniss in der Judenfrage'. Not surprisingly, he criticized those who sought to construct a barrier between Jews and Germans. Anticipating his later manifesto from 1915 *Deutschtum und Judentum*, Cohen acknowledged the deep affinity between Judaism and Protestantism, on one hand, and Judaism and Kantianism, on the other.

But then he turned his anger on a most unlikely target, his former teacher Graetz, already under attack. Graetz represented a form of particularism that Cohen found at odds with his harmonious vision of German Judaism. He called this perspective 'Palestinian', a somewhat bewildering choice of words for someone who was usually precise in using them. Graetz did in fact visit Palestine in 1872, but he would not make Jewish settlement there a major focus of his scholarly or public activity. Cohen clearly had something else in mind: 'Palestinian' connoted a narrow, parochial and material understanding of Jewishness, quite at odds with his own more ethereal conception of Judaism as an exalted spiritual force. Not only did he criticize Graetz for this narrowness of perspective; in a related gibe, he also accused his former teacher of 'a frightening perversity of emotional judgments'. Graetz's colourful and impassioned portrayals of historical actors clearly marked, for Cohen, a triumph of the sensory over the rational.[14] It also represented the second-order pursuit of historians, who were capable of grasping only that which was accessible to the physical senses rather than seeking out the a priori laws that constitute existence. Graetz's superficial historicism, on this reading, stood in contrast to the 'transcendental method' that Cohen had begun to explore already in 1871 in *Kants Theorie der Erfahrung*.

In analysing Cohen's oddly timed attack, it is hard to separate the personal from the methodological from the larger contextual consideration. He was clearly separating from his one-time teacher, as well as from his youthful infatuation with history as he sought to articulate his vision of the elegance and superiority of philosophy. For Cohen, philosophy held to the kind of precise norms of procedure that befitted a noble *Geisteswissenschaft*. It was sober and scientific as opposed to history's inescapable surrender to subjectivity and the sensory.

There was also an element of cultural judgement in Cohen's critique. Graetz's barely concealed tendentiousness in his historical writing fortified a kind of Jewish particularism that upset Cohen's vision of a universal spiritual Judaism consonant with loyalty to the German nation. In an era of constant tumult, and especially in 1880 in a moment of unsettling antisemitic agitation, Cohen felt compelled to take Graetz to task for his excess of 'emotional judgements'. The historian's withering assessments of both deviant Jews and unsympathetic non-Jews did not serve the cause of combating antisemitism.

Something of the heaviness of the cultural pessimism of the day lay over this critique. Unlike Nietzsche, who was the era's great prophet of pessimism, Cohen believed in and wrote about the prospect of a better day for humanity. But the *Zeitgesit* sowed the seeds of rebellion against the old verities and optimism of the Enlightenment. There was, as Carl Schorske described it in his classic study of *fin-de-siècle* Vienna, an emerging 'politics in a new key'. Even Hermann Cohen, whose Kantian mooring affirmed many of those verities, was swept up into the sharp polemical culture of the day.

Towards the end of his life, Cohen returned to the subject of his teacher, and the nature of his historical thinking. In 1917, he published an analysis of Graetz's philosophy of Jewish history. The passage of nearly forty years had brought massive change to the Continent, accelerated by the epoch-changing Great War. Although different in nature from the earlier age of *Kulturpessimissmus*, the current era was beset by its own anxiety and pessimism. The enormity of destruction of the war induced a new scepticism about existing political and cultural conventions. Long-standing theological and epistemological premises were challenged or discarded, leading to a sharp 'crisis consciousness'.[15]

In this state of crisis, history once again came under scrutiny. The previous efforts of Wilhelm Dilthey – in debate with the Southwest School of Neo-Kantians – to shore up the methodological foundations of the discipline in the late nineteenth century were revisited. Once again, Hermann Cohen weighed in, juxtaposing his own disciplinary practice to Heinrich Graetz' historical method and vision of Jewish history. Thus, the latter was drawn to 'the succulent fruit of national-political Judaism', while regarding the philosopher's 'sublimated idealized Judaism' as a 'dried-out husk'. Engaging in his own creative misprision, Cohen asserted that Graetz was intent on demonstrating that Judaism was at heart a 'political constitution' rather than a 'messianic religion'. This was especially galling to Cohen because it echoed the perspective of one of Cohen's great intellectual foils Baruch Spinoza.[16] As he had done earlier in 1880, the seventy-five-year-old Marburg philosopher grated against the subjective, sensory features of Jewish history, on which he believed Graetz's base historicism singularly focused. But Cohen was himself in an awkward spot, since the very winds of change that brought renewed criticism to the practice of history had begun to sweep away the ground on which his own neo-Kantian philosophy stood.

Franz Rosenzweig

If Hermann Cohen proffered a critique of a lower-order historicism from the heart of the philosophical establishment in nineteenth-century Germany, his student, Franz Rosenzweig, took aim at the prominence of history from his perspective as a theological renegade in the tumultuous Weimar era. The two men represented different generations of German Jews; one was beholden to the ideal of a seamless German-Jewish harmony and the other to a more dialectical relationship that one historian has called 'dissimilation'. That said, they joined forces at a crucial moment in their respective lives. After Cohen retired from Marburg, he devoted himself with greater urgency to Jewish thought and philosophy. He moved to Berlin, where he began to teach at the Lehranstalt für die Wissenschaft des Judentums. There he met Franz Rosenzweig in one of his seminars in 1913, a fateful year in Rosenzweig's life when he was close to following the path of a number of colleagues and relatives by converting from Judaism to Protestantism. Cohen had a galvanizing effect on Rosenzweig, demonstrating to him the intellectual seriousness and vivacity of serious study of Judaism. The two actually joined forces a number of years later to conceive of a new institution of learning, to be called the Akademie für die Wissenschaft des Judentums, in which the boundary between academic and Jewish communal interests would be consciously traversed. This plan never reached fruition, at least as Cohen and Rosenzweig imagined it. That is, the Akademie did take rise, but as the antithesis of their vision – as a centre of purely academic research.

Notwithstanding their partnership, Rosenzweig had a totally different outlook in terms of method and cultural politics. Unlike the establishmentarian Cohen, he was a rebel fighting on multiple fronts. The story of his pushback against the aridity of historicism commences with his erstwhile historical studies in 1908 at the University of Freiburg with Friedrich Meinecke and Heinrich Rickert, two of the leading figures (and opponents) in scholarly debates about the nature of historicism. Four years later, Rosenzweig completed a dissertation on Hegel and the state that combined intellectual biography with an analysis of Hegel's political thought.[17] But in the middle, in 1910, Rosenzweig began to express reservations about the meaning and significance of history. In a letter to his mentor and cousin, Hans Ehrenberg, Rosenzweig wrote: 'God does not redeem man through History, but actually as the God of Religion.'[18]

Rosenzweig's decision to leave behind historical study was something different from Hermann Cohen's rationale; it was not the philosopher's dismay with the historian's subjective surrender to the senses or failure to grasp experience on the basis of objective a prioris. It was the theologian's unwillingness to tolerate the atomizing quality of historicism, which shattered sacred sources of faith into minute contextual shards. In travelling his own path away from Freiburg and historical studies with Meinecke, Rosenzweig was anticipating what would become by the 1920s an 'anti-historicist revolution' fronted by leading Protestant theologians such as Karl Barth, Rudolf Bultmann and Friedrich Gogarten.[19] Having witnessed the effects of the 'Historical Jesus' debate in the nineteenth century, these scholars were deeply sceptical of the redemptive, or even minimally salutary, power of history to illuminate what the past offered. They rejected that historicist ethos that reduced all historical phenomena to the same rank, in line with Ranke's famous aphorism that 'every epoch is immediate to God'.

As in the case of Cohen, Rosenzweig's path away from history and historicism was not disconnected from his own emerging Jewish world view. A particularly important experience for him, along with his encounter with Cohen in Berlin in 1913, was his deployment with the German army in the First World War, during which time he came face-to-face with Southern and Eastern European co-religionists. The effects were dramatic, affording Rosenzweig a startling new perspective on a holistic mode of Jewish existence that he had never experienced in his native Germany.

With that vital mode uppermost in his mind and while still serving as a soldier, Rosenzweig set about to imagine a new Jewish intellectual and educational world of which he himself, who only recently embraced his Jewish identity, could be part. In 1917, he drafted a proposal and sent it as a letter to Hermann Cohen. It became the basis of their joint efforts to create an innovative academy of Jewish learning. As noted, the institution of their vision did not take rise, at least not in Berlin. Cohen died in 1918, and Rosenzweig decamped to Frankfurt where, in 1920, he opened the 'Lehrhaus', which embodied some of the key ideas in his and Cohen's plan. In particular, the new centre sought to erase the boundaries between teacher and student, centre and periphery, with the goal of enfranchising and invigorating the disaffected young generation of German Jews.

It is important to recall the moment in which Rosenzweig acted. There was a palpable sense of gloom and despondency in the waning years of the Great War and its aftermath, as Germany took stock of its staggering loses. At the same time, there was a glimmer of possibility, as if the War's massive destruction had cleared away old structures to allow space for new ones to surface. It was in the midst of this ambience that Rosenzweig wrote his proposal cum letter to Cohen, which was published in 1918 as 'Zeit ists' (It is Time). It was also in this ambience that Roseznweig drafted in epistolary form what is known as the 'Urzelle', a blueprint for his major work of Jewish thought that was published in 1919 as *Stern der Erlösung*.[20]

From the moment of his spiritual crisis in 1913 when he contemplated conversion until the publication of the *Stern*, Rosenzweig underwent a remarkably rapid transformation. In the course of those six years, he developed an impressive degree of Jewish knowledge, theological sophistication and faith. As he laid it out in the 'Urzelle', his personal belief and larger theological system were logically centred on Revelation, which he described as 'a fixed immovable centrepoint' that was itself the source of a 'pure factuality' (*reine Tatsächlichkeit*).[21]

This version of factuality was very different from the facticity upon which the work of the historian was based. It was not a matter of collecting small factual stones and assembling them into an edifice that was subject to the corrosive effects of time. Rosenzweig's notion of the *Tatsächlichkeit* of Revelation did not operate at the whim of historicism's normal rules of causality. It transcended the shackles of time and space, much as the Christ of faith did for opponents of the 'Historical Jesus' school.

On Rosenzweig's view, the Jewish people also had that capacity to soar through time and space. In a lecture that he gave in his hometown of Kassel in the fall of 1919, Rosenzweig juxtaposed the idea of *Geist* (spirit) to that of *Epochen* (epochs). He noted that '(h)istory exercises it powers over the nations via epochs, through which they pass from childhood to adulthood to old age and then death'. 'But', he continued, 'it is this power of history over the life of nations that is denied here'. Indeed, on his view, one nation resists that power, 'one that is free from the constraint of time, that same constraint to which all other nations are subject. A nation at once unique and eternal among the nations.' This was the Jewish nation, which was guided by a *Geist* that 'breaks through the shackles of time'. The Jewish *Geist* 'disregards the omnipotence of time. Indeed, it walks unperturbed through history.'[22]

In arriving at this view, Rosenzweig was taking his place among a generation of theological upstarts in Germany, neo-traditionalists who were seeking to claw back to a meaningful concept of religious faith after the perceived assault of irreligious (or to use a term not yet in vogue, secular) modernizers. In one of his earliest essays, 'Atheistic Theology' from 1914, Rosenzweig scored both Protestant and Jewish thinkers in the modern age for apotheosizing this decidedly this-worldly phenomenon. Both were smitten, he lamented, by 'the curse of historicity'.[23] Herein lay a key early moment in Rosenzweig's critique of the culture of historicism that sacralized the profane and profanated the sacred.

The Great War, with its unprecedented scale of destruction, seemed to render impossible belief in a benign god, reinforcing instead the sense of an all-powerful, uncontrollable and soulless modern technological monster. Facing this grave theological challenge, Rosenzweig and his fellow seekers attempted to reconstruct the foundations of faith, taking aim at the common target of historicism. Both symbolically and as a matter of scholarly practice, historicism was seen as a pernicious tool of fragmentation and relativization that dismantled the essential values on which religious faith was built. It was necessary to overcome the ubiquity of historicism in order to capture anew the holism of sacred texts, figures and events.

This current of theological rebellion was but one rivulet in a larger sea of opposition and innovation that characterized the culture of the Weimar Republic. The Republic took rise in November 1918 amid the simmering ashes of the War, buoyed by a new spirit of optimism and weighed down by the pain of massive loss (of life, property and territory, in the case of Germany). This clash of vectors, accentuated by the political upheaval and economic volatility of the early 1920s, invited convention-defying initiatives in art, music, and ideas.

Franz Rosenzweig was a product of that age and its guiding spirit. He revolted against the complacent secularism of his elders, whose very sense of the sacred was being eroded before their eyes, aided by the chiselling effects of historicism. His own illuminating life journey was a compressed passage that brought him in short order from the centre of power of historicism to a position of sharp dissent. Tellingly, in 1920, his one-time mentor, Friedrich Meinecke, approached him about the possibility of taking up a lectureship at the University of Freiburg. Rosenzweig had already left behind the world of history. He confessed to Meinecke that he had had a stark turning point, a crisis, in 1913. In the wake of that moment, he came to realize that 'history to me was a purveyor of forms, no more' – lacking an essential and organic quality of its own. In light of this realization, it is no surprise that Rosenzweig's unmooring from history coincided with – indeed, enabled – an intense quest that would define and impart meaning to the rest of his life: the discovery of a living connection to what he called 'my Judaism'.[24] In this respect, Rosenzweig participated in a highly personal path of return to Jewish tradition. At the same time, he contributed to a cross-denominational, theologically driven critique of historicism that sought to restore a sense of holism to a broken age.

Yosef Hayim Yerushalmi

A guiding theme up to this point has been the basic proposition that powerful cultural (and political) crises shake the foundations of disciplinary and epistemological systems. Crisis can impel scholars to travel well beyond their methodological origins to seek new intellectual sources of authority. In the cases of Hermann Cohen and Franz Rosenzweig, the tumult of their respective days coincided with – and may well have induced in them – a certain disdain for history, from which they moved away in search of deeper philosophical or theological meaning.

Cohen and Rosenzweig serve as bookends of the modernist revolt against an Enlightenment-born modernity. Cohen's rise to philosophical prominence – and attack on Heinrich Graetz – occurred in the Nietzschean moment of cultural pessimism, one with which he himself was not fully comfortable, but which inspired other thinkers and artists to overturn prevailing norms and ideals. This revolt reached full strength in the second and third decades of the twentieth century. Indeed, in the waning years of the First World War and at the outset of the Weimar era, Franz Rosenzweig rose to prominence along with a diverse band of cultural creators who, in a decidedly modernist, vein, deviated from the staid, bourgeois platitudes of their parents' generation.

Just as a modernist sensibility helped to instigate intellectual rebellion, including against the practices and methodological presumptions of history, the postmodern era served as the contextual bed for a third critique at century's end. The intrigue in this third case is that the chief protagonist was none other than an historian himself, the towering scholar of Jewish history, Yosef Hayim Yerushalmi (1932–2009), best known as the author of *Zakhor: Jewish History and Jewish Memory* (1982).[25]

Yerushalmi was neither a declared postmodernist nor an admirer of that which went under its name.[26] But he lived in an age dominated by postmodernism's concerns. As Jean-François Lyotard noted in *The Postmodern Condition*, 'postmodern' meant 'incredulity toward metanarratives', which generated both scepticism and fear of the totalizing (and totalitarian) inclinations contained therein.[27] Postmodernism also trained new attention on the process of literary (and historical) representation, challenging the belief that one could achieve a degree of interpretive fixity or, in the terms of the historian, objectivity.

While many critics tended to regard postmodernism as an act of wilful nihilism advanced by ill-intentioned promoters, it, of course, had its own history. Lyotard famously situated the postmodern problem of representation as a conundrum born in the wake of Auschwitz: 'Suppose that an earthquake destroys not only lives, buildings, and objects but also the instruments used to measure earthquakes directly and indirectly.'[28] With shattered instruments, the task of accurate representation, especially of an event of the magnitude of the Shoah, becomes nearly impossible.

Indeed, the post-Holocaust era posed serious epistemological and hermeneutical challenges. Postmodernism, as it emerged in the late 1970s and 1980s, was, at least in part, a belated response to these challenges. It triggered its own sense of intellectual and cultural crisis which, in my view, helps set the stage for Yerushalmi's *Zakhor*, arguably the most important book to be published in Jewish studies over the past half century.

In this brief, 100-page volume, the Columbia historian masterfully summarizes the *longue durée* of Jewish collective memory from antiquity, noting the diverse rituals and liturgy that conveyed it. Collective memory, he demonstrated, had indeed been a vital connective tissue of Jews throughout their journey through history. This story of continuity comes to an abrupt end in *Zakhor*'s fourth chapter when Yerushalmi arrived at the modern period and the birth of a new critical historical sensibility – the very sensibility that guided him throughout his career as an historian of the Jews.

At that point, Yerushalmi adopted a dolorous and longing tone, as he juxtaposed the richness of pre-modern collective memory and the cold dissecting labours of the modern historian. Historicism offered neither a warm communal embrace nor deep consolation. Echoes of both Nietzsche and Rosenzweig reverberate throughout the chapter, as Yerushalmi observes that the Jewish historian was called upon to provide little more than 'faith to fallen Jews'.[29] The historian's guiding practice both marked and widened the rupture of modernity, dissolving the bonds of memory that linked Jews to one another previously.

Lyotard's comment about the instruments destroyed in the rubble of Auschwitz is relevant here. Although Yerushalmi did not explicitly describe himself in these terms, he stood in the long shadow of the Holocaust. He knew well that in late antique and medieval times, Jews had developed reliable methods of memorializing the past, especially the tragedies that had befallen them and their ancestors. But this capacity weakened in modern times, owing both to the lingering effects of genocidal destruction and to the 'acceleration of history', as Pierre Nora described it, that contributed to observers knowing more and more about less and less.[30] Stitching together the fabric of memory anew – and in the process, generating meaning out of history – was no longer the mandate of the historian. Modern historical research provided neither remembrance nor consolation.

Yerushalmi's *cri de coeur* echoed powerfully, in no small measure because the criticism he offered was directed inward. Within the field of Jewish studies, it inaugurated a vigorous debate about the relationship between history and memory that reverberates to this day, as scholars produced a more detailed map of the history of historiography, interrogated his conclusion about the rupture induced by modern historical research and pondered their own subject positions as historians.[31] At the same time, *Zakhor* inspired, coincided and was in conversation with important new work on memory formation after the Holocaust produced by a diverse array of researchers, including Saul Friedlander, Lawrence Langer, Shoshana Felman, Geoffrey Hartman, James Young and Annette Wieviorka. More generally, Yerushalmi's interest belonged to a broader moment of scholarly engagement with memory, among whose key foci in Europe were the *lieux de mémoire* approach of Pierre Nora and Mona Ozouf in France (1984) and the study of cultural memory by Jan Assmann and Aleida Assmann in Germany at the turn of the last century.

This late twentieth-century milieu was a postmodern moment. As in the case of Yerushalmi, not all caught up in it subscribed to deconstructionist or related literary methods or presuppositions; in fact, a good number actively fought what they perceived as the pernicious nihilism of postmodernism. And yet, for all its sins, real or imagined, the postmodern moment induced a degree of reflexivity about scholarly method and the interpretive process that humanistic scholarship in general – and historicism in particular – sometimes neglected.

Yerushalmi's own meditations joined in that moment in at least two regards. First, he offered in *Zakhor* a healthy measure of scepticism about history and its utility for life, although his lament may well have drawn more from Nietzsche than Derrida. Second, he engaged in the sort of methodological self-reflection that the intellectual Zeitgeist encouraged and even demanded. And his example was a powerful one. Many others – students, admirers, and critics – followed him down this reflexive path.

The enduring impact of Yerushalmi's example was not to deliver the last word on historicism, but in fact to stimulate a robust, thirty-five-year debate among historians, philosophers, theologians and literary critics over the function of history. This is perhaps the final irony in our story about crises of historicism. They induce fear of change – of desiccation, distortion and desacralization. This fear often induces rigorous polemics. In some cases, the polemics end in a methodological dead-end. But in other cases, they can defy expectations and lead to both enhanced self-reflection and a reinvigoration of historical practice itself.

Notes

1 Calvin R. Rand, 'Two Meanings of Historicism in the Writings of Dilthey, Troeltsch, and Meinecke', *Journal of the History of Ideas* 25, no. 4 (1964): 503–18.
2 Thomas Albert Howard, *Religion and the Rise of Historicism: W. M. L. de Wette, Jacob Burckhardt, and the Theological Origins of Nineteenth-Century Historical Consciousness* (New York: Cambridge University Press, 2000), 14.
3 Paul R. Mendes-Flohr, 'The Study of the Jewish Intellectual: A Methodological Prolegomenon', in *Divided Passions: Jewish Intellectuals and the Experience of Modernity* (Detroit, MI: Wayne State University Press, 1991), 37, 42.
4 Joanne B. Ciulla, 'Handmaiden and Queen: What Philosophers Find in the Question: "What Is a Leader?"', in *Leadership Studies: The Dialogue of Disciplines*, ed. Michael Harvey and Ronald E. Riggio (Cheltenham: Edward Elgar Publishing, 2011), 54.
5 Lydia Patton, 'Methodology of the Sciences', in *The Oxford Handbook of German Philosophy in the Nineteenth Century*, ed. Michael Forster and Kristin Gjesdal (Oxford: Oxford University Press, 2015), 594–606.

6 Frederick C. Beiser, *The German Historicist Tradition* (New York, NY, and Oxford: Oxford University Press, 2011).
7 Stephen Kalberg, 'The Origin and Expansion of Kulturpessimismus: The Relationship between Public and Private Spheres in Early Twentieth Century Germany', *Sociological Theory* 5, no. 2 (1987): 150.
8 Wilhelm Marr, *Der Sieg des Judenthums über das Germanenthum* (Bern: Rudolph Costenoble, 1879), 38.
9 Joshua Foa Dienstag, 'Nietzsche's Dionysian Pessimism', *The American Political Science Review* 95, no. 4 (2001): 935.
10 Friedrich Nietzsche, *On the Advantage and Disadvantage on Life*, trans. Peter Preuss (Indianapolis, IN: Hackett Publishing Company, 1980), 2.
11 Hermann Cohen, 'Ein Gruß der Pietät an das breslauer Seminar', in *Jüdische Schriften*, vol. 2, ed. Bruno Strauss (Berlin: C. A. Schwetschke & Sohn, 1924), 420.
12 David N. Myers, 'Hermann Cohen and the Problem of History at the Fin de Siècle', chap 2, in *Resisting History: Historicism and Its Discontents in German-Jewish Thought* (Princeton, NJ: Princeton University Press, 2003).
13 Michael A. Meyer, 'Great Debate on Antisemitism: Jewish Reaction to New Hostility in Germany 1879-1881', *The Leo Baeck Institute Year Book* 11, no. 1 (1966): 145.
14 Myers, 'Hermann Cohen', 53.
15 Robert J. Rubanowice, *Crisis in Consciousness: The Thought of Ernst Troeltsch* (Tallahasee: University Presses of Florida, 1982).
16 Quoted in Myers, 'Hermann Cohen', 56.
17 See Josiah B. Simon, 'Franz Rosenzweig's Hegel and the State: Biography, History and Tragedy' (PhD diss., University of Oregon, 2014).
18 Franz Rosenzweig, *Briefe und Tagebücher*, ed. Rachel Rosenzweig and Edith Rosenzweig-Scheinmann, vol. 1 of *Franz Rosenzweig: Der Mensch und sein Werk; Gesammelte Schriften* (The Hague: Martinus Nijhoff, 1979), 112-13.
19 See Friedrich Wilhelm Graf, 'Die "antihistorische Revolution" in der protestantischen Theologie der zwanziger Jahre', in *Vernunft Wissenschaftliche Theologie und kirchliche Lehre*, ed. Jan Rohls and Gunther Wenz (Göttingen: Vanndenhoeck & Ruprecht, 1988), 377-405; as well as Kurt Nowak, 'Die "antihistorische Revolution": Symptome und Folgen der Krise historische Weltorientierung nach dem Ersten Weltgrieg', in *Umstrittene Moderne: die Zukunft der Neuzeit im Urteil der Epoche Ernst Troeltschs*, ed. H. Renz and F. W. Graf (Gütersloh: Gütersloher Verlagshaus, 1987), 133-71.
20 A. Udoff and B. E. Galli, ed., *Franz Rosenzweig's 'The New Thinking'* (Syracuse, NY: Syracuse University Press, 1999), 45.
21 Udoff and Galli, *Franz Rosenzweig's 'The New Thinking'*, 57, 62-3. Meanwhile, on the ambience for Jewish intellectuals in this period, see Ulrich Sieg, *Jüdische Intellektuelle im Ersten Weltkrieg: Kriegserfahrungen, weltanschauliche Debatten und kulturelle Neuentwürfe* (Berlin: Akademie Verlag, 2001).

22 Franz Rosenzweig, 'Geist und Epochen der jüdischen Geschichte', in *Zweistromland: Kleinere Schriften zu Glauben und Denken*, ed. A. Mayer and R. Mayer, vol. 3 of *Franz Rosenzweig: Der Mensch und sein Werk; Gesammelte Schriften* (Dordrecht: Springer Verlag, 1984), 533, 537–8.
23 Franz Rosenzweig, 'Atheistische Theologie', in *Zweistromland: Kleinere Schriften zu Glauben und Denken*, ed. A. Mayer and R. Mayer, vol. 3 of *Franz Rosenzweig: Der Mensch und sein Werk; Gesammelte Schriften* (Dordrecht: Springer Verlag, 1984), 686.
24 Nahum G. Glatzer, *Franz Rosenzweig: His Life and Thought* (New York, NY: Farrar, Strauss and Young, 1953), 95–6.
25 Yosef Hayim Yerushalmi, *Zakhor: Jewish History and Jewish Memory*, with a new preface and postscript by the author (New York, NY: Schocken Books, 1989).
26 Y. H. Yerushalmi, 'Jüdische Historiographie und Postmodernismus: Eine abweichende Meinung', in *Geschichtsschreibung heute: Themen, Positionen, Kontroversen*, ed. Michael Brenner and David N. Myers (Munich: C. H. Beck Verlag, 2002), 75–94.
27 Jean-François Lyotard, *Postmodern Condition: A Report on Knowledge* (Minneapolis: University of Minnesota, 1984), xxiv.
28 Jean-François Lyotard, *The Differend: Phrases in Dispute* (Minneapolis: University of Minnesota, 1988), 56.
29 Yerushalmi, *Zakhor*, 98. It is interesting to contrast this portrait of the historian to Cohen's rendering of Graetz, who was cast in somewhat one-dimensional terms a pure subjective emotionalism.
30 Pierre Nora, 'Between Memory and History: Les Lieux de Mémoire', *Representations*, no. 26 (Spring 1989): 7.
31 Perhaps the most important of Yerushalmi's respondents was Amos Funkenstein, 'Collective Memory and Historical Consciousness', *History and Memory* 1, no. 1 (1989): 5–26.

Bibliography

Bambach, Charles R. *Heidegger, Dilthey, and the Crisis of Historicism*. Ithaca, NY: Cornell University Press, 1995.
Beiser, Frederick C. *The German Historicist Tradition*. New York, NY, and Oxford: Oxford University Press, 2011.
Beiser, Frederick C. *Hermann Cohen: An Intellectual Biography*. Oxford: Oxford University Press, 2018.
Ciulla, Joanne B. 'Handmaiden and Queen: What Philosophers Find in the Question: "What Is a Leader?"'. In *Leadership Studies: The Dialogue of Disciplines*, edited by Michael Harvey and Ronald E. Riggio, 54–65. Cheltenham: Edward Elgar Publishing, 2011.

Cohen, Hermann. 'Ein Gruß der Pietät an das breslauer Seminar'. In *Jüdische Schriften*, vol. 2, edited by Bruno Strauss, 418–24. Berlin: C. A. Schwetschke & Sohn, 1924.
Dienstag, Joshua Foa. 'Nietzsche's Dionysian Pessimism'. *The American Political Science Review* 95, no. 4 (2001): 923–37.
Funkenstein, Amos. 'Collective Memory and Historical Consciousness'. *History and Memory* 1, no. 1 (1989): 5–26.
Glatzer, Nahum N. *Franz Rosenzweig: His Life and Thought*. New York, NY: Farrar, Strauss and Young, 1953.
Graf, Friedrich Wilhelm. 'Die "antihistorische Revolution" in der protestantischen Theologie der zwanziger Jahre'. In *Vernunft Wissenschaftliche Theologie und kirchliche Lehre*, edited by Jan Rohls and Gunther Wenz, 377–405. Göttingen: Vanndenhoeck & Ruprecht, 1988.
Howard, Thomas Albert. *Religion and the Rise of Historicism: W. M. L. de Wette, Jacob Burckhardt, and the Theological Origins of Nineteenth-Century Historical Consciousness*. New York, NY: Cambridge University Press, 2000.
Kalberg, Stephen. 'The Origin and Expansion of Kulturpessimismus: The Relationship between Public and Private Spheres in Early Twentieth Century Germany'. *Sociological Theory* 5, no. 2 (1987): 150–64.
Lyotard, Jean-François. *The Postmodern Condition: A Report on Knowledge*. Translated by Geoff Bennington and Brian Massumi. Minneapolis: University of Minnesota, 1984.
Lyotard, Jean-François. *The Differend: Phrases in Dispute*. Minneapolis: University of Minnesota, 1988.
Marr, Wilhelm. *Der Sieg des Judenthums über das Germanenthum*. Bern: Rudolph Costenoble, 1879.
Mendes-Flohr, Paul R. 'The Study of the Jewish Intellectual: A Methodological Prolegomenon'. In Mendes-Flohr, *Divided Passions: Jewish Intellectuals and the Experience of Modernity*, 23–53. Detroit, MI: Wayne State University Press, 1991.
Meyer, Michael A. 'Great Debate on Antisemitism: Jewish Reaction to New Hostility in Germany 1879–1881'. *The Leo Baeck Institute Year Book* 11, no. 1 (January 1966): 137–70.
Myers, David N. 'Hermann Cohen and the Problem of History at the Fin de Siècle'. In Myers, *Resisting History: Historicism and Its Discontents in German-Jewish Thought*. Princeton, NJ: Princeton University Press, 2003.
Myers, David N. *The Stakes of History: On the Use and Abuse of Jewish History for Life*. New Haven, CT: Yale University Press, 2018.
Nietzsche, Friedrich. *On the Advantage and Disadvantage on Life*. Translated by Peter Preuss. Indianapolis, IN: Hackett Publishing Company, 1980.
Nora, Pierre. 'Between Memory and History: Les Lieux de Mémoire'. *Representations*, no. 26 (Spring 1989), 7–24.
Nowak, Kurt. 'Die "antihistorische Revolution": Symptome und Folgen der Krise historische Weltorientierung nach dem Ersten Weltgrieg'. In *Umstrittene Moderne:*

die Zukunft der Neuzeit im Urteil der Epoche Ernst Troeltschs, edited by H. Renz and F. W. Graf, 133–71. Gütersloh: Gütersloher Verlagshaus, 1987.

Patton, Lydia. 'Methodology of the Sciences'. In *The Oxford Handbook of German Philosophy in the Nineteenth Century*, edited by Michael Forster and Kristin Gjesdal, 594–606. Oxford: Oxford University Press, 2015.

Rand, Calvin G. 'Two Meanings of Historicism in the Writings of Dilthey, Troeltsch, and Meinecke'. *Journal of the History of Ideas* 25, no. 4 (1964): 503–18.

Rosenzweig, Franz. *Briefe und Tagebücher*, edited by Rachel Rosenzweig and Edith Rosenzweig- Scheinmann. Vol. 1 of *Franz Rosenzweig: Der Mensch und sein Werk; Gesammelte Schriften*. The Hague: Martinus Nijhoff, 1979.

Rosenzweig, Franz. 'Atheistische Theologie'. In *Zweistromland: Kleinere Schriften zu Glauben und Denken*, edited by A. Mayer and R. Mayer, 687–97. Vol. 3 of *Franz Rosenzweig: Der Mensch und sein Werk; Gesammelte Schriften*. Dordrecht: Springer Verlag, 1984.

Rosenzweig, Franz. 'Geist und Epochen der jüdischen Geschichte'. In *Zweistromland: Kleinere Schriften zu Glauben und Denken*, edited by A. Mayer and R. Mayer, 527–38. Vol. 3 of *Franz Rosenzweig: Der Mensch und sein Werk; Gesammelte Schriften*. Dordrecht: Springer Verlag, 1984.

Rubanowice, Robert J. *Crisis in Consciousness: The Thought of Ernst Troeltsch*. Tallahasee: University Presses of Florida, 1982.

Schorske, Carl E. *Fin-de-Siècle Vienna: Politics and Culture*. New York, NY: Alfred A. Knopf, 1979.

Sieg, Ulrich. *Jüdische Intellektuelle im Ersten Weltkrieg: Kriegserfahrungen, weltanschauliche Debatten und kulturelle Neuentwürfe*. Berlin: Akademie Verlag, 2001.

Simon, Josiah B. 'Franz Rosenzweig's Hegel and the State: Biography, History and Tragedy'. PhD diss., University of Oregon, 2014.

Udoff A. and Galli, B. E., ed. *Franz Rosenzweig's "The New Thinking"*. Syracuse, NY: Syracuse University Press, 1999.

Volkov, Shulamit. 'The Dynamics of Dissimilation: Ostjuden and German Jews'. In *The Jewish Response to German Culture: From the Enlightenment to the Second World War*, edited by Jehuda Reinharz and Walter Schatzberg, 195–211. Hanover, NH: University Press of New England, 1986.

Yerushalmi, Yosef Hayim. *Zakhor: Jewish History and Jewish Memory*, with a new preface and postscript by the author. New York, NY: Schocken Books, 1989.

Yerushalmi, Yosef Hayim. 'Jüdische Historiographie und Postmodernismus: Eine abweichende Meinung'. In *Geschichtsschreibung heute: Themen, Positionen, Kontroversen*, edited by Michael Brenner and David N. Myers, 75–94. Munich: C. H. Beck Verlag, 2002.

2

Historicism as a modern theological problem

Gary Dorrien

Abstract

This chapter argues that the sort of questions typically associated with 'historicism' and its alleged 'crisis' in Troeltsch's and Barth's generation – questions of historical method, developmental thinking and historical relativism – had been key issues in modern theology since the early nineteenth century. It shows, more generally, how and why the relation between *Geschichte* and *Glaube* had been a central theme in modern theological thinking since Friedrich Schleiermacher. Only against this background does it become intelligible why theologians after the First World War devoted hundreds of learned pages to the 'problems' of historicism and their possible 'overcoming'.

Introduction

Historicism is one of the chief things that modern theologians fight about, along with idealism, naturalism, post-colonialism and cultural privilege. Indeed, all modern theologians claim to take historicism seriously: they disqualify for inclusion in the category of modern theology if they do not do so. But what exactly historicism entails, and to what degree it should be endorsed or defended, is something modern theologians disagree about. This is because, as I will argue in this chapter, liberal theologians since the early nineteenth century have continuously been rethinking the relation between historical enquiry and theological reflection. It may suffice to illustrate this with some brief comments on the gods of modern theology in nineteenth- and twentieth-century Europe: Immanuel Kant, Friedrich Schleiermacher, G. W. F. Hegel, Albrecht Ritschl, Adolf von Harnack, Ernst Troeltsch and Karl Barth.[1]

Instead of tracing the occurrence and different meanings of the term 'historicism', my aim is to show that the sort of questions typically associated with historicism and its alleged 'crisis' in Troeltsch's and Barth's generation – questions of historical method, developmental thinking and historical relativism – had been key issues in modern theology since the early nineteenth century. Instead of zooming in on the specific meanings of historicism in Troeltsch or Barth, I will try to show how and why, more generally, the relation between *Geschichte* and *Glaube* had been a central theme in modern theological thinking since Schleiermacher. Only against this background does it become intelligible why theologians after the First World War devoted hundreds of learned pages to the 'problems' of historicism and their possible 'overcoming'.[2]

What is liberal theology?

England had the first trickle of liberalizing theologies, but no full-fledged movement of liberal theology until the end of the nineteenth century. Germany had the first full-fledged movement of liberal theology, and in both contexts religion was distinctly problematic for liberal ideology. To the liberal traditions in England and Germany associated with Locke and Kant, the liberal state was naturally tolerant by virtue of deriving from a rational social contract, it existed to protect the natural rights of citizens and religion had to be constrained by modern rationality. In the United States, Thomas Jefferson and Benjamin Franklin espoused a liberalism of this sort, where it competed with a latter-day Puritan notion deriving from John Milton that the state has a sacred duty to protect liberty – the seed of what became the American social gospel.

In all these cases, the liberal rhetoric of freedom was shot through with hypocrisy, because precious few liberals included all human beings in the rights of humanity. Liberalism arose as an ideological justification of capitalism and as tolerant relief from the religious wars of the seventeenth century. Liberals designed a supposedly natural political economy based on self-interested market exchanges that protected the interests of the capitalist class. They afforded liberal rights only to white male owners of property, branding all others as disqualified. Some liberals opposed all such exclusions and hypocrisy, but they had to be called radical liberals or liberal socialists to distinguish them from what liberalism usually meant.

Liberal theology arose as an aspect of this story. In Germany the Kantians contended that they were the only liberals. Later usage was more generous, which

I shall adopt, counting as liberal or modern the schools of Kant, Schleiermacher, Hegel, Ritschl and Troeltsch, plus similar traditions in Britain and the United States. Until the modern era, every Christian theology operated within a house of authority. The external authority of the Bible and Christian tradition established what had to be believed about very specific things. Liberal theology broke away from authority-based religious thinking by refusing to establish or compel religious beliefs on the basis of a bare authority claim, seeking a third way between orthodox over-belief and secular disbelief, accepting the historical critical approach to the Bible, allowing science to explain the physical world, looking beyond the church for answers and seeking to make faith relevant to the modern world.

These six planks have held up through the centuries and from place to place, effectively defining what liberal theology has been and still is. But no essential anything truly passes from one time and place to another, the meaning of everything is constantly reinterpreted and there was a seventh plank that played a fateful role in modern theology: the social consciousness of the Progressive era. In theology it was variously called social Christianity, Christian socialism or the social gospel, and it played out differently in England, Germany and the United States. In England, Christian socialism was overwhelmingly Anglo-Catholic and liberal theology was rationalistic and elitist. In Germany, liberal theology became wholly identified with Culture Protestantism, the civil religion of an expanding German Empire, which set up liberal theology for a devastating crash. In the United States, the social gospel was politically activist and mostly progressive, it had a much broader impact than its European counterparts and it fused completely with what is still called 'liberal theology' in the United States.

The Hegelian School

I have begun by historicizing modern theology, but I need to get rolling on historicism *in* modern theology. The iconic traditions of modern theology are German. Kantian theologians grounded Christian truth entirely in the moral concerns of practical reason, conceiving theology as freethinking critical reflection on moral faith. Religion is important as support for moral religion, and false and distracting as anything else. The school of Schleiermacher said that religion is about awe, mystery and the infinite, not moral control. Kantian philosophy is mostly correct, but Kantian religion is superficial. The essence of religion is religious feeling *(Gefühl)*. All religions construe the whence of human existence and dependence, and Christianity is about the experience of redemption in Jesus Christ. Schleiermacher granted that religious philosophy is a legitimate enterprise – he was a post-Kantian objective idealist. But he insisted that theology has nothing to do with it. Theology is the Christian community's interpretation of its experience of divinity and redemption, period. Everything else belongs to other disciplines. The school of Hegel said it was disastrous for theologians to reduce the truth of Christianity to their feelings about it. Hegel's metaphysical system rehabilitated the Christian worldview on modern terms. Christianity is a picture story about the movement of self-certain Spirit abandoning its unity nature to embrace the suffering of the world and return to itself. It apprehends in pictorial form the universal process by which Spirit redeems the world by desiring, sundering, suffering, reconciling and coming to know itself.

All three of these theological schools, and the Mediating versions of them, said that historical criticism is valuable and necessary to a point. It deconstructs superstitious traditions and ascertains historical probabilities. The Kantians thought they were covered on this subject because they invented historical criticism in the first place. Early Enlightenment rationalists took the Bible as a flat text and corrected it from the standpoint of their own naturalistic worldview. They exposed discrepant accounts, or harmonized them; rejected miracle stories, or provided naturalistic explanations; stressed that the Bible contains myths, or deduced a rational system from the Bible, conceiving interpretation as taxonomy.

A bit later, in the 1760s, the German founders of historical criticism – Johann Semler, Johann Eichhorn, Johann Griesbach – made a course correction by deconstructing the history of the text itself. They studied the Bible from a scientific standpoint ostensibly stripped of dogmatic premises, revolutionizing biblical scholarship by deciphering the historical development of the Bible. They had no nation, yet they had far more historical consciousness than scholars from the mighty nations of France and England. These German scholars were the first to call themselves 'liberal theologians', until Kant came along in the early 1780s, after which they called themselves Kantians. Heinrich Paulus, Wilhelm de Wette and other Kantians took pride in their historical methods without believing it established good theology. Historical criticism was just a tool, and mostly negative. Kantians, the Schleiermacher school and Hegelians agreed about that. They were careful not to contradict whatever came from historical criticism, but the establishing role belonged to something else: moral faith, religious experience or the truth of Christian ideas.

The Hegelian School played the leading role in this area, because it dominated mid-nineteenth-century theology and it had more at stake in the question of history. Hegel said that what matters in Christianity is the nature and movement of God as spirit, the death of God on Calvary as a moment in the life of God and the consummated self-realization of Spirit. The community of faith adopts this story and sustains it; there is no life of faith without the community. But only philosophy can justify its content, not bishops or history. What matters is the content in and for itself, not the transmission of church doctrine. Only philosophy can adequately express the content of true religion, because philosophy deals with concepts and religion deals with pictures. Hegel mixed two concepts of history in expounding this argument, *Geschichte* and *Historie*: 'Only by philosophy can this simply present content be justified, not by history (*Geschichte*). What spirit does is no history (*Historie*). Spirit is concerned only with what is in and for itself, not something past, but simply what is present.'[3]

Hegelian theologians fiercely debated what that meant, especially after Hegel died in 1831. Had Hegel used the term *Historie* in both sentences, he might have been construed as saying that history as bare literal fact justifies nothing and is not the point. Many of his more orthodox followers took him that way. As it was, he used the term *Geschichte* – interpreted history, or the meaning of history – in the first sentence, which raised unsettling questions about the extent to which he regarded *any* historical basis as being intrinsic to Christian truth.

Hegel did not say that philosophy should replace religion or that the historical core of Christianity is entirely dispensable. He taught that philosophy is originally dependent upon and must continue to be fed by religious experience. But he was careful not to say how much of the gospel narrative must be historically credible if Christianity is to be accepted as the true religion. The logic of his argument pressed in the direction of minimizing historicity. He could be evasive, as in the foregoing example, although most of the time he spoke of 'divine history', asserting that God *is* the eternal history. But on historical enquiry itself, Hegel was brutally frank. He said he respected what historical critics did with ancient texts and not what they did with religious truth, for historical knowledge is pitifully low grade. To be a theologian and aspire to mere historicism is as pitiful as you can get. It is to adopt the mentality of a counting-house clerk. A clerk keeps the ledgers and accounts of other people's wealth. At least Kant and Schleiermacher spoke out of something they knew personally. Hegel let his followers decide how much they needed to believe about past historical events. But historicist theology was the most pitifully shallow and reductionist strategy of them all.

The Ritschlian School

This conviction grated on the founder of the Ritschlian School, Albrecht Ritschl, whose followers swept the field of theology in the late nineteenth century. Ritschl was born to the Prussian Union Church as the son of a conservative Lutheran bishop. He studied under Ferdinand Christian Baur at Tübingen in 1845, and his relationship with Baur was stormy, competitive, brief and formative. Baur taught his students to interpret Christianity in Hegel's fashion as a total historical reality. He employed the conventional thesis-antithesis-synthesis version of Hegel's dialectic, conceiving early Christianity as a struggle between the church's 'Judaizing' and 'Hellenizing' factions, represented respectively by the Jerusalem-based apostles (especially Peter) and the Hellenistic Gentile converts championed by Paul.[4]

In his early career Ritschl espoused Baur's brand of historicism and his rendering of early Christian history, but in 1850 he turned against Baur's dictum that pure historicism is impossible. Ritschl offended Baur and his disciples by claiming that philosophy gets in the way of understanding what happened in early Christianity; it is better to interpret history without a philosophy. Accusations of bad faith ensued back and forth. Baur said the Johannine literature is a synthesis of the conflict between Judaizers and Hellenizers, which led to Catholicism. Ritschl said Catholicism was no synthesis, but rather a negation of Judaism by a triumphant Hellenistic faction that redefined Christianity in its own image. Catholicism stood for corruption and deracination, erasing the Jewish character of Christianity.[5]

Ritschl grieved that German theologians routinely denigrated the Jewish aspects of Christianity. He had Martin Luther against him on this subject, but Ritschl enlisted Luther to his side by emphasizing Luther's polemic against the 'Babylonian captivity' of the church and playing down Luther's violent polemics against Jews. In Ritschl's later career at Göttingen, he acquired an eminent colleague, Paul de Lagarde, the founder of the history of religions school, who was a vile anti-Semite, very proud of it, and vehemently anti-Ritschl on this basis.[6]

To Ritschl, historicism was the golden key that made metaphysical speculation unnecessary. From 1846 to 1864, he taught at Bonn; in 1857, he left church history to become a theologian; in 1864, he moved to Göttingen and changed the field of theology. Ritschl combined Kant on moral religion, Schleiermacher on religious experience and himself on social-ethical consciousness. He argued that Christianity is fundamentally a socio-historical movement with a distinct social-ethical character founded on Christian faith alone. Ritschlian theology was geared to solve two problems: the challenge of Darwinian evolution and the bitter disputes between pietists and confessionalists in the Prussian church. As a theologian, Ritschl sought to avoid religious conflicts with science; as a Prussian churchman, he was appalled at the erosion of the church's moral and social authority. His solution to the first problem came straight from Kant: science describes the way things are or appear to be, while theology is about the way things should be. Religious knowledge is never disinterested; it consists of value judgements about reality, especially judgements contributing to personal and social good.[7]

The goal of true religion is to attain the highest possible good. In Christianity, Ritschl argued, this good is found in the central ideas of the apostolic tradition, a job for historical criticism. The point is not to uncover what Jesus really said. Quests of the historical Jesus kept getting this wrong, feeding the impression that Christianity should be based on whatever historical critics discovered about the Jesus of history. Ritschl implored that what matters is to uncover the collective Christian experience of value inspired by Jesus.

What makes a religion good is its concern with value. Historical research shows that the essence of Christianity is the kingdom of God as valued by the Christian community. But the kingdom is valued as absolute only by those who follow Jesus. Outsiders don't care what Jesus taught about sin, redemption or the kingdom. Ritschl stressed the logical upshot: Christian truth cannot be grasped outside the Christian community, for Christian faith is knowable only to faith. It is comprehensible only within the inner history of the church's life and practices. Personal redemption and social religion go together in the gospel. Ritschl famously described this double character as an ellipse determined by two foci, personal redemption and the kingdom of God. The mark of true Christianity is its mutually relational double character in which the religious and ethical dimensions perpetually interact.

Adolf von Harnack

The Ritschlian School offers the rare example of a school outshining its founder. Ritschl was short on personal magnetism, his writing style was clumsy and verbose, his German nationalism embarrassed the social gospel Americans that he influenced and Adolf von Harnack soared far beyond him. Harnack grew up in a Russian majority town in Livonia where he belonged to a German-speaking Prussian nationalist elite. His Prussian aristocratic identity cast a long shadow over his legacy. He wrote massive scholarly works that detailed the Hellenization of Christian doctrine, won a coveted position at Berlin in 1888 and popularized Ritschlian theology. Britons and North Americans flocked to Berlin to hear him, marvelling at his knack for cutting through tangled webs of doctrine and historical detail. Harnack tempered his aristocratic bearing with a kindly, charming personality and a sincere evangelical piety, telling audiences that Jesus Christ is the central fact of human history. All that came before and after Jesus must be interpreted in light of his creative personality.[8]

Harnack's disciplined clarity was a central factor in his vast influence and productivity. He taught that historical theology breaks the power of traditions that fossilized Christianity into something alien to the gospel of Jesus. The gospel writers made no pretence of presenting disinterested historical accounts. The gospels are testimonies of faith composed by Jewish Christian communities in the last stages of their absorption by the Hellenistic church. To treat them as history or myth is to miss their unique character as the faith literature of a disappearing community of memory. With the triumph of Hellenistic Christianity, the peculiar gospel blend of faith and tradition became alien to the church. It was no longer a living possession. The gospels became alien texts, though not lacking in historical material. Harnack judged that the gospel picture of the life and teaching of Jesus is basically reliable. Jesus taught that the kingdom of God is coming, the human soul is infinitely valuable under the rule and love of God and believers hold the promise of righteousness and eternal life.[9]

Harnack's voice was so commanding that he obscured for many that other kinds of liberal theology existed. He taught that theology separates the gospel kernel from various historical husks, and that Germany's greatness rested on two pillars: the German Army and German scholarship. The First World War began for him on 1 August 1914, when the Emperor asked him to compose a call to war. The enemy nations, when Harnack began, were France and Russia. Before he had finished, he was told to add England, which stunned him; Harnack prized his British friends. Within a month he had lost most of them. Some British scholars distinguished between bad Prussian militarism and good-but-cowardly German scholarship. Harnack trembled with rage at reading such things, refusing to accept moral criticism from acolytes of the British Empire. He believed that Western Christian civilization was at stake in

Germany's fate, and he signed public declarations saying it defiantly, including the one that famously repulsed Karl Barth.[10]

For all his iconic status, Harnack was never at the cutting edge of the Ritschlian School, and his eminence was misleading. One would not have guessed from his writings that the Ritschlian School seethed internally with controversy. At the very time that Harnack spoke with commanding assurance to a global audience, Ritschlian theologians sharply debated whether they had any ground of certainty or should want one. Wilhelm Herrmann and Ernst Troeltsch played the star roles in this drama.

Wilhelm Herrmann and Ernst Troeltsch

Herrmann was a pietist liberal who taught at Marburg and pushed Ritschl on three topics: metaphysics, Kant and historical evidence. He protested that Kant and Ritschl did not sufficiently expunge metaphysics from theology, and Ritschl wrongly let Kant define what religion is about. True religion is not a branch of moral reasoning; it is an independent power through which God saves a lost human being. We are saved by faith, as Luther taught, not by moral achievement. Through faith we learn that God is unique, mysterious and transcendent. The reality known to true faith is knowable only to faith, not to any other kind of cognition.[11]

For thirty years Herrmann equivocated on how far *he* should go. Are *all* apologetic arguments illegitimate? From the beginning, Herrmann was a Lutheran fideist – faith is its own basis. No one has ever been saved by information. What saves is the person of Jesus as we encounter and experience him. In faith we meet the living presence of Jesus, not the historical Jesus sought by historians. But Herrmann hedged on how he said it because Ritschlian theology was deeply vested in arguments about the historical character of Christianity. In the early twentieth century, he and Troeltsch dramatically debated this issue, which drove Herrmann to say it unequivocally: revelatory experience cannot be established by something else. True religion is a special kind of knowing, period.[12]

That was never an option for Troeltsch, even though he and Herrmann had the same theological hero, Schleiermacher. Troeltsch said that Herrmann was wilfully incoherent, bordering on intellectual dishonesty. As soon as you give an inch to historical criticism, it takes a mile. Herrmann grasped the problem, so he lurched to an indefensible answer that has no future in the academy. Troeltsch implored that the only viable option for theologians is to go all the way with historicism. Just as Ritschl marked an advance on Baur, the History of Religions marked an advance on Ritschl. Troeltsch began as a protégé of Ritschl at Göttingen, moved into Lagarde's circle and accepted the History of Religions argument that real historicism – that is, objective historical enquiry – does not favour any religion. The Ritschlians practised a rigged historicism that privileged Christianity at the outset. Real historicism proceeds in scientific fashion, studying religions by an objective criterion not derived from any particular religion. Troeltsch denied that theology and the History of Religions were incompatible. His ambition was precisely to formulate a Christian theology based on History of Religions scholarship.[13]

Troeltsch was a battler, always fighting with someone, even as he aspired to scientific objectivity. He taught at Heidelberg from 1894 to 1915 and despaired at being surrounded by mediocrities. He made his friends on the conference lecture circuit, notably Harnack and Max Weber, who implored Troeltsch to relinquish his snotty attitude about politics and social problems. Thus did Troeltsch acquire a second major project, studying how Christianity formulated its social teaching. Always he taught that everything historical is relative, there is no independent Christian entity and historical relativism is not the final truth. In his early career Troeltsch was a neo-Hegelian, arguing that humanity has a common dynamism of spirit that advances in different ways through the mysterious movement of divine Spirit in and through the human spirit. The more that religions advance towards their goal, the more they strive for the fullness of truth, moving beyond the spell of nature and local mythology. Buddhism, neo-Platonism and Christianity are the most advanced, but Buddhism is too pessimistic and otherworldly to be a universal religion of redemption, and neo-Platonism is too mystical. Only Christianity gets to universal redemption: God is experienced in the individual heart and the outward social world, and all people are included in God's plan.[14]

Christianity, on this telling, overcame its tribal origins through two strategies: Pauline theology and Logos theology. Paul construed Christianity as a new, independent, universal religious power, but he relied on Judaism and his unrepeatable inner experiences in theorizing what Christianity is about. Later generations had no recourse to Paul's vision of Christ, his inner struggle with the limits and demands of Jewish law, or his ecstatic experiences of the Spirit. To make Christianity intelligible to Christians and outsiders, the church formulated doctrines of revelation and the incarnation that led to Logos theology: All moments of truth in the world's religions and philosophies are expressions of the mind of God, and which Christ incarnated.

Troeltsch decidedly favoured Logos theology over Paul, but he was too historicist to keep saying that Logos theology apprehends the essence of religion, and he tired of struggling with Hegel's system. Modern history knows nothing of an all-inclusive principle that regulates the emergence of everything individual and constitutes the essence of all value. It knows only concrete, individual things conditioned by their context. Historical consciousness may grasp ideas that are said to be universally valid, but it knows no values that coincide with actual universals. Rather, it knows ideas that appear in individual form and make their claim for universal validity by resisting other ideas. So Troeltsch concluded that idealistic theories of graded progression miss what actually happens. Real history offers no evidence of gradual progression to higher orientations. Moreover, Harnack's kernel and husk strategy works no better, because the absolute and the relative are not readily separated. The truest parts of Christianity are not things that can be lifted above history. Being historical means that even the retrograde aspects of Christianity have a place in it.

True historicism focuses on the particularities of historical periods and the interrelationships of cultural structures. Baur developed a scale-oriented theory about early Christianity and Catholicism, but real history does not unfold in schemes about logically related members of ascending series. For that reason, Troeltsch gave up the Hegelian idea of an absolute working itself out through the permutations of history. In mid-career he adopted the neo-Kantian value theory of Heinrich Rickert, reasoning that critical consciousness does not exclude norms. Critical history discerns the individual value orientations that occur in history – forms of striving towards a goal. These relative, situated tendencies may be construed as a unified whole, even as they never realize the goal. Religion is about cultivating and realizing value orientations, and some religions do it better than others.[15]

Thus, his post-Ritschlian project had not changed. Troeltsch still railed against aimless exploring and imagined a history of religions theology. He said it would be absurd – a capitulation to nihilism – if theologians refused to discern value orientations in history and make value judgements about them. Historical reason identifies orienting goals and ideals, not universal principles. In his landmark work, *The Social Teaching of the Christian Churches* (1912), Troeltsch argued that Western Christianity had produced only two comprehensive social philosophies in its entire history: medieval Catholicism and Calvinism. Both were spent forces by the nineteenth century, Christianity desperately needed an alternative and Christian Socialism was too naïve and left wing to be the answer.[16]

Christianity needed a modern, critical, effective and inspiring way of engaging the world, though Troeltsch admitted he did not know what it was. All he knew was that Christianity provides a strong basis for personality and individuality, and only Christianity does so. This is what Christianity contributes to a better world – the belief in personality as a universal principle and value. Christianity invented the idea of an individual person imbued with sacred dignity. Only Christianity embraces and unites all human souls, through its concept of Divine Love. Historically and ethically, only Christianity solved the problem of inequality, by conceiving all people as children of God loved by God. Troeltsch did not believe that these 'only' claims were problematic for his universalism – until the end of his life. During the First World War, he gave raving nationalist pro-war speeches, but when he wrote theology he espoused Christian personalism as a universal creed.

Then the war ended, Troeltsch tried to write a philosophy of history, and he got impaled on the problem of claiming universality for a Christian idea. He argued for a universal history leading to a modern cultural synthesis resting on the ancient Hebraic tradition, classical Greece, the Hellenistic-Roman period and medieval Europe. Troeltsch had no real interest in anything outside Western history, but he realized that this attitude was problematic for his project. In his last book, published in 1924 after his death, he said the dream of a universal history must be relinquished. We know nothing of 'humanity' or a common Spirit; all we know are particular groups, families, races, classes, schools and sects from six thousand years, a tiny fraction of the human experience. Any idea claiming universality is as thoroughly particular and historical as any other idea. No historically conscious European has an idea of universality or a concept of values that is not European.[17]

In the end he said the idea of personality is too Christian to be universal, and he regretted having claimed otherwise. In place of his vision of historical development as the shaping of community life in accordance with a universal norm epitomized in Christianity, Troeltsch settled for what he called 'Europeanism'. Europeanism has a vital, scientific and liberating historical individuality, he reasoned. It valorizes individuality and critical rationality more than any other culture, and its carryover into the United States was a major point in its favour. Troeltsch took pride that Americans looked to Europe for high culture and intellectual leadership, filling their museums with European art. He said that America's ascendancy had a chance of being good for Europeanism – which was not an easy thing to say in the aftermath of the First World War.[18]

Barthian crisis theology

The Ritschlians had unified over Culture Protestantism, not theology; then Troeltsch gave jingoistic rally speeches imploring Germans to defeat their godless mongrel enemies. Karl Barth's contempt for *that* record seethed through everything he said about the Ritschlian School. After the war, Barth routed the Ritschlian establishment with a dramatic Expressionist rhetoric about the wrath of a Wholly Other God. Barthian 'crisis theology' was vehemently eschatological and anti-historicist. Pauline theology, Barth said, hurtles through the centuries as a fire alarm about the corruption of the world and the coming of a new age of the kingdom. Pauline radicalism about faith was the answer to the crisis and trauma of the church. Barth took many of its planks from his teacher Herrmann, without crediting Herrmann: revelation is divine self-revealing, theology is the explication of self-authenticating revelation, history is not a basis or subject of faith (that would amount to 'historicism') and Christian faith is not a worldview. Paul Tillich, emerging from the war, agreed with Barth about Pauline faith and the Ritschlian School, but not about the liberal tradition. Two dominant ways of construing liberal theology flowed from what Barth and Tillich said about it. Barth said the tragedy of liberal theology began with Kant and Schleiermacher; Tillich said it began with the Ritschlian School.

Liberal theology went down with the Ritschlian School. According to Barth, liberal theology betrayed Christ by construing faith as a human work and reducing God to an aspect of the world process. Ritschl was not worth refuting, having baptized the German bourgeois order. Harnack was a more scholarly version of Ritschl. Troeltsch trivialized theology by reducing it to the ponderings of historicist onlookers. Hegel was great, but his system was a poor substitute for Christian revelation. Schleiermacher was great, but he founded a bad thing, liberal theology. Tillich countered that liberal theology *was* the Ritschlian School, and Schleiermacher and Hegel should not be blamed for it.[19]

Both versions of this polemical rendering were enormously influential to the end of the twentieth century. Yet liberal theology is still creatively refashioning itself a century after the First World War. Barth's repudiation of it, for all his tremendous emotive and intellectual force, was never a fair description, and neither was Reinhold Niebuhr's subsequent polemic against American liberalism. They showed that ridicule is a powerful weapon, but Barth did not demonstrate that liberals addressed irrelevant questions or produced faulty scholarship, and the later Niebuhr confessed that of course he was a liberal theologian, what else could he be? It was only the idealistic versions that he hated. The fact that Barth famously turned against his liberal teachers after reading their names on a pro-war manifesto registered what was really at issue. If Harnack and Herrmann supported a baleful political cause, how did that refute two centuries of liberal scholarship about biblical criticism, epistemology, historicism, the scientific world picture and Darwinian evolution?[20]

Conclusion

If Barth, in the second edition of his *Römerbrief*, identified 'historicism' as one of the two main enemies of Christian theology as he conceived of it ('psychologism' being the other one), he framed this as an attack on the entire German liberal tradition. Yet as this chapter has made clear, the charge of historicism was anything but new: it emerged out of a century of liberal theological debate over questions regarding the relation between *Geschichte* and *Glaube*. Although the term 'historicism' entered theologians' vocabulary only in the decades around 1900, the issues at stake had already been debated for almost a century. As this chapter has tried to show, three clusters of questions had been especially prominent in nineteenth-century liberal theology: questions about biblical criticism (how and why the Bible should be subjected to critical scholarly study), questions about historical development (how a Hegelian or Darwinian account of progress should be evaluated theologically) and questions about historical relativism (whether and how Christianity could be said to be superior to other religions). Only against the background of these long-standing debates does it become possible to understand, not only what 'historicism' meant to various theologians in Wilhelmine or Weimar Germany, but also why the issues at stake were important to any modern theologian worth the name.

Notes

1   For detailed renderings of arguments summarized in this chapter, see Gary Dorrien, *The Word as True Myth: Interpreting Modern Theology* (Louisville, KY: Westminster John Knox Press, 1997); Gary Dorrien, *Kantian Reason and Hegelian Spirit: The Idealistic Logic of Modern Theology* (Oxford: Wiley-Blackwell, 2012); Gary Dorrien, *In a Post-Hegelian Spirit: Philosophical Theology as Idealist Discontent* (Waco, TX: Baylor University Press, 2020).

2 Ernst Troeltsch, *Der Historismus und seine Probleme* (Berlin: Rolf Heise, 1924); Ernst Troeltsch, *Der Historismus und seine Überwindung* (Berlin: Rolf Heise, 1924), English edition; Ernst Troeltsch, *Christian Thought: Its History and Application*, ed. F. von Hügel (1923; repr., New York, NY: Meridian Books, 1957).
3 G. W. F. Hegel, *Lectures on the Philosophy of Religion*, vol. 3, ed. Peter C. Hodgson, trans. R. F. Brown, Peter C. Hodgson and J. M. Stewart (Berkeley: University of California Press, 1985), 232–3.
4 F. C. Baur, *Das Christenthum und die christliche Kirche der drei ersten Jahrhunderte* (Tübingen: L. F. Fues, 1853), 133; F. C. Baur, *Ausgewählte Werke in Einzelausgaben*, vol. 1, ed. Klaus Scholder (Stuttgart: Friedrich Fromann Verlag, 1963), 313; F. C. Baur, *Die christliche Gnosis, oder die christliche Religions-Philosophie in ihrer geschichtlichen Entwicklung* (Tübingen: C. F. Osiander, 1835); Horton Harris, *The Tübingen School: A Historical and Theological Investigation of the School of F. C. Baur* (Grand Rapids, MI: Baker Book House, 1990), 101–12; Otto Ritschl, *Albrecht Ritschls Leben*, 2 vols. (Freiburg: J. C. B. Mohr, 1892–1896).
5 Albrecht Ritschl, *Die Entstehung der altkatholischen Kirche* (Bonn: Adolph Marcus, 1850).
6 Rolf Rendtorff, 'Die jüdische Bibel und ihre antijüdische Auslegung', in *Auschwitz: Krise der christlichen Theologie: Eine Vortragsreihe*, ed. Rolf Rendtorff and Ekkehard Stegemann (Munich: Christian Kaiser, 1980), 99–116; Lou H. Silberman, 'Wellhausen and Judaism', *Semeia* 25 (1982): 75–82; Martin Luther, 'The Babylonian Captivity of the Church', in *Martin Luther's Basic Theological Writings*, ed. Timothy F. Lull (Minneapolis, MN: Fortress Press, 1989), 267–313; Paul A. de Lagarde, *Gesammelte abhandlungen* (Leipzig: F. A. Brockhaus, 1866); Paul A. de Lagarde, *Librorum Veteris Testamenti canonicorum* (Göttingen: Prostat in aedibus Dieterichianus Arnoldi Hoyer, 1883); Paul A. de Lagarde, *Onomastica sacra* (Hildesheim: G. Olms, 1887); Paul A. de Lagarde, *Schriften für das deutsche Volk* (1878; repr., Munich: J. F. Lehmann, 1934).
7 Albrecht Ritschl, *The Christian Doctrine of Justification and Reconciliation*, ed. H. R. Mackintosh and A. B. Macaulay (Edinburgh: T & T Clark, 1902), 1–13.
8 Agnes von Zahn-Harnack, *Adolf von Harnack*, 2nd ed. (Berlin: Walter de Gruyter, 1951); Kurt Nowak et al. eds., *Adolf von Harnack: Christentum, Wissenschaft und Gesellschaft* (Göttingen: Vandenhoeck & Ruprecht, 2003); Adolf von Harnack, *History of Dogma*, trans. Neil Buchanan, 7 vols. (Boston, MA: Little, Brown, and Company, 1905).
9 Adolf von Harnack, *What Is Christianity?*, trans. Thomas Bailey Saunders (1900; repr., Philadelphia, PA: Fortress Press, 1957), 8–10, 30–52; Adolf von Harnack, 'The Evangelical Social Mission in the Light of the History of the Church', in Adolf von Harnack and Wilhelm Herrmann, *Essays on the Social Gospel*, trans. G. M. Craik (New York, NY: G. P. Putnam's Sons, 1907), 3–91.

10 'Declaration of Professors in the German Reich' (23 October 1914), Humanities Web Documents, www.humanitiesweb.org; 'Manifesto of Ninety-Three German Intellectuals to the Civilized World' (3 October 1914), Humanities Web Documents, www.humanitiesweb.org. The latter document is often misdated, as on this site.

11 Wilhelm Herrmann, *Die Metaphysik in der Theologie* (Halle: Max Niemeyer, 1876); Wilhelm Herrmann, *Die Religion im Verhältnis zum Welterkennen und zur Sittlichkeit* (Halle: Max Niemeyer, 1879); Wilhelm Herrmann, 'Der evangelische Glaube und die Theologie Albr. Ritschls', in *Gesammelte Aufsätze*, ed. F. W. Schmidt (Tübingen: J. C. B. Mohr, 1923), 1–25; Hermann Timm, *Theorie und Praxis in der Theologie Albrecht Ritschls und Wilhelm Herrmanns* (Gütersloh: Gerd Mohn, 1967), 98; Gustav Ecke, *Die theologische Schule Albrecht Ritschls und die Evangelische Kirche der Gegenwart* (Berlin: Reuther & Reichard, 1897); Johannes Rathje, *Die Welt des freien Protestantismus: Ein Beitrag zur deutsch-evangelischen Geistesgeschichte, dargestellt an Leben und Werk von Martin Rade* (Stuttgart: Ehrenfried Klotz Verlag, 1952), 102–3.

12 Wilhelm Herrmann, *Faith and Morals*, trans. Donald Matheson and Robert W. Stewart (New York, NY: G. P. Putnam's Sons, 1904); Wilhelm Herrmann, 'Kants Bedeutung für das Christentum', in *Schriften zur Grundlegung der Theologie*, vol. 1., ed. Peter Fischer-Appelt (Munich: Chr. Kaiser Verlag, 1966), 104–22; Wilhelm Herrmann, 'Hermann Cohens Ethik', 'Die Auffassung der Religion in Cohens und Natorps Ethik', and 'Der Begriff der Religion nach Hermann Cohen', in *Schriften zur Grundlegung der Theologie*, vol. 2., ed. Peter Fischer-Appelt (Munich: Chr. Kaiser Verlag, 1967), 88–113, 206–32, 318–23; Wilhelm Herrmann, 'Die Auffassung der Religion in Cohens and Natorps Ethik', in *Gesammelte Schriften*, ed. Friedrich Wilhelm Schmidt (Tübingen: J. C. B. Mohr, 1923), 377–405; Wilhelm Herrmann, *Ethik*, 5th ed. (Tübingen: J. C. B. Mohr, 1921), 90–6; Theodor Mahlmann, 'Das Axiom des Erlebnisses bei Wilhelm Herrmann', *Neue Zeitschrift für systematische Theologie und Religionsphilosophie* 4, no. 1 (1962): 11–18; Peter Fischer-Appelt, *Metaphysik im Horizont der Theologie Wilhelm Herrmanns* (Munich: Chr. Kaiser, 1965); Paul Natorp, *Religion innerhalb der Grenzen der Humanität*, 2nd ed. (Tübingen: J. C. B. Mohr, 1908).

13 Ernst Troeltsch, 'Historical and Dogmatic Method in Theology', trans. Ephraim Fischoff, in *Religion in History*, ed. James Luther Adams (Minneapolis, MN: Fortress Press, 1991), 10–32; Wilhelm Herrmann, 'Die Bedeutung der Geschichtlichkeit Jesu für den Glauben: Eine Besprechung des gleichnamigen Vortrags von Ernst Troeltsch', in *Schriften zur Grundlegung*, vol. 2., 282–9. See Wilhelm Herrmann, 'Die Lage und Aufgabe der evangelischen Dogmatik in der Gegenwart', in *Gesammelte Aufsätze*, 95–6, 126–38; reprinted in Wilhelm Herrmann, *Schriften zur Grundlegung*, vol. 1, 1–89.

14 Ernst Troeltsch, *Gesammelte Schriften*, 4 vols. (Tübingen: J. C. B. Mohr, 1912–1925); Ernst Troeltsch, 'Christianity and the History of Religion', in *Religion in*

History, 78–83; Ernst Troeltsch, 'Historical and Dogmatic Method in Theology', trans. Ephraim Fischoff, and 'The Dogmatics of the History-of-Religions School', trans. Walter E. Wyman, Jr., in *Religion in History*, 11–32, 87–108; Ernst Troeltsch, 'Geschichte und Metaphysik', *Zeitschrift für Theologie und Kirche* 8 (1898): 1–69.

15 Ernst Troeltsch, *Die Absolutheit des Christentums und die Religionsgeschichte* (Tübingen: J. C. B. Mohr, 1902), English edition, *The Absoluteness of Christianity and the History of Religions*, trans. David Reid (Louisville, KY: Westminster John Knox Press, 2005), 45–59, 67–94; Heinrich Rickert, *Die Grenzen der naturwissenschaftlichen Begriffsbildung: Eine logische Einleitung in die historischen Wissenschaften* (Tübingen: J. C. B. Mohr, 1902); Heinrich Rickert, *Kulturwissenschaft und Naturwissenschaft* (Tübingen: J. C. B. Mohr, 1921); Heinrich Rickert, *Zur Lehre von der Definition* (Tübingen: J. C. B. Mohr, 1915).

16 Ernst Troeltsch, *The Social Teaching of the Christian Churches*, 2 vols., trans. Olive Wyon (Louisville, KY: Westminster John Knox Press, 1992); Troeltsch, 'Die Bedeutung des Protestantismus für die Enstehung der modernen Welt', *Historische Zeitschrift* 97 (1906): 1–66; English edition, Troeltsch, *Protestantism and Progress: The Significance of Protestantism for the Rise of the Modern World*, trans. J. Montgomery (Philadelphia, PA: Fortress Press, 1986).

17 Troeltsch, *Historismus und seine Probleme*, 677, 765–7; Troeltsch, *Christian Thought*, 123–36, 218–22; Robert Rubanowice, *Crisis in Consciousness: The Thought of Ernst Troeltsch* (Tallahassee: Florida State University Press, 1982), 62–98.

18 Troeltsch, *Historismus und seine Probleme*, 702–20; Troeltsch, *Christian Thought*, 121–44.

19 Karl Barth, *Protestant Theology in the Nineteenth Century: Its Background and History* (Valley Forge, PA: Judson Press, 1973), 425–73, 654ff; Paul Tillich, *A History of Christian Thought* (New York, NY: Simon and Schuster, 1968), 411–31, 504–19.

20 Reinhold Niebuhr, *Moral Man and Immoral Society* (New York, NY: Scribners, 1932); Reinhold Niebuhr, *An Interpretation of Christian Ethics* (New York, NY: Harper & Brothers, 1935); Reinhold Niebuhr, 'Reply to Interpretation and Criticism', in *Reinhold Niebuhr: His Religious, Social, and Political Thought*, ed. Charles W. Kegley and Robert W. Bretall (New York, NY: Macmillan, 1956), 441; Reinhold Niebuhr, 'The Quality of Our Lives', *The Christian Century* 77, no. 19 (11 May 1960): 568.

Bibliography

Barth, Karl. *Protestant Theology in the Nineteenth Century: Its Background and History.* Valley Forge, PA: Judson Press, 1973.

Baur, F. C. *Ausgewählte Werke in Einzelausgaben*, vol. 1, edited by Klaus Scholder. Stuttgart: Friedrich Fromann Verlag, 1963.

Baur, F. C. *Das Christenthum und die christliche Kirche der drei ersten Jahrhunderte.* Tübingen: L. F. Fues, 1853.

Baur, F. C. *Die christliche Gnosis, oder die christliche Religions-Philosophie in ihrer geschichtlichen Entwicklung.* Tübingen: C. F. Osiander, 1835.

Dorrien, Gary. *In a Post-Hegelian Spirit: Philosophical Theology as Idealist Discontent.* Waco, TX: Baylor University Press, 2020.

Dorrien, Gary. *Kantian Reason and Hegelian Spirit: The Idealistic Logic of Modern Theology.* Oxford: Wiley-Blackwell, 2012.

Dorrien, Gary. *The Word as True Myth: Interpreting Modern Theology.* Louisville, KY: Westminster John Knox Press, 1997.

Ecke, Gustav. *Die theologische Schule Albrecht Ritschls und die Evangelische Kirche der Gegenwart.* Berlin: Reuther & Reichard, 1897.

Fischer-Appelt, Peter. *Metaphysik im Horizont der Theologie Wilhelm Herrmanns.* Munich: Chr. Kaiser, 1965.

Harnack, Adolf von. 'The Evangelical Social Mission in the Light of the History of the Church'. In Adolf von Harnack and Wilhelm Herrmann, *Essays on the Social Gospel*. Translated by G. M. Craik. New York: G. P. Putnam's Sons, 1907.

Harnack, Adolf von. *History of Dogma.* Translated by Neil Buchanan. 7 vols. Boston, MA: Little, Brown, and Company, 1905.

Harnack, Adolf von. *What Is Christianity?* Translated by Thomas Bailey Saunders. Philadelphia, PA: Fortress Press, 1957. First published 1900.

Harris, Horton. *The Tübingen School: A Historical and Theological Investigation of the School of F. C. Baur.* Grand Rapids, MI: Baker Book House, 1990.

Hegel, G. W. F. *Lectures on the Philosophy of Religion*, vol. 3, edited by Peter C. Hodgson. Translated by R. F. Brown, Peter C. Hodgson and J. M. Stewart. Berkeley: University of California Press, 1985.

Herrmann, Wilhelm. 'Der evangelische Glaube und die Theologie Albr. Ritschls'. In Wilhelm Herrmann, *Gesammelte Aufsätze 1–25*, edited by F. W. Schmidt. Tübingen: J. C. B. Mohr, 1923.

Herrmann, Wilhelm. 'Die Auffassung der Religion in Cohens und Natorps Ethik'. In *Gesammelte Schriften*, edited by Friedrich Wilhelm Schmidt, 377–405. Tübingen: J. C. B. Mohr, 1923.

Herrmann, Wilhelm. *Die Metaphysik in der Theologie.* Halle: Max Niemeyer, 1876.

Herrmann, Wilhelm. *Die Religion im Verhältnis zum Welterkennen und zur Sittlichkeit.* Halle: Max Niemeyer, 1879.

Herrmann, Wilhelm. *Ethik.* 5th ed. Tübingen: J. C. B. Mohr, 1921.

Herrmann, Wilhelm. *Faith and Morals.* Translated by Donald Matheson and Robert W. Stewart. New York: G. P. Putnam's Sons, 1904.

Herrmann, Wilhelm. *Schriften zur Grundlegung der Theologie*, vol. 1, edited by Peter Fischer-Appelt. Munich: Chr. Kaiser Verlag, 1966.

Herrmann, Wilhelm. *Schriften zur Grundlegung der Theologie*, vol. 2, edited by Peter Fischer-Appelt. Munich: Chr. Kaiser Verlag, 1967.

Lagarde, Paul A. de. *Gesammelte abhandlungen*. Leipzig: F. A. Brockhaus, 1866.
Lagarde, Paul A. de. *Librorum Veteris Testamenti canonicorum*. Göttingen: Prostat in aedibus Dieterichianus Arnoldi Hoyer, 1883.
Lagarde, Paul A. de. *Onomastica sacra*. Hildesheim: G. Olms, 1887.
Lagarde, Paul A. de. *Schriften für das deutsche Volk*. Munich: J. F. Lehmann, 1934. First published 1878.
Luther, Martin. 'The Babylonian Captivity of the Church'. In *Martin Luther's Basic Theological Writings*, 267–313, edited by Timothy F. Lull. Minneapolis, MN: Fortress Press, 1989.
Mahlmann, Theodor. 'Das Axiom des Erlebnisses bei Wilhelm Herrmann'. *Neue Zeitschrift für systematische Theologie und Religionsphilosophie* 4, no. 1 (1962): 11–88.
Natorp, Paul. *Religion innerhalb der Grenzen der Humanität*. 2nd ed. Tübingen: J. C. B. Mohr, 1908.
Niebuhr, Reinhold. *An Interpretation of Christian Ethics*. New York, NY: Harper & Brothers, 1935.
Niebuhr, Reinhold. *Moral Man and Immoral Society*. New York, NY: Scribners, 1932.
Niebuhr, Reinhold. 'The Quality of Our Lives'. *The Christian Century* 77, no. 19 (11 May 1960): 568–72.
Niebuhr, Reinhold. 'Reply to Interpretation and Criticism'. In *Reinhold Niebuhr: His Religious, Social, and Political Thought*, 434–6, edited by Charles W. Kegley and Robert W. Bretall. New York, NY: Macmillan, 1956.
Nowak, Kurt, Otto Gerhard Oexle, Trutz Rendtorff and Kurt-Victor Selge, eds. *Adolf von Harnack: Christentum, Wissenschaft und Gesellschaft*. Göttingen: Vandenhoeck & Ruprecht, 2003.
Rathje, Johannes. *Die Welt des freien Protestantismus: Ein Beitrag zur deutsch-evangelischen Geistesgeschichte, dargestellt an Leben und Werk von Martin Rade*. Stuttgart: Ehrenfried Klotz Verlag, 1952.
Rendtorff, Rolf. 'Die jüdische Bibel und ihre antijüdische Auslegung'. In *Auschwitz: Krise der christlichen Theologie: Eine Vortragsreihe*, 99–116, edited by Rolf Rendtorff and Ekkehard Stegemann. Munich: Christian Kaiser, 1980.
Rickert, Heinrich. *Die Grenzen der naturwissenschaftlichen Begriffsbildung: Eine logische Einleitung in die historischen Wissenschaften*. Tübingen: J. C. B. Mohr, 1902.
Rickert, Heinrich. *Kulturwissenschaft und Naturwissenschaft*. Tübingen: J. C. B. Mohr, 1921.
Rickert, Heinrich. *Zur Lehre von der Definition*. Tübingen: J. C. B. Mohr, 1915.
Ritschl, Albrecht. *The Christian Doctrine of Justification and Reconciliation*, edited by H. R. Mackintosh and A. B. Macaulay. Edinburgh: T. & T. Clark, 1902.
Ritschl, Albrecht. *Die Entstehung der altkatholischen Kirche*. Bonn: Adolph Marcus, 1850.
Ritschl, Otto. *Albrecht Ritschls Leben*. 2 vols. Freiburg: J. C. B. Mohr, 1892–1896.
Rubanowice, Robert. *Crisis in Consciousness: The Thought of Ernst Troeltsch*. Tallahassee: Florida State University Press, 1982.

Silberman, Lou H. 'Wellhausen and Judaism'. *Semeia* 25 (1982): 75–82.
Tillich, Paul. *A History of Christian Thought*. New York, NY: Simon and Schuster, 1968.
Timm, Hermann. *Theorie und Praxis in der Theologie Albrecht Ritschls und Wilhelm Herrmanns*. Gütersloh: Gerd Mohn, 1967.
Troeltsch, Ernst. *Christian Thought: Its History and Application*, edited by F. von Hügel. New York, NY: Meridian Books, 1957. First published 1923 by University of London Press (London).
Troeltsch, Ernst. *Der Historismus und seine Probleme*. Berlin: Rolf Heise, 1924.
Troeltsch, Ernst. *Der Historismus und seine Überwindung*. Berlin: Rolf Heise, 1924. English edition.
Troeltsch, Ernst. *Die Absolutheit des Christentums und die Religionsgeschichte*. Tübingen: J. C. B. Mohr, 1902. English edition, *The Absoluteness of Christianity and the History of Religions*. Translated by David Reid. Louisville, KY: Westminster John Knox Press, 2005.
Troeltsch, Ernst. 'Die Bedeutung des Protestantismus für die Enstehung der modernen Welt'. *Historische Zeitschrift* 97 (1906): 1–66. English edition, Troeltsch, *Protestantism and Progress: The Significance of Protestantism for the Rise of the Modern World*. Translated by J. Montgomery. Philadelphia, PA: Fortress Press, 1986.
Troeltsch, Ernst. *Gesammelte Schriften*. 4 vols. Tübingen: J. C. B. Mohr, 1912–1925.
Troeltsch, Ernst. 'Geschichte und Metaphysik'. *Zeitschrift für Theologie und Kirche* 8 (1898): 1–69.
Troeltsch, Ernst. *Religion in History*. Edited by James Luther Adams. Minneapolis, MN: Fortress Press, 1991.
Troeltsch, Ernst. *The Social Teaching of the Christian Churches*. 2 vols. Translated by Olive Wyon. Louisville, KY: Westminster John Knox Press, 1992.
Zahn-Harnack, Agnes von. *Adolf von Harnack*. 2nd ed. Berlin: Walter de Gruyter, 19.

Part Two

Travels through space

3

Historicism and positivism in sociology: From Weimar Germany to the contemporary United States

George Steinmetz

Abstract

This chapter traces the relations between the words 'historicism' and 'positivism' and underlying epistemological ideas associated with them since the 1880s. By retracing the encounters between historicism and positivism specifically in the social sciences, the chapter encourages modern scholars to renew their interest in what modern historicism had to offer as a counterbalance to the persistent pressure of positivism.

Introduction

Raymond Williams wrote that positivism is a 'swear-word by which nobody is swearing', but he immediately added that 'the real argument is still there'.[1] Conflicts around positivism continue to roil the social sciences. The same can be said of 'historicism', a word that has long been used a weapon. Here too there are still 'real arguments' around the epistemic assumptions associated with the concept of historicism, even when the word itself is not used. This chapter will examine these two concepts and the fundamental social scientific positions they designate. I will argue that the historicism and positivism have tended to move together since the 1880s. They usually figure as semantic opposites. Most importantly, the epistemic stances to which these words refer have long structured the deepest polarizations within social scientific fields, starting with the so-called 'conflict over methods' in German economics in the 1880s. The polarization became more explicit during the Weimar Republic, when the terms *Historismus* and *Positvismus* attained their clearest and most polarized definitions. By contrast, the word 'historicism' played a different and subordinate role in the postwar positivism dispute in German sociology, having been radically and idiosyncratically redefined in the meantime by Karl Popper, one of the key figures in the dispute.[2] Surprisingly, the terms 'historicism' and 'positivism' reemerged as opposites in American sociology during the 1980s and 1990s. Here they are understood in terms nearly identical to the Weimar discussion.

According to Rothacker, the word *Historismus* 'was already widespread in the middle of the nineteenth century'.[3] The earliest evidence for use of the word *Historismus* in German has been traced to Friedrich Schlegel.[4] Yet the word had extremely heterogeneous meanings. At the same time, a variety of authors (Möser, Herder, Humboldt and Savigny) expressed epistemic positions that foreshadowed post-1880s German anti-naturalist philosophy and 1920s sociological historicism, even if the word *Historismus* was not systematically used to describe these views.[5] The word *Historismus* then disappeared, only to reemerge in Carl Menger's polemic against the German historical school of economics in 1884, *Die Irrthümer des Historismus in der deutschen Nationalökonomie* (The Errors of Historicism in the German School of National Economics).[6] The so-called *Methodenstreit* in German economics involved a conflict between the 'younger historical school of German national economics', led by Gustav Schmoller, and the generalizing, abstract approach associated with Menger. Although Schmoller did not describe his own position as 'historicist' but simply as 'historical', Menger's label stuck.[7]

By 1922 Ernst Troeltsch wrote that Historismus was in a crisis, perhaps a terminal one.[8] Yet Troeltsch defended historicism against positivism throughout *Der Historismus und seine Probleme*. Other social scientists and humanists have continued to deploy the word 'historicism', and even more importantly, they have drawn on the basic ideas encompassed in the modern reformulation of historicism.[9] As with positivism, the real argument around historicism is still there.

Social scientists rarely discuss epistemology or ontology explicitly. More often, they engage in intradisciplinary conflicts by drawing on subcutaneous, spontaneous theories of science. Bourdieu perceptively remarked that a map of the US sociology field would be mainly structured around epistemological differences, rather than, say, theoretical or political differences.[10] But these epistemic assumptions often lie deeply buried in scholars' scientific unconscious and scholarly habitus.[11] Epistemological battles are carried out in obscure and shadowy theatres and are couched in languages of euphemism, deflection, denial and vulgar insult.[12] This chapter is part of a broader effort to entice some of these murky specimens out of hiding and into the light of day.

The most profound disagreement among contemporary social scientists is one that opposes modern historicism and modern positivism. Positivism and historicism capture a basic polarization of the Weimar and contemporary American sociological fields more accurately than terms such as 'positivism versus nonpositivism' or 'quantitative versus qualitative sociology'.

This may seem like a surprising claim, given the obvious disagreement on definitions of the words 'historicism' and 'positivism'. But as I will argue here, there has been widespread agreement about these definitions among sociologists, in both the Weimar Republic and the contemporary United States.[13] Definitions of concepts are specific to time, place and discipline or intellectual field, as the German history of concepts project has long shown. Yet this does not prevent us from discerning dominant definitions in particular situations, or from comparing these definitions to our own contemporary understandings. This polarization may also seem startling to readers accustomed to thinking of both terms as meaning the same thing: 'fact grubbing' empiricism ('*Faktenhuberei*').[14] This elision of the two terms, however, 'contradicts the self-understanding of historicism'. As philosopher Manfred Riedel pointed out, the opposition to positivism was part of 'the fixed inventory of the mode of thought of the nineteenth-century "historical school"'.[15] This elision also contradicts the self-understanding of philosophical positivism since Comte, which was oriented towards discovering abstract, general laws and was therefore sharply opposed to a naïve empiricism.

As suggested by other chapters in this volume, historicism has had a strong presence in the humanities, including philosophy, history, theology, art history and literary criticism. In the social sciences, historicism has been most explicitly represented within German economics, law, ethnology, political theory and sociology before 1933.[16] I focus here on sociology in the Weimar Republic, which was one of the most exciting moments in the discipline's history[17] and the moment at which historicism was defended most explicitly. Broadly speaking, German sociology produced the most sustained defence of historicist and culturalist sociology, while US sociology has long produced the most influential forms of non-historical, non-cultural positivism. I look at thinkers who have tried to formulate careful definitions of both terms, historicism and positivism. It is important to keep in mind that we are talking about 'modern' historicism as it was redefined between 1900 and 1933, rather than Ranke's historical method or Popper's drastic redefinition of historicism. By the same token, I am speaking of 'modern' social science positivism as it was understood in German sociology before 1933, and in the United States since roughly the 1960s, rather than Comte's positivism, logical positivism or the 'positivism' of historians' untheoretical fact-mongering.

In the rest of this chapter, I first briefly examine the frequency of these two terms in German social science between 1890 and 1933. I also briefly examine the American sociology and history disciplines in the twentieth century. This selection of 'cases' makes sense. There has been a great deal of emigration and 'remigration' of positivist and historicist ideas and scholars between these two countries since the 1930s. Troeltsch and other Weimar scholars saw the United States, UK, and France as the heartland of modern positivism and Germany as the seedbed of modern historicism. My main findings in this section are: (1) the word 'historicism' appeared and moved together with 'positivism' in Weimar social science; (2) the word 'positivism' was much more familiar to American sociologists than the word 'historicism' until the 1980s; and (3) since the 1980s, the two terms have tended to appear together in American sociological discourse. This is a somewhat startling echo of the Weimar period, especially since most US sociologists are unaware of the repetition. My explanation for the first finding is that sociologists have usually defined historicism as the antonym of positivism. My explanation for the second finding is that American scholarship, even in the humanities, has been powerfully subjected to positivist understandings of knowledge. And I explain the adoption of the historicism versus positivism polarity in recent US sociology in terms of a belated emergence of Weimar sociological constellations, which migrated to the United States after 1993 but long remained in submerged 'exile' there.[18]

This quantitative exercise can only provide a superficial introduction. The rest of the chapter looks more closely, first, at definitions of historicism and positivism (parts 2 and 3), in order to discern the ways different authors respond to their contemporaries and predecessors. I identify an overall shift in definitions starting around 1880, when the polarization between historicism and positivism began to harden and the meanings of the two terms began to approach the forms I call 'modern historicism' and 'modern positivism'. These concepts are neither averages, nor 'ideal types', but are 'real type' concepts, extracted from the writings of contemporaries.[19] The chapter's last section looks at the reception of historicism in German sociology and its elimination after 1933.

Historicism and positivism in American and German sociology and history

As a first approach to these questions, we might want to know how familiar the words 'historicism' and 'positivism' were to contemporary social scientists and historians. Here we need to pay attention to timing, since the two words entered different languages and disciplines at different moments. For Germany I focus on the 1890–1933 period, the high point of interest in historicism among social scientists. Another reason for focusing on this period is that historicist sociology was eviscerated in Nazi Germany and disparaged in postwar Germany. This helps explain some of the peculiar vicissitudes of the word 'historicism' after 1945.

Let's first examine the number of mentions of the words *Historismus* and *Positivismus* in the *Archiv für Sozialwissenschaft und Sozialpolitik* between 1888 (when it was still called *Archiv für soziale Gesetzgebung und Statistik*) and 1933, when it suspended publication.[20] This was the most influential social science journal in Wilhelmine and Weimar Germany. It was founded by Max Weber, Werner Sombart and Edgar Jaffé; its other editors were Alfred Weber, Joseph Schumpeter and Emil Lederer.

The first observation about Figure 1 is that the two words were used with some frequency. Moreover, historicism and positivism moved in tandem. Mentions of both words rose after the journal's editorship was taken over by Sombart and Weber in 1904. Sombart was even more strongly opposed than his teacher Schmoller to positivism, arguing that economists should not focus on general or repeated events but on the unique, singular, concrete and individual.[21] Weber famously adopted the neo-Kantian philosophical position of Heinrich Rickert concerning the differences between the natural and human sciences, including the possibility of explaining unique events or 'historical individuals'. Weber attacked the 'wrong-headed claim of historians who argue that scientific knowledge is identical with uncovering laws'.[22]

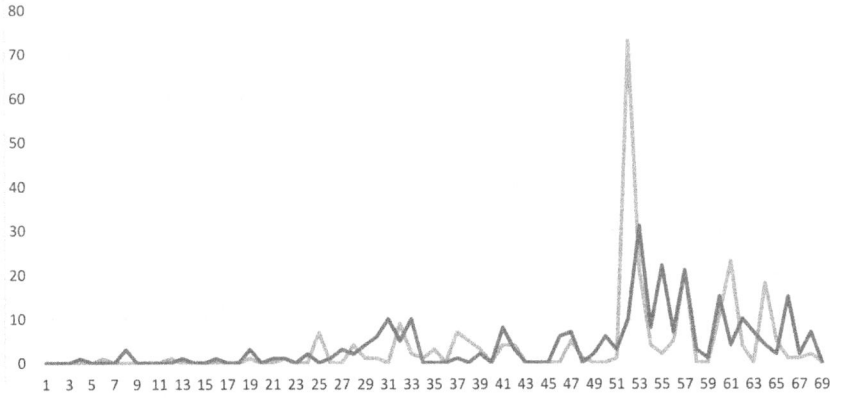

Figure 1 **Number of mentions per volume of the words** *Historismus* **(grey) and** *Positivismus* **(black), plus declensions,** *Archiv für Sozialwissenschaft und Sozialpolitik* **(vols. 1–69, 1888–1933).** Generated using JSTOR.

Sociological interest in historicism peaked during the early 1920s around the relevant publications by Troeltsch and Mannheim. Mentions then slowly tapered off until the demise of the Weimar Republic.[23]

As discussed below, German sociology moved sharply away from historicism after 1933, and this continued after 1945. Although the *Archiv* was never refounded, the *Kölner Zeitschrift* was recreated, but it was still controlled by Leopold von Wiese, whose opposition to historical sociology remained unshaken. A new sociology journal, *Soziale Welt*, was launched in 1949, but the word 'historicism' has been mentioned only 26 times since then, and has never been used in the title of an article.[24] Other sociology journals did not begin publishing until the 1970s (*Soziologie, Zeitschrift für Soziologie, Leviathan*). Here again the word *Historismus* was almost never used. The engagement with historicism, in other words, virtually disappeared from most German sociology after 1933.

American sociology reveals a very different pattern (Figure 2). In the oldest journal of sociology, *American Journal of Sociology (AJS)*, the words 'historicism' and 'historicist' have *never* appeared in the title of a single article or book review. And while the word *historicism* (with its various declensions) has been used 198 times since the journal's beginnings, *positivism* has been mentioned 947 times.[25] Use of the previously unfamiliar word *historicism* peaked during the mid-1980s,

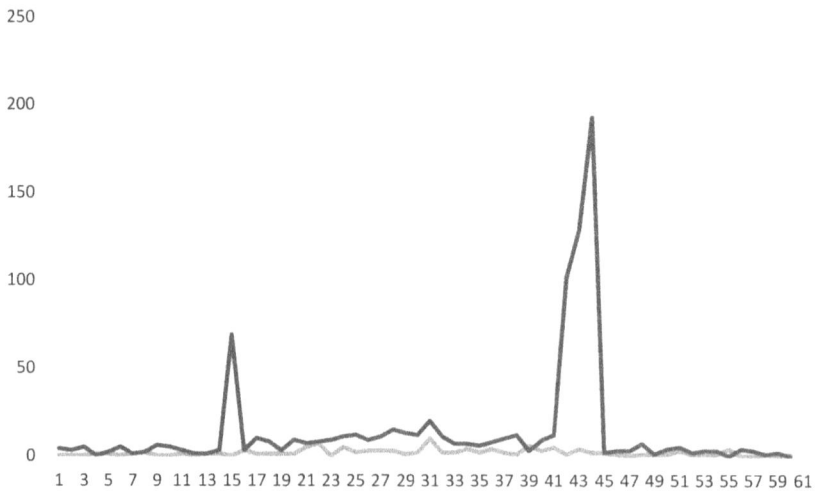

Figure 2 Number of mentions per issue of the words 'historicism'/'historicist' (grey) and 'positivism' (black), *American Journal of Sociology*, **1956–2015.** Generated using JSTOR.

when historical sociology was roiled by conflicts around efforts to align it with the precepts of methodological positivism.[26]

History journals suggest a different contrast between the United States and Germany. Articles and book reviews in the *American Historical Review* used the terminology of positivism 699 times and historicism 518 times between 1895 and 2014.[27] German historians, by contrast, mention historicism more often than positivism. Articles and book reviews in *Historische Zeitschrift* used the word *Historismus* (plus declensions) 812 times in the same time span (1895–2014), while the word *Positivismus* (plus declensions) was used 684 times. These numbers suggest two hypotheses. First, the conflict within sociology between historicism and positivism is often homologous with the relation between the history and sociology disciplines. In Germany, historians and sociologists only interacted intensively during the Nazi period, whereas the high point of interdisciplinary interaction in the United States was the 1970s–1980s.[28] Most historians in Wilhelmine and Weimar Germany were adamant about distinguishing their work from sociology, and vice versa. Second, American historians are located between US sociologists and German historians in terms of their use of the two keywords. They seem to be pulled towards the positivist pole by the general field of the human and social sciences, which tilts more towards positivism in the United States.

This quantitative exercise would have little meaning without a closer reading of the authors and their arguments.

Historicism

It is crucial to historicize historicism in the present context. Historicism continued to evolve during the 1880s, with each author adding or subtracting certain elements of preceding definitions, disagreeing with some and agreeing with other aspects of predecessors. But there was some convergence around a set of precepts that I characterize as *modern historicism*.[29] To understand this redefined concept, we need first to briefly examine some of the central features of the older historicism(s). Here again, I focus on Germany, for reasons of space, and because the German social science historicists mainly drew on German predecessors.

The three central tenets of historicism in general are the omnipresence of historical change, individualization and holism.[30] According to Ankersmit, classical historicism is an attitude 'centred around history, which saw most spheres of intellectual life as permeated by history'. Historicism insists that the 'nature of a thing is to be found in its history'.[31] As Troeltsch argued, historicism entails the 'fundamental historicization of all of our thinking about mankind, its culture and its values.' According to Annette Wittkau, historicism is 'nothing other than the ... process of becoming conscious of the historical genesis (*Gewordenheit*) of man and the world'.[32] Historicism was not just about the past, but was the study of the human world in general, including the present, construed as a historically produced moment.

What is classical historicism's understanding of historical change? Herder's historicism already broke with the idea that 'there is a single uniform set of values for all nations', and that they would all follow the same evolutionary path, although he allowed that 'each nation takes from the past, and gives to posterity, according to its own individual nature'.[33] This vision still contained an idea of progress, but Herder was writing before the Napoleonic occupation of Germany, which led many German thinkers to reject the idea of universal progress. As Mannheim argued, German Romanticism and historicism were responses to the French Revolution and its vision of universal historical progress through ever-increasing rationality.[34] Early German historicism rejected stadial accounts of history and universal theories of social evolution, and this included the account of three fixed stages by the founder of Positivism, Augste Comte. One hundred and fifty years after Herder, Alfred Weber argued that the unity of world history had to be broken up in a plurality of world-historical cultures.[35] As Gary Dorrien points out in his contribution to this volume, Troeltsch's last book also relinquished the dream of universal history. Progress had been dealt another set of severe blows in the meantime by the First World War and its aftermath, and by the widely read *Der Untergang des Abendlandes* (1918–1923) by Oswald Spengler.[36] Historicists used concepts like 'development' (*Entwicklung*) or 'particular development' to counter the rationalist-teleological notion of the idea of progress and as alternatives to the natural science conception of evolution.[37]

This turn away from the idea of progress was accompanied by the further deepening of the historicity of historicism, embodied in new accounts of human subjectivity and practice in Nietzsche, Dilthey and Husserl, and the wider trends of *Lebensphilosophie*.[38] Social processes were no longer simply seen merely as being historical but as being fully processual, even 'in their molecular structure', as Freyer put it.[39] Historical social process, according to Alfred Weber, had to be conceived of as a 'life stream' (*Lebensstrom*), not as a snapshot or a series of discrete events, much less as universal, teleological trajectories.[40] Mannheim spoke of the 'the reality of the fluid basis' (*Faktum der gleitenden Basis*) in human existence, in thought, in philosophy', defending a position he called 'dynamic relationalism'.[41] These positions differed not only from teleological narratives of historical progress but from positivism, which requires ontological stability in order to ground its 'constant conjunctions of events' or 'covering laws'.

The second feature of historicism in both its older and modern forms is that it is *individualizing*. Meinecke identified the 'essence of historicism [in] the substitution of a process of individualising observation for a generalizing view of human forces in history'.[42] The individual subject of history is 'irrational', in the language of the time, insofar as it cannot be fully described by concepts or explained by general causal laws. Hegel had already spoken of world historical individuals making history, and Nietzsche emphasized 'the importance of individuality in history'.[43] But historicist individualization was not restricted to great men. In the older historicism, individualization was often linked to highly specific contexts and places, monarchies, nation states or 'geographic individuals'. As Tessitore writes,

> Individuality has a double meaning in historicism. On the one hand, it refuses to permit an abstract universalism to which individualities are subsumed. On the other hand, it understands individuality not simply as a separation from the general but more importantly as something that embodies (*trägt*) and realizes the general.[44]

According to Carlo Antoni, 'the historico-social sciences' had been 'emancipated by the work of the Historical School' – emancipated, that is, from scientistic naturalism. But they were 'still lacking philosophical justification'.[45] A philosophical justification for the individualizing approach to the human sciences was provided by the Southwest German neo-Kantians Windelband, Lask and especially Rickert, who elaborated the concept of the 'historical individual'. An historical individual could be anything from a specific society, state, city or place, to a single event, a process or an individual person. This was a crucial intervention in creating a systematic alternative to naturalizing positivism.

Such extreme individualization might seem to stand in conflict with a third principle of historicism, *holism*. Historicists argued that a given society, culture or historical epoch is not a mere aggregate or composite of atomized realities, but an integrated whole. According to Mannheim, what historicism undertakes in the individual historico-cultural spheres is that it exhibits these different spheres of culture, not in their immanent exclusiveness, but as an integrative part of a totality ... that analyzing, atomizing, isolating tendency which dominated the other sciences and which led to the endeavor to build up the most complex structures out of the simplest elements, is being supplanted by the recognition of 'complexes' and 'totalities' as primary and irreducible data, as given, for example, in perceptions of *Gestalt*.[46]

In another essay Mannheim illustrated the difference between historicist and positivist approaches as follows:

The conservative [i.e. historicist] picture of things as a whole is like the inclusive sort of picture of a house which one might get by looking at it from all possible sides, a concrete picture of the house in all its detail from every angle. But the progressive [i.e. positivist] is not interested in all this detail; he makes straight for the ground plan of the house and his picture is suitable for rational analysis rather than for intuitive representation.[47]

As Mandelbaum wrote, 'historicism demands that we reject the view that historical events have an individual character which can be grasped apart from viewing them as embedded within a pattern of development' or a 'stream of history'.[48] Historicism often seeks to identify the dominant or core idea of an epoch or social constellation, such as liberalism, conservatism, positivism, or historicism, and then to connect acts, events and individuals to this idea. These totalities are unique configurations or assemblages, 'individual totalities', in Troeltsch's terms, and not 'essential totalities' à la Althusser.[49] Similar ideas were proposed by other historicists. The idea of cultural *constellation* was proposed by Max Weber and propagated by Alfred Weber, the idea of *figuration* was popularized by Norbert Elias and the ideas of *Gestalt* and field (*Feld*) were introduced to social science by psychologist Kurt Lewin and used by Mannheim and others. Historicist holism is thus a radical form of contextual relationalism.

Holism also means that the whole may have effects on its parts. This is related to discussions of ontological emergence. Emergent phenomena are those that can be 'said to arise out of and be sustained by more basic phenomena, while at the same time exerting some sort of "top-down" control, constraint or some other influence upon those very sustaining processes'.[50] Historicist holism thus rejects atomism or methodological individualism. This is another important link to non-positivist social science.

German historicism's transformations, c. 1880–1933

One of the important changes in historicism over the course of the nineteenth century is that it separated from its association with conservatism. Droysen, the historian who launched the most sustained historicist critique of positivism in the mid-nineteenth century, connected reactionary post-1848 Prussian politics with positivism.[51] Schmoller and other members of the historical school of economics criticized 'Manchester Liberalism' and offered a programme for reforming capitalism. Sombart rejected the idea of any objective hierarchy in the value of different nations or peoples.[52] Max Weber, a liberal, famously advocated the principle of value freedom. Alfred Weber was also a liberal but became a Social Democrat after 1945. Mannheim was close to Lukács and Marxism. Meinecke's politics followed a 'zig-zag path' between right and liberal-left over the course of different regimes and political conjunctures.[53] Historicism continued to have conservative and far right tendencies. Freyer and Schmitt collaborated with the Nazis, and Spann joined the Nazi Party. Like positivism, historicism is orthogonal to political positions in the long term and across different national and disciplinary settings. German historicism from the mid-nineteenth century onwards encompassed a strong tendency to separate politics from science in an effort to align history with scientific objectivity.[54] This makes it highly misleading to speak of an 'epistemological left' or 'epistemological right' in any universal sense.

These statements may seem surprising in light of postwar criticism of historicism. Historian Thomas Nipperdey called historicism 'unmodern, unscientific, ideological', and, most importantly here, 'reactionary'.[55] Sociologist René König, a leading 'modernizer' of postwar German sociology, attacked historicism as 'reactionary' and 'antiquarian', although he also insisted contradictorily that there was an 'almost perverse alliance' between historicism and the 'newest developments in Marxism', especially after 1945.[56] Marxist Georg Lukács suggested in 1954 that German historicism had helped to create 'a mental climate favourable to the acceptance of the Nazi mystique of the Führer', and added for good measure (and quite absurdly) that Mannheim was one of the 'forerunners' of 'Anglo-Saxon imperialism'.[57]

Mannheim and Troeltsch argued that historicism had emerged in many European countries in response to the French Revolution.[58] Mannheim explained that German historicism diverged after 1815 and became 'dynamic historicism' under the conditions of a conservative-dominated government in which the bourgeoisie was excluded from power.[59] Because the German bourgeoisie was committed to static theories of natural right, non-bourgeois conservatism was pushed towards a more dynamic vision of history. German historicism thus became attuned to the incessant flux, cultural heterogeneity and incommensurable value conflicts characteristic of emerging modernity. Rather than a life-sapping, backwards-looking antiquarianism, as Nietzsche and König argued, historicism was connected to the fluid chaos of the present.

Modern historicism accepted the key features of the older historicism: extreme historicization, individualization and holism. What was added was, first, a rigorous philosophical analysis of the problems of individualization and generalization. Three additional foci emerged: contingency and crisis; relativism; and the need for interpretation or a hermeneutic method, in addition to a causal or explanatory one.

With respect to individualization and generalization, Windelband distinguished between idiographic and nomothetic sciences, aligning history with the former.[60] The natural or nomothetic sciences subsume events under general laws, he argued, while the human or idiographic sciences analyse events as part of a specific totality or concrete universal. Windelband understood sociology as a nomothetic science, due to the positivistic orientation of most sociology at the time of his writing. Windelband's student Heinrich Rickert opened the door to a wider spectrum of possibilities between universal laws and singular events. According to Rickert, the object of the cultural sciences (*Kulturwissenschaften*) is the 'historical individual', not the average case or the general law. Mannheim called Conservatism a historical individual. This language spread to human science disciplines. Carl Ritter described the Earth as a 'cosmic individual', Emil Hözel discussed 'geographical individuals', Troeltsch suggested that the entire Earth was a 'individual singularity' (*individuelle Einmaligkeit*) and Freyer argued that reality itself was a historical individual.[61]

For Rickert, the realities studied by the natural sciences were just as singular, complex and overdetermined as those in the human sciences. The difference was located not in the scientific object itself but in epistemology: historians have an individualizing intent or value orientation, while natural scientists have a generalizing orientation. Historiography is a *Wirklichkeitswissenschaft*, a science of reality, because it deals with phenomena in all of their real concreteness, rather than abstracting from the concrete particularities of each phenomenon in order to construct a general concept, as in the natural sciences.[62] History is no less scientific than natural science, and is indeed more 'realistic', but it 'diverges logically from natural science in essential points concerning its concept formation'.[63] There may be a 'unity of science', Rickert concluded, but that unity is 'never to be understood as meaning the uniformity of all its branches' with respect to methods or scientific aims.[64]

Discussions of historicism starting in the last decades of the nineteenth century insisted on the ideas of *contingency* and *crisis*.[65] Contingency is a reformulation of the ancient Greek idea of chance and the disorder of the 'sublunary sphere', in contrast to necessity, the 'severe rule of laws, forms, and concepts'.[66] Medieval theologians assigned the idea of contingency (*contingens*) to the arbitrary and wilful interventions of God in the temporal world.[67] Contingency came then to mean the factual and accidental in contrast to conceptual necessity and lawfulness'.[68] Kant reaffirmed this ancient dualism as the necessity of categories versus the contingency of experience. The natural sciences were a world of law-like, noumenal regularities, standing in tension with the contingencies of experience and the idea of a free or self-determining will. The Kantian distinction underpinned the historicist sociologists' distinction between the law-like and ahistorical natural and logical sciences (*Naturwissenschaften* and *Logoswissenschaften*), on the one hand, and *Geisteswissenschaften* on the other.[69] In Windelband's first book in 1870 he defined contingency or accident (*Zufall*) as the 'shadow of necessity'. But necessity soon became the shadow of contingency. Windelband redeployed Schopenhauer's idea of 'relative contingency', which he distinguished from the idea of a complete lack of causality: relative contingency was not 'causeless' (*ursachenlos*) but 'lawless' (*gesetzlos*). Relative contingency did not negate causality, but pointed to the irregular, unexpected, singular forms of overdetermination, the tying together (*Verknüpfung*) of two facts that are each themselves 'fully caused', though not by the same causal determinant.[70]

According to Troeltsch, the 'full meaning of contingency' was only recognized once the irrational was introduced into the heart of rationality. This occurred across various philosophies and theories starting with Nietzsche. Max Weber focused on the omnipresence of 'irrational' values (habit, tradition and 'value rationality') alongside formal rationality in 'social action'. More significantly, Weber introduced contingency against generalization in social science.[71] Weber's first metatheoretical work, 'Roscher and Knies', criticized positivists who conflate 'necessitation and nomological regularity'.[72] Schmitt emphasized the aleatory moment in which leadership might direct society and the state in unforeseen directions.[73] Troeltsch noted that new scientific theories emphasized the mutability and contingency even of natural laws.[74] In reality, he argued, there is a plurality of laws operating simultaneously; the historical individual only becomes explicable when we take into account the joint effect of this combination of laws.[75] For Alfred Weber, social structures became constraints but not determinants of social practice, and historical prediction ('cultural prognoses') therefore became impossible. Sociology could provide some sort of 'orientation' by accounting for the complex paths leading up to the present.[76]

Epistemic contingency was linked to the idea of *crisis* in society and within sociology. Scientific crisis, for Freyer, was a 'productive chaos'.[77] Crises stemming from the coincidence of a series of singular causal paths figure in Alfred Weber's thinking as moments of *Kairos*, shaping the history of a people or nation for centuries to come.[78] Raymond Aron echoed the German sociologists in describing crises as moments of possibility.[79] Weimar-era German sociology itself came to be described as a 'crisis science'.[80] Contingency and crisis have figured centrally in theories of modernity ever since.[81]

Another feature of modern historicism is *relativism*, which has both ethical and epistemic dimensions. Ethical relativism was at the centre of the 'crisis of historicism' according to Troeltsch, and was the only aspect of modern relativism he tried to overcome. This relativism was the chief target of liberal and Marxist critics of historicism. Ethical relativism was equated with the 'anarchy of values' stemming from modernity and capitalism and from the historicist break with enlightenment philosophies. Historicism's commitment to individuality was said to lead inexorably to a relativity of values.[82] At the same time, Troeltsch insisted, recognizing the *relativity* of values was not the same thing as embracing full-scale *relativism*. The historical relativity of values has a 'certain analogy to the doctrine of psychical relativity' in Einstein, Troeltsch argued, but as in ethics, the latter was 'no unlimited relativism, since the system of relations can be calculated from each position and the relationship to the other objects can be mathematically described despite its mobility'.[83] Troeltsch adumbrated a method of immanent critique whereby values would be aligned with the commitments of a given historical community. Troeltsch also insisted that positivism and naturalism were themselves normatively relativistic, and could therefore not provide a standpoint for rejecting historicism. The fact that naturalists, despite their 'orientation towards general laws of being, always reach different conclusions' about timeless values showed how flawed their approach was, as did the fact that their 'natural laws' were always loaded with the ideals of their own national history or politics.[84] One could not answer the question of ethical relativity by embracing positivism,

Mannheim argued that modern historicism '*veers away from relativism*' by combining the value position of the observer and the observed, or as we might say today, emic and etic positions. According to Mannheim,

> The mere fact that every item of historical knowledge is determined by a particular positional perspective ... in no way implies the relativity of the knowledge so obtained. The *concrete values* which serve as a standard have *developed* in their fullness of meaning *organically out of the same historical process* which they have to help interpret ... Troeltsch introduces an idea ... that besides the application of standards based upon the historical position of perspective of the observer, *one may also describe and evaluate past epochs in terms of their own standards and values* ... Historians indeed may grasp past epochs from those epochs' own centres., a mode of interpretation called *the immanent critique and representation of the past.*[85]

This idea of the immanent critique of a historical community's values marks a clear link between interwar historicism and postwar critical theory, which seeks norms via imminent criticism of social practice.[86] Whether critical theory has been able to avoid the extremes of ethical relativism and universalism is a different question, as recent critics have suggested.[87]

Scientific relativism also provoked unease. For centuries historians and philosophers had described science as progressing inexorably. The historicity of natural science appeared as a conceptual shock, a *concept-quake*, in Nietzsche's sense, during the 1920s.[88] This relativizing approach to scientific knowledge was set in motion by a variety of intellectual and social processes, including historicism.[89] Simmel, who was both an anti-historicist and a participant in sociology's historicist turn, introduced the problem of *Nichtwissen* or non-knowledge. *Nichtwissen* was juxtaposed to knowledge, including scientific knowledge, but it also opened doorways between the two. The contextualized history of science, which emerged around 1930, showed that the most exalted forms of scientific knowledge production were permeated by factors that could be called 'non-knowledge'.[90]

Scientific relativism generated an array of efforts to rethink scientific discovery, not all of which amounted to admitting defeat and accepting that 'anything goes'. Rickert's argument that there were absolute values within given communities was relevant to the debates on ethics and science.[91] Henri Bergson and other philosophers met with Einstein in 1922 to discuss the implications of his theory for their own work, and Gaston Bachelard took Einstein's lessons to heart in his historical philosophy of science.[92] The earliest fully contextual explanations of discovery in the natural sciences appeared in the first half of the 1930s in publications by Boris Hessen, Ludwik Fleck and others.[93] Bachelard and Popper opened up the context of scientific discovery to the entire gamut of historical, social and psychological influences, even if the 'context of justification' was still, for Popper at least, subject to strict rules of falsification.[94]

A final change in historicism concerns the relationship between scientific explanation (*Erklären*) and interpretation (*Verstehen*). Interpretation was initially linked to idiographic descriptions of historical individuals, and was understood as an alternative to explanation and causal regularity. After reading Rickert, however, Weber glimpsed an alternative in which singular events could be causally explained without being fitted into a supposedly universal causal law. (As we saw above, Windelband had made a similar argument in 1870.) Weber's historical studies on ancient Rome, religion and capitalism support this reading. Weber makes causal, explanatory claims, without reducing history to law-like 'constant conjunctions of events'. Weber explains historical events as resulting from contingent, singular conjunctions or combinations of heterogeneous causal factors. Interpretation and explanation are no longer mutually exclusive here but need to be combined. Weber's conceptual introduction in *Economy and Society* ('Basic Sociological Terms') states this unequivocally: Sociology is defined here as 'a science concerning itself with the interpretive understanding of social action and thereby with a causal explanation of its course and consequences'.[95]

The discussion of historicism in German sociology came to end after 1933. But this did not mean that historicism had disappeared completely from sociology. Instead, it had migrated overseas. Before getting into that later story, however, I want to briefly survey historicism's main Other in the social sciences: positivism.

Modern Positivism and its presence in Germany

In 1909 Max Weber contrasted Historismus à la Schmoller with the 'natural science' approach to social science, and criticized the monstrous 'changelings' (*Wechselbälge*) that he said were 'spawned when "Sociology" was *raped* by technocrats schooled only in the natural sciences'.[96] This provocative comment is a good introduction to the rhetorical intensity of discussion in this domain. German historians had been riven by struggles over positivism since the second half of the nineteenth century, but historicists maintained the upper hand.[97] This configuration was transferred into the nascent field of sociology, although positivism had a stronger position there than in history discipline due to peculiarities of German sociology's nineteenth-century development.[98]

There is much disagreement nowadays among sociologists not just about the definition of positivism but its very existence. Yet while positivism has indeed has had as many different definitions as historicism,[99] there is significant convergence in definitions of 'modern' social science positivism. Neither this is Auguste Comte's original positivism, nor is it derived from logical positivism, although it is not entirely incompatible with either of those earlier positions, and to some extent emerged out of them. Social science positivism today maps closely onto the position that German historicists called positivism, starting around 1900. German sociologists were referring to the roughly same position during the 1960s 'positivism dispute'.[100]

This modern form of positivism was defined in 1908 by Edgar Jaffé, cofounder with Weber and Sombart of the *Archiv*. According to Jaffé, German idealism's earlier struggle against Comtian positivism had been overtaken by a new struggle: 'The one-sidedness of the current of thought that is individualistic and only takes note of political history in the narrow and narrowest sense led to a counter-current, promoted by the rise of the natural sciences and the formation of the theory of evolution after Darwin, which also seeks generally valid laws for history'.[101] In 1911, sociologist Max Adler labelled this approach 'modern positivism'.[102] I adopt Adler's label here. Troeltsch defined 'Anglo-French positivism' in similar terms. This approach modelled itself on the natural sciences, Troeltsch wrote, emphasizing the 'abstraction of the general law' and the reduction of peculiarities to 'general laws', the 'arranging of singles into groups', and the identification of 'successions of changes which ever repeat themselves and therefore allow for a ... prediction of the future'.[103] Positivism was also oriented towards the ideas of 'progress' and 'universal history' and adopted a 'teleological philosophy of history', even though that 'did not prevent it from despising teleology' à la Hegel.[104] Yet while positivism claimed to seek universal theories, positivists in each country tended to identify 'human progress with their own national values', Troeltsch observed: 'thus now American democracy, now English Parliamentarism, now the French glory of the Revolution are praised as the essence of humanity and of natural-lawful progress'.[105]

Modern social science positivism is first and foremost the tenet 'that all sciences, including the social sciences, are concerned with developing explanations in the form of universal laws or generalizations'.[106] Philosophers have called this position *regularity determinism* because it assumes that variables are linked to one another in universal, law like ways.[107] Positivism has been associated with this idea of historical 'constant conjunctions of events' for more than a century.[108]

Social scientific versions of positivism are also often called 'natural science' approaches, or *naturalism*. Strong versions of naturalism argue that social objects can be studied in the same way as natural objects. This is connected to the thesis of the unity of the natural and social sciences.[109] Naturalist social science often adopts methods that mimic the exact sciences. Hayek defined this mimicry as *scientism*, a 'slavish imitation' of the 'method and language' of physical science.[110]

Modern positivism often combines these first two assumptions, regularity determinism and scientistic naturalism, with a third tenet, *empiricism*. Empiricism is the position that restricts science to observables and prohibits any reference to theoretical or unobservable causes. This is one of the most confusing aspects of the differentiation between positivism and historicism, since rigorous emphasis on empirical facts was also used to define historicism à la Ranke (see above). In modern social scientific positivism, however, empiricism often plays a secondary role. One of the most influential alternatives to historicism in Weimar sociology, for example, was the *Formalism* associated with Simmel and von Wiese. This approach was organized around universal, a priori categories or social structures and was neo-Kantian, not empiricist.[111] Yet Formalist sociology was positivist in terms of the two other defining aspects of modern positivism: regularity determinism and scientific naturalism.[112] In contrast to the neo-Kantian Rickert, who did not expect the human sciences to seek general laws, formal sociology followed Kant in eschewing this distinction. As Freyer wrote, formal sociology 'denaturalizes its object profoundly; it transforms it from a reality bound to a specific temporal moment into a formation from which time has been totally removed'.[113] A different form of non-empiricist positivism in the social sciences is represented by some versions of rational choice theory.[114] Modern positivism is often ontologically atomistic. Larger social aggregates, if they are allowed at all, have no emergent properties and are merely the product of combining individual-level phenomena. At the same time, however, individual facts are not of interest in themselves, for methodological individualists, but are subsumed under general categories and fitted into law-like statements.

Modern positivism is also strongly linked to the notion of axiological neutrality or value freedom. At one extreme, positivism led to a variety of 'art history in which the word "beautiful" is not used', as Rothacker quipped.[115] As noted above, historicism was accused of relativism but was better equipped to argue for norms that, while not claiming universality, were also not arbitrary. Weber's 'value freedom' encompassed a hyper-individualistic, Nietzschean wilfulness around the selection and framing of research topics, even if values were supposed to be bracketed when carrying out empirical research.

German sociology, 1900–1933: The rise and demise of historicist historical sociology

Positivism maintained a strong presence in the nineteenth-century German human sciences, including early, pre-disciplinary sociology.[116] Yet German sociology underwent a startling transformation in the decades before 1933: positivists' dominance over the field was challenged by self-proclaimed historicists. Erich Rothacker's *Einleitung in die Geisteswissenschaften* (1920) codified the dominant struggle in the German human sciences since Hegel as pitting historicism against positivism. Sociologist Johann Plenge wrote in the *Archiv* that 'we have to humbly accept that we find ourselves in an era of Historicism and that we cannot ask for anything else'.[117] Max Scheler, the founder of German sociology of knowledge, insisted that 'our German mentality is anti-positivist and anti-utilitarian'.[118] According to Freyer, Alfred Weber immersed himself in 'modern historicism' and emerged as the leading proponent of 'cultural sociology' and 'historical sociology'.[119] In 1926 another scholar declared in the pages of the *Archiv* that that the 'positivist *Imperium* is finished ... the necessity of a revolution in our epistemological ideals is being recognized more and more'.[120] Alfred Vierkandt, who held the first sociology chair at Berlin University, aligned himself with Troeltsch and the historicists and asserted in 1926 that 'the human sciences have always been immune to positivism in their praxis'.[121] According to Vierkandt, the Austrian sociologist 'Othmar Spann was the first of the German sociologists to declare war on positivism' already in 1914, followed by 'an entire list of German sociologists such as Hans Freyer, Theodor Litt, Spranger, Ernst Troeltsch, myself, and others have come around in the meantime to this same standpoint, opposed to positivism'.[122] Von Wiese, leader of the anti-historicist camp in sociology, wrote that according to Vierkandt and others, positivism was 'accursed' (*fluchbeladen*).[123] In the years following Troeltsch's declaration that historicism was in crisis it had become dominant within German sociology.

The high point of this explicitly historicist wave was Mannheim's 'Historicism', which appeared as the lead article in the *Archiv* in 1924. Mannheim asserted here that historicism had 'developed into an intellectual force of extraordinary significance' and had become the 'real foundation' (*der wirkliche Träger*) epitomizing 'our Weltanschauung'. It was a 'principle that not only organizes the work of the cultural sciences (*Geisteswissenschaften*) like an invisible hand, but that permeates everyday life'. Historicism was 'an intellectual force with which we must come to grips, whether we want to or not. Just as in Athens, Socrates was morally obliged to define his position vis-a-vis the Sophists, because the intellectual outlook of the latter corresponded to the socio-cultural conditions of the contemporary world … so today we are under a moral obligation to seek a solution to the problem of historicism.'[124] Sociologists referred repeatedly to this essay in the remaining years of the Weimar Republic.

Nazism largely eliminated historicism within the discipline. Most of the historicists were forced into exile or to leave their teaching and research posts. Paul Eppstein, a sociologically oriented economist who used the phrase 'historicist sociology' and compared 'historicist' and 'empiricist-positivistic' forms of Marxism, was killed at Theresienstadt.[125] Another historicist sociologist, Ernst Grünfeld, was driven to suicide.[126] According to Rauschning, Hitler claimed that Nazism was 'the final step in the defeat of Historicism' and its replacement by a 'purely biological' worldview. Rauschning is unreliable as a source of direct quotes, but suggestive of Nazi understandings of historicism.[127]

Postwar West German sociology continued to distance itself from the Weimar traditions. 'Americanizing' or applied forms of sociology gained the upper hand, or rather perpetuated the Nazi-era emphasis on applied, presentist and quantitative forms of sociology.[128] Hans Albert, a postwar sociological modernizer, explained in the pages of the *Kölner Zeitschrift für Soziologie* that 'positivism was the only legitimate scientific foundation for sociology'.[129] Dietrich Rueschemeyer dismissed Karl Mannheim's 'historicist hypotheses' that could never be 'operationalized in a form appropriate to industrial-style research'.[130] Adorno formed a temporary alliance with 'Americanizing' forms of sociology in the 1950s and argued in 1952 that 'sociology is not a *Geisteswissenschaft*'.[131] But the philosopher Hans Blumenberg,[132] a philosopher who had suffered under the Nazis, wrote later that 'I have always felt the charge of "historicism" to be an honorable one.'[133]

Despite these attempts to destroy Weimar sociological historicism, it has survived to some extent outside dominant regimes of knowledge, and has had lasting effects on present-day discussions in the United States. Its influence on historical sociologists is not limited to those who are aware of the Weimar legacy.

Conclusion: From spontaneous positivism to modern historicism, and beyond

The history of social science has shown that a number of excellent social theories, concepts, works and thinkers have been collectively forgotten, often due to the conflictual dynamics that shape scientific history rather than any decisive test of strength or disconfirming evidence. This chapter has tried to construct one of these repressed memoires, in broad strokes: interwar German sociological historicism and its diasporic marginalization in exile. I have also alluded to a second site of amnesia: the fading away of explicit discussion of the philosophy of (social) science. Sociologists' indifference to philosophical grounding presents a risk of unwittingly adopting spontaneous philosophies of science without even being aware of the existence of alternatives. In the present, such spontaneous scientific philosophies tend to be 'modern positivist' ones. Contemporary forms of governmentality prioritize predictable laws of human behaviour. Capitalism structures human relations as relations between commodities, which are commensurated by the homogenizing value form. And as the natural sciences become ever better at shaping and predicting human behaviour, scholars in the social sciences and even in the humanities lose self-confidence about the distinctiveness of their objects, methods and epistemologies and are pulled towards scientism. Modern scientistic positivism is in some sense the natural default stance for scholarship lacking an explicit counter-epistemology.

Historicism was not primarily a philosophical movement, but it has the advantage for social scientists of having been linked from the start to social research. It also has the advantage over other non-positivist social epistemologies of being firmly grounded in historical research. This allows social scientists to better see how such a quasi-philosophical approach can transform, or justify, their research practices, and how they can defend themselves against the misleading charge that any approach other than positivism is non-scientific and non-explanatory. The advantage of modern historicism as a starting point becomes clear if we compare it with critical realism, one of the most powerful critiques of the positivist philosophy of science. Whatever its merits – and they are many – most critical realists have not been interested in historical research.[134] This does not mean that Rickert, Weber, Troeltsch, Mannheim or any of the others discussed in this chapter can be taken as the final word on alternatives to social science positivism. Yet social scientists could do much worse than to return to the pre-1933 *Archiv für Sozialwissenschaft und Sozialpolitik*, where these issues are discussed at a high level among specialists from various disciplines. The time is ripe to bring these debates back into the social scientific polis.

Notes

1. Raymond Williams, 'Positivist', in *Keywords* (New York: Oxford University Press, 1983), 238–9.
2. Karl R. Popper, *The Poverty of Historicism* (London: Routledge and K. Paul, 1957). On the positivism dispute see, most recently, Marius Strubenhoff, 'The Positivism Dispute in German Sociology, 1954–1970', *History of European Ideas* 44, no. 2 (2018): 260–76.
3. Erich Rothacker, 'Das Wort Historismus', *Zeitschrift für deutsche Wortforschung* 16 (1960): 3. Heussi claimed that the word came to use in only the last three decades of the nineteenth century, a point Rothacker disputes. Karl Heussi, *Die Krisis des Historismus* (Tübingen: J. C. B. Mohr, 1932), 2. Heussi is an unreliable guide to this entire discussion.
4. Georg G. Iggers, 'Historismus: Geschichte und Bedeutung eines Begriffs: eine kritische übersicht der neuesten Literatur', in *Historismus am Ende des 20. Jahrhunderts: eine internationale Diskussion*, ed. Gunter Scholtz (Berlin: Akademie-Verlag, 1997), 103. A search of WorldCat provides no hits for the word 'historicism' before 1939 in the titles of English language publications, and the majority of titles through the 1960s refer to German thinkers.
5. Frederick C. Beiser, *The German Historicist Tradition* (Oxford: Oxford University Press, 2011).
6. Heinrich Dilly, 'Entstehung und Geschichte des Begriffs "Historismus" – Funktion und Struktur einer Begriffsgeschichte', in *Geschichte allein ist zeitgemäss. Historismus in Deutschland*, ed. Michael Brix und Monika Steinhauser (Lahn-Giessen: Anabas-Verlag Kämpf, 1978), 14.
7. Carl Menger, *Die Irrthümer des Historismus in der deutschen Nationalökonomie* (Wien: A. Hölder, 1884); Gustav Schmoller, *Grundriß der allgemeinen Volkswirtschaftslehre* (Leipzig: Duncker & Humblot, 1901); there is a vast literature on the entire dispute, but see especially Erik Grimmer-Solem, *The Rise of Historical Economics and Social Reform in Germany, 1864–1894* (Oxford: Clarendon Press; 2003), ch. 7.
8. Ernst Troeltsch, 'Die Krise des Historismus', *Die Neue Rundschau* 33 (1922): 572–90.
9. On use of the language of historicism by historical sociologist Charles Tilly, see George Steinmetz, 'Charles Tilly, Historicism, and the Critical Realist Philosophy of Science', *American Sociologist* 41, no. 4 (2010): 312–36.
10. I confirmed this hypothesis in my analyses of American sociology and it has been reconfirmed quantitatively in a recent study of US sociology using correspondence analysis: Tomasz Warczok and Stephanie Beyer, 'Between the Global and the Local. The Field of American Sociology', forthcoming.

11 I first proposed the notion of a *positivist unconscious* in American sociology in a paper entitled 'The Long Revolution in Sociology's Positivist Unconscious: A History of the Present', at the meetings of the Social Science History Association in 1999. The concept was developed further in subsequent publications; George Steinmetz, 'The Genealogy of a Positivist Haunting: Comparing Prewar and Postwar U.S. Sociology', *boundary 2*, vol. 32, no, 2 (2005): 107–33.

12 For a recent heavy-handed example, see Kieran Healy, 'Fuck Nuance', *Sociological Theory* 35, no. 2 (2017): 118–27. For an earlier polemic against non-positivist social science, see Ludwig von Mises, 'Soziologie und Geschichte', *Archiv für Sozialwissenschaft und Sozialpolitik* 61 (1929): 465–512. For a simplistic dismissal of any alternative to positivism as inherently anti-scientific, see James S. House, 'The Culminating Crisis of American Sociology and Its Role in Social Science and Public Policy: An Autobiographical, Multimethod, Reflexive Perspective', *Annual Review of Sociology* 45 (2019): 1–26.

13 Edward Kiser and Michael Hechter argue that 'comparative-historical sociologists have serious methodological disagreements: some are best considered historicists, whereas others are generalists'. Kiser and Hechter's 'Generalists', as I will argue below, are modern positivists. Edgar Kiser and Michael Hechter, 'The Role of General Theory in Comparative-Historical Sociology', *American Journal of Sociology* 97 (1997): 10.

14 Michael Schlott, 'Mythen, Mutationen und Lexeme. "Historismus als Kategorie der Geschichts- und Literaturwissenschaft', *Scientia poetica: Jahrbuch für Geschichte der Literatur und der Wissenschaften* 3 (1999): 163. For a nuanced discussion of the conflation of positivism and historicism, see Manfred Riedel, 'Positivismuskritik und Historismus. Über den Ursprung des Gegensatzes von Erklären und Verstehen im 19. Jahrhundert', in *Positivismus im 19. Jahrhundert. Beiträge zu seiner geschichtlichen und systematischen Bedeutung*, ed. Jürgen Blühdorn und Joachim Ritter (Frankfurt a. M.: V. Kostermann, 1971), 81–91.

15 Riedel, 'Positivismuskritik', 81.

16 On the multidisciplinary reach of German historicism see Annette Wittkau, *Historismus: Zur Geschichte des Begriffs und des Problems* (Göttingen: Vandenhoeck & Ruprecht, 1992).

17 David Kettler and Colin Loader, 'Weimar Sociology', in *Weimar Thought: A Contested Legacy*, ed. John P. McCormick and Peter E. Gordon (Princeton: Princeton University Press, 2013), 15–34.

18 George Steinmetz, 'Ideas in Exile: Refugees from Nazi Germany and the Failure to Transplant Historical Sociology into the United States', *International Journal of Politics, Culture, and Society* 23, no. 1 (2020): 1–27; more generally see Pierre Bourdieu, 'The Social Conditions of the International Circulation of Ideas', in

Bourdieu. A Critical Reader, ed. Richard Shusterman (Oxford: Blackwell, 1999), 220–8.

19 I reintroduced the notion of *real types* in George Steinmetz, 'American Sociology's Epistemological Unconscious and the Transition to Post-Fordism: the case of Historical Sociology', in *Remaking Modernity: Politics, Processes and History in Sociology*, ed. Julia Adams, Elisabeth Clemens and Ann Orloff (Durham, NC: Duke University Press, 2005), 109–57. I discuss the differences between my use of the term *real type* and Menger's use, and the differences from Weber's Ideal Type concept, in George Steinmetz and Phil Gorski, 'Ideal Types vs. Real Types', https://www.youtube.com/watch?v=OOr5jvUJtQk/.

20 I include mentions of adjectival forms of *Historismus* (*historistisch* with endings -e, -er, -em and -es) and Positivismus (*positivistisch*, with the same endings) as well as the nouns *Positivist(-en), Historismen,* and *Historizimus* (a neo-neologism based on the German translation of Popper's *The Poverty of Historicism*, which was never used).

21 Ewald Schams, 'Der "zweite" Nationalökonomie: Bemerkungen zu Werner Sombarts Buch "Die drei Nationalökonomien"', *Archiv für Sozialwissenschaft und Sozialpolitik* 64 (1930): 453–91.

22 Max Weber, *Collected Methodological Writings*, ed. Hans Henrik Bruun and Sam Whimster (London: Routledge, 2012), 169, note 1.

23 There were other German language sociology journals in this period but they were more specialized, less prominent, and did not publish anywhere as many pages as the *Archiv*. The two dedicated sociology journals in Weimar Germany were dominated by the theoretical stance of their editors: Von Wiese's *Kölner Vierteljahrshefte für Soziologie* and Richard Thurnwald's *Sociologus*. Von Wiese's 'formalism' was positioned against the Weberian and historicist schools in German sociology. Thurnwald was an ethnologist trying with mixed success to gain recognition as a sociologist during the Weimar and Nazi periods, and his journal's contributors were not located at the centre of the emerging sociology discipline. *Schmollers Jahrbuch*, finally, focused on economics, treated historically. Aron, *La Sociologie allemande contemporaine* (Paris: Alcan, 1935); George Steinmetz, 'La sociologie et l'empire: Richard Thurnwald et la question de l'autonomie scientifique', *Actes de la recherche en sciences sociales* no. 185 (December 2010), 12–29.

24 According to an online search using JSTOR.

25 Data from JSTOR.

26 Craig Calhoun, 'The Rise and Domestication of Historical Sociology', in *The Historic Turn in the Human Sciences*, ed. Terrence J. McDonald (Ann Arbor: University of Michigan Press, 1996), 305–38. 'Methodological positivism' is my term for the specific epistemology that dominated American sociology in the

postwar period and that still maintains a strong position. George Steinmetz, 'Positivism and Its Others in the Social Sciences', in *The Politics of Method in the Human Sciences: Positivism and Its Epistemological Others*, ed. George Steinmetz (Durham, NC: Duke University Press, 2005), 1–56.

27 The meaning of this pattern can be determined only through closer analysis, of course, in order to determine what is being designated by the words 'historicism' and 'positivism'.

28 George Steinmetz, 'Field Theory and Interdisciplinary: Relations between History and Sociology in Germany and France during the Twentieth Century', *Comparative Studies in Society and History* 59, no. 2 (April 2017): 477–514.

29 Others have analysed the transformations of historicism in the late nineteenth and early twentieth centuries, with slightly different accents. Oexle calls the new formation 'Historismus II.' Otto Gerhard Oexle, *Geschichtswissenschaft im Zeichen des Historismus* (Göttingen: Vandenhoeck & Ruprecht, 1996).

30 Beiser, *The German Historicist Tradition*, 3–6.

31 F. R. Ankersmit, 'The Necessity of Historicism', *Journal of the Philosophy of History* 4, no. 2 (2010): 226–40; Friedrich Engel-Jánosi, *The Growth of German Historicism* (Baltimore: The Johns Hopkins Press, 1944), 13.

32 Troeltsch, *Der Historismus und seine Probleme* (Tubingen: Mohr, 1922), 102; Wittkau, *Historismus*, 150.

33 Beiser, *The German Historicist Tradition*, 137.

34 Karl Mannheim, 'Conservative Thought', in *Essays on Sociology and Social Psychology*, ed. Paul Kecskemeti (New York: Oxford University Press, 1953), 74–164.

35 Freyer, *Soziologie als Wirklichkeitswissenschaft* (Leipzig: B. G. Teubner, 1930), 137.

36 Julia Hell, *The Conquest of Ruins: The Third Reich and the Fall of Rome* (Chicago: The University of Chicago Press, 2019).

37 Troeltsch, *Der Historismus*, ch. III.

38 On Dilthey's role in German historicism see Beiser, *German Historicist Tradition*, ch. 8; Antonio Negri, *Saggi sullo storicismo tedesco. Dilthey e Meinecke* (Milano: Feltrinelli, 1959).

39 Freyer, *Soziologie als Wirklichkeitswissenschaft*, 171.

40 Alfred Weber, *Ideen zur Staats- und Kultursoziologie* (Karlsruhe: G. Braun, 1927), 16–17, 39. Weber's concept of *Lebensstrom*, or social life as vital process, can be traced to Schopenhauer and Nietzsche. Troeltsch also referred to the 'historical stream of life', in *Christian Thought* (London: University of London Press, 1923), 67. For a contemporary critique of vitalism see Heinrich Rickert, *Die Philosophie des Lebens. Darstellung und Kritik der philosophischen Modeströmungen unserer Zeit*, 2nd ed. (Mohr: Universitäts- und Landesbibliothek, 1922).

41 Reinhard Laube, *Karl Mannheim und die Krise des Historismus: Historismus als wissenssoziologischer Perspektivismus* (Göttingen: Vandenhoeck & Ruprecht, 2002), 47, quoting from Mannheim, 'Zur Problematik der Soziologie in Deutschland', *Neue Schweizer Rundschau* 36, no. 37 (1929), 820–9.

42 Friedrich Meinecke, *Historism: The Rise of a New Historical Outlook* (London: Routledge and K. Paul, 1972 [1959]), lv.

43 Troeltsch, *Der Historismus*, 140; Ludwig Marcuse, *Die Individualität als Wert und die Philosophie Friedrich Nietzsches* (Berlin: Schmitz & Bukofzer, 1917).

44 Fulvio Tessitore, 'Die Frage des Historismus in Deutschland nach dem zweiten Weltkriege', in *Kritischer Historismus: Gesammelte Aufsätze* (Köln: Böhlau, 2005), 113.

45 Carlo Antoni, *From History to Sociology: The Transition in German Historical Thinking* (Detroit, CT: Wayne State University Press, 1959).

46 Mannheim, 'Historicism', in *Essays on the Sociology of Knowledge*, ed. Paul Kecskemeti (London: Routlege and Kegan Paul, 1952), 95–6.

47 Mannheim, 'Conservative Thought', 111. Althusser's theories, especially his idea of 'structure in dominance' (*structure à dominante*) and his late 'aleatory Marxism', are ironically compatible with Mannheim's modern historicism. Althusser failed to recognize this, however, and echoed Popper's idiosyncratic definition of historicism as teleological and essentialist. See Althusser, 'Marxism Is Not a Historicism'; and *For Marx* (London: NLB, 1977). E. P. Thompson recognized this mistake; see 'The Poverty of Theory', in *The Poverty of Theory and Other Essays* (New York: Monthly Review Press, 1978), 5.

48 Maurice Mandelbaum, *History, Man, and Reason. A Study in Nineteenth-Century Thought* (Baltimore: Johns Hopkins Press, 1971), 43.

49 Troeltsch, *Der Historismus*, 32, 71.

50 Antonella Corradini and Timothy O'Connor, 'Introduction', in *Emergence in Science and Philosophy*, ed. Antonella Corradini and O'Connor (New York: Routledge, 2010), xi.

51 Riedel, 'Positivismuskritik', 87; Beiser, *The German Historicist Tradition*, 297.

52 Patrick Henßler and Josef Schmid, *Bevölkerungswissenschaft im Werden. Die geistigen Grundlagen der deutschen Bevölkerungssoziologie* (Wiesbaden: VS Verlag für Sozialwissenschaften, 2007), 103; Werner Sombart, *Vom Menschen. Versuch einer geistwissenschaftlichen Anthropologie* (Berlin: Duncker & Humblot, 1956), 273.

53 More precisely, Meinecke's underlying political stance across the many political transitions was one of 'conservative-liberal German nationalism and imperial patriotism'. Immanuel Geiss, "Kritischer Rückblick auf Friedrich Meinecke', in *Studien über Geschichte und Geschichtswissenschaft* (Frankfurt am Main: Suhrkamp, 1972), 102.

54 Tessitore, 'Die Frage des Historismus'.
55 Thomas Nipperdey, 'Historismus und Historismuskritik heute', in *Die Funktion der Geschichte in unserer Zeit*, ed. Eberhard Jäckel and Ernst Weymar (Stuttgart: Klett, 1975), quoted in Tessitore, 'Die Frage des Historismus', 114.
56 René König, 'Soziologie in Berlin um 1930', in *Soziologie in Deutschland: Begründer, Verfechter, Verächter* (Munich: Hanser, 1987), 274; René König, 'Die deutsche Soziologie im Jahre 1955', *Kölner Zeitschrift für Soziologie und Sozialpsychologie* 8 (1956): 3, 6.
57 György Lukács, *The Destruction of Reason* (Atlantic Highlands, NJ: Humanities Press, 1980), 631, 640. Mannheim had provoked Lukács by suggesting that the latter's critique of *Verdinglichung* (reification) was connected to same strands of modern conservative thought as Historicism and *Lebensphilosophie*. Mannheim, 'Conservative Thought', 162, note 1.
58 Mannheim, 'Conservative Thought', 82; Troeltsch, *Der Historismus*, 8. The role of French Revolution in the genesis of German historicism is confirmed by Ulrich Muhlack, *Geschichtswissenschaft im Humanismus und in der Aufklärung: die Vorgeschichte des Historismus* (München: Beck, 1991).
59 Karl Mannheim, *Conservatism: A Contribution to the Sociology of Knowledge* (London: Routledge & Kegan Paul, 1986), 128.
60 Wilhelm Windelband, 'History and Natural Science', *History and Theory* 19 (1980): 165–8.
61 Guy Oakes, 'Weber and the Southwest German School: The Genesis of the Concept of the Historical Individual', in *Max Weber and His Contemporaries*, ed. Theodor Mommsen and Jürgen Osterhammel (London: Unwin Hyman, 1987), 434–46; Emil Hözel, 'Das geographische Individuum bei Karl Ritter und seine Bedeutung für den Begriff des Naturgebietes und der Naturgrenze', pts. 1 and 2, *Geographische Zeitschrift* 2, no. 7 (1896): 378–96; no. 8 (1896): 433–44; Ernst Troeltsch, 'Die Bedeutung des Begriffs der Kontingenz', in *Gesammelte Schriften 2* (Tubingen: J. C. B. Mohr, 1913), 774; Volker Kruse, 'Historische Soziologie als 'Geschichts- und Sozialphilosophie' – Zur Rezeption der Weimarer Soziologie in den fünfziger Jahren', in *Erkenntnisgewinne, Erkenntnisverluste Kontinuitaten und Diskontinuitäten in den Wirtschafts-, Rechts- und Sozialwissenschaften zwischen den 20er und 50er Jahren*, ed. Karl Acham (Stuttgart: F. Steiner, 1998), 86–7.
62 Thomas Burger, *Max Weber's Theory of Concept Formation: History, Laws, and Ideal Types* (Durham, NC: Duke University Press, 1976), 42.
63 Rickert, *The Limits of Concept Formation in Natural Science: A Logical Introduction to the Historical Sciences* (Cambridge: Cambridge University Press, 1986), 47.
64 Rickert, *Science and History. A Critique of Positivist Epistemology* (Princeton, NJ: Van Nostrand, 1962), xii–xiii.

65 Peter Vogt, *Kontingenz und Zufall: eine Ideen- und Begriffsgeschichte* (Berlin: Akademie Verlag, 2011).
66 Troeltsch, 'Die Bedeutung', 772; Rüdiger Bubner, 'Die Aristotelische Lehre vom Zufall. Bemerkungen in der Perspektive einer Annäherung der Philosophie an die Rhetorik', in Rüdiger Bubner et al., eds., *Kontingenz* (Göttingen: Vandenhoeck & Ruprecht, 1985), 3–21.
67 Troeltsch, 'Die Bedeutung', 772; Albrecht Becker-Freyseng, *Die Vorgeschichte des philosophischen Terminus 'contingens': die Bedeutungen von 'contingere' bei Boethius und ihr Verhältnis zu den Aristotelischen Möglichkeitsbegriffen* (Heidelberg: F. Bilabel, 1938); Joachim Roland Söder, *Kontingenz und Wissen: die Lehre von den Futura contingentia bei Johannes Duns Scotus* (Munster: Aschendorff, 1999).
68 Troeltsch, 'Die Bedeutung', 771–2.
69 Freyer, *Soziologie als Wirklichkeitswissenschaft*.
70 Wilhelm Windelband, *Die Lehren vom Zufall* (Berlin: F. Henschel, 1870), 5, 26–7.
71 Kari Palonen, *Das 'Webersche Moment': zur Kontingenz des politischen* (Wiesbaden: Springer, 1998), 102.
72 Max Weber, *Roscher and Knies: The Logical Problems of Historical Economics* (New York: Free Press, 1975), 97. Kruse, 'Historische Soziologie', 91 note 23.
73 On Schmitt as a theorist of contingency see Michael G. Festl, *Scheitern an Kontingenz: politisches Denken in der Weimarer Republik* (Frankfurt: Campus Verlag, 2019), ch. 8.
74 Troeltsch, *Der Historismus*, 475.
75 Troeltsch, 'Die Bedeutung', 774.
76 Weber, *Ideen zur Staats- und Kultursoziologie*, 9.
77 Freyer, *Soziologie als Wirklichkeitswissenschaft*, 295.
78 Albert Salomon, 'The Place of Alfred Weber's "Kultursoziologie" in Social Thought', *Social Research* 3, no. 1/4 (1936): 497.
79 Mannheim, 'German Sociology (1918–1933)', *Politica* (February 1934): 12–33; Nicolas Baverez, *Raymond Aron: un moraliste au temps des ideologies* (Paris: Flammarion, 1993), 76, 80; Marcotte-Chenard, this volume. Aron argued in 1937 that the Weberians 'accept the Comtian definition of sociology as seeking to discern the laws of history'. This may have been partly true of Weber at the very end of his life, but it directly contradicts all of his explicitly 'methodological' writings between 1903 and the First World War and all of the historicists discussed in the present chapter. Raymond Aron, *Introduction à la philosophie de l'histoire: Essai sur les limites de l'objectivité historique* (Paris: Gallimard, 1938), 34. Either Aron was blinded by the French positivist tradition or he was trying to make Weber palatable to a hostile French readership.
80 David Frisby, *The Alienated Mind* (London: Heineman, 1992), 107ff.; Johannes Weiß, 'Negative Soziologie', *Ethik und Sozialwissenschaften* 6 (1995): 241–6.

81 Arnd Hoffmann, *Zufall und Kontingenz in der Geschichtstheorie* (Frankfurt am Main: V. Klostermann, 2005); Markus Holzinger, *Der Raum des Politischen: politische Theorie im Zeichen der Kontingenz* (München: Wilhelm Fink, 2006).
82 Troeltsch, *Der Historismus*, 11.
83 Troeltsch, *Der Historismus*, 219.
84 Troeltsch, *Der Historismus*, 209, 142.
85 Mannheim, 'Historicism', 104.
86 Michael Bock, 'Die "kritische Theorie" als Erbin der geisteswissenschaftlichen Soziologie der Zwischenkriegszeit', in *Erkenntnisgewinne, Erkenntnisverluste Kontinuitaten und Diskontinuitäten in den Wirtschafts-, Rechts- und Sozialwissenschaften zwischen den 20er und 50er Jahren*, ed. Karl Acham (Stuttgart: F. Steiner, 1998), 223–49; Titus Stahl, *Immanente Kritik: Elemente einer Theorie sozialer Praktiken* (Frankfurt: Campus, 2013).
87 Amy Allen, *The End of Progress: Decolonizing the Normative Foundations of Critical Theory* (New York: Columbia University Press, 2016); George Steinmetz, 'Inheriting Critical Theory: Amy Allen's "The End of Progress"', *Current Perspectives in Social Theory* 36 (2019): 37–48.
88 George Steinmetz, 'Concept-Quake: Toward a Historical Sociology of Social Science', in Didier Fassin and George Steinmetz, eds., *The Social Sciences through the Looking-Glass. Studies in the Production of Knowledge* (forthcoming).
89 Laube, *Karl Mannheim,* 41.
90 Matthias Gross, '"Objective Culture" and the Development of Nonknowledge: Georg Simmel and the Reverse Side of Knowing', *Cultural Sociology* 6, no. 4 (2012): 422–37.
91 Hans Henrik Bruun, *Science, Values and Politics in Max Weber's Methodology* (Aldershot, England: Ashgate, 2007), 28.
92 'La théorie de la relativité', séance du 6 avril 1922, *Bulletin de la Société Française de Philosophie* 22, no. 3 (1922): 91–113; Henri Bergson, *Durée et simultanéité, à propos de la théorie d'Einstein* (Paris: F. Alcan, 1922); Monika Wulz, 'Vom Nutzen des Augenblicks für die Projekte der Wissenschaft', *Berichte zur Wissenschaftsgeschichte* 35, no. 2 (2012): 131–46.
93 Steinmetz, 'Concept-Quake'.
94 Karl R. Popper, *Logik der Forschung: zur Erkenntnistheorie der modernen Naturwissenschaft* (Vienna: J. Springer, 1935).
95 Max Weber, *Economy and Society*, vol. 1 (Berkeley: University of California Press, 1978), 4.
96 My emphasis. Max Weber, 'Energetische Kulturtheorien', *Archiv für Sozialwissenschaft und Sozialpolitik* 29 (1909): 576–7.
97 Steinmetz, 'Field Theory'.

98 Riedel, 'Positivismuskritik'. On scientism in German protosociology, see Peter M. Hejl, *Protosoziologie: wissenschaftliches Selbstverständnis und Beziehungen zur Biologie der deutschsprachigen Soziologie bis 1914* (Siegen: LUMIS, 1998); on epistemological discussions in German sociology before 1933 see also Eckehard Kühne, 'Historisches Bewusstsein in der deutschen Soziologie: Untersuchungen zur Geschichte der Soziologie von der Zeit der Reichsgründung bis zum Ersten Weltkrieg auf wissenssoziologischer Grundlage' (PhD diss., Marburg/Lahn, 1971); Harald Homann, 'Gesetz und Wirklichkeit in den Sozialwissenschaften: vom Methodenstreit zum Positivismusstreit' (PhD diss., Tübingen, 1989).
99 Peter Halfpenny, *Positivism and Sociology: Explaining Social Life* (London: Allen & Unwin, 1982).
100 Theodor W. Adorno et al., *The Positivist Dispute in German Sociology* (New York: Harper & Row, 1976).
101 Edgar Jaffé, review of *Lehrbuch der Historischen Methode und der Geschichtsphilosophie*, by Ernst Bernheim, *Archiv für Sozialwissenschaft und Sozialpolitik* 27 (1908): 829.
102 Max Adler, 'Mach und Marx. Ein Beitrag zur Kritik des modernen Positivismus', *Archiv für Sozialwissenschaft und Sozialpolitik* 33 (1911): 348–400.
103 Troeltsch, *Der Historismus*, 378.
104 Troeltsch, *Der Historismus*, 379, 381.
105 Troeltsch, *Der Historismus*, 382.
106 Norman Blaikie, 'Positivism', in *The SAGE Encyclopedia of Social Science Research Methods*, ed. Michael S. Lewis-Beck, Alan Bryman and Tim Futing Liao (Thousand Oaks, CA: Sage, 2004), 837–8.
107 Roy Bhaskar, *Scientific Realism and Human Emancipation* (London: Verso, 1986).
108 Erich Rothacker, *Einleitung in die Geistewissenschaften* (Tübingen: Mohr, 1920), 195.
109 Othmar Spann, 'Ein Wort an meine Gegner auf dem Wiener Soziologentage', *Kölner Vierteljahrshefte für Soziologie* 6, no. 4 (1927): 312–13.
110 F. A. von Hayek, 'Scientism and the Study of Society (Part 1)', *Economica* 9 (1942): 268–9.
111 This is particularly clear in the case of Simmel, the progenitor of formalistic German sociology. Simmel's discussion of the philosophy of history is ambiguous about whether singular events that cannot be 'deduced from general laws' can be explained at all, and his discussion of the idea of 'Historicism' is even more confused. Yet he suggests there 'that his main purpose is the refutation of historicism'. Georg Simmel, *Die Probleme der Geschichtsphilosophie*, 2nd ed. (Leipzig: Duncker & Humbolt, 1905), 72, note 1; Guy Oakes, 'Introduction', in Georg Simmel, *The Problems of the Philosophy of History: An Epistemological Essay* (New York: Free Press, 1977), 5.

112 Siegfried Landshut, *Kritik der Soziologie: Freiheit und Gleichheit als Ursprungsproblem der Soziologie* (München and Leipzig: Duncker & Humblot, 1929); Freyer, *Soziologie als Wirklichkeitswissenschaft*, 84.
113 Freyer, *Soziologie als Wirklichkeitswissenschaft*, 159.
114 Some historical sociologists and game theorists accept the ontology of human rationality but reject regularity determinism; see Ivan Ermakoff, *Ruling Oneself Out: A Theory of Collective Abdications* (Durham: Duke University Press, 2008).
115 Rothacker, *Einleitung*, 196.
116 Heinz Maus, 'Geschichte der Soziologie', in *Handbuch der Soziologie*, ed. Werner Ziegenfuss (Stuttgart: F. Enke, 1956), 39.
117 Johan Plenge, 'Realistische Glossen zu einer Geschichte des Deutschen Idealismus', *Archiv für Sozialwissenschaft und Sozialpolitik* 32 (1911): 9.
118 Max Scheler, *Nation und Weltanschauung* (Leipzig: Neue Geist-Verlag, 1923), 64.
119 Freyer, *Soziologie als Wirklichkeitswissenschaft*, 137; Alfred Weber, *Alfred-Weber-Gesamtausgabe*, vol. 8, *Schriften zur Kultur- und Geschichtssoziologie (1906–1958)* (Marburg: Metropolis, 1997).
120 Friedrich Seifert, review of *Der Mythos von Orient und Occident: eine Metaphysik der alten Welt*, by Johann Jakob Bachofen, in *Archiv für Sozialwissenschaft und Sozialpolitik* 56 (1926): 812.
121 Alfred Vierkandt, 'Die Überwindung des Positivismus in der deutschen Soziologie der Gegenwart', *Jahrbuch für Soziologie* 2 (1926): 70.
122 Vierkandt, 'Die Überwindung des Positivismus', 68.
123 Leopold von Wiese, 'Der zweite Band des Jahrbuchs für Soziologie', *Kölner Vierteljahrshefte für Soziologie* 5, no. 2 (1926), 159.
124 Karl Mannheim, 'Historismus', *Archiv für Sozialwissenschaft und Sozialpolitik* 52, no. 1 (June 1924): 1.
125 Paul Eppstein, 'Die Fragestellung nach der Wirklichkeit im historischen Materialismus', *Archiv für Sozialwissenschaft und Sozialpolitik* 60 (1928): 449–507; Claus-Dieter Krohn, 'Eppstein, Paul', in *Biographisches Handbuch der deutschsprachigen wirtschaftswissenschaftlichen Emigration nach 1933*, ed. Harald Hagemann and Claus-Dieter Krohn (München: K.G. Saur, 1999), 142–3.
126 Ernst Grünfeld, *Die Peripheren: Ein Kapitel Soziologie* (Amsterdam: N. v. Noord-hollandsche uitgevers mij, 1939).
127 Hermann Rauschning, *Gespräche mit Hitler* (New York: Europa Verlag, 1940), 219. I am grateful to Jakob Borchers for identifying this quotation, widely misidentified and always treated as authentic.
128 Carsten Klingemann, *Soziologie und Politik: Sozialwissenschaftliches Expertenwissen im Dritten Reich und in der frühen westdeutschen Nachkriegszeit* (Wiesbaden: VS Verlag für Sozialwissenschaften, 2009).
129 Hans Albert, 'Entmythologisierung der Sozialwissenschaften: Die Bedeutung der analytischen Philosophie für die soziologische Erkenntnis', *Kölner Zeitschrift*

für Soziologie und Sozialpsychologie 8 (1956): 234–70, glossed by Volker Kruse, 'Historische Soziologie', 77.
130 Henrika Kuklick, summarizing an unpublished paper by Rueschemeyer from 1977 in 'The Sociology of Knowledge: Retrospect and Prospect', *Annual Review of Sociology* 9 (1983): 291.
131 Theodor Adorno, 'Zur gegenwärtigen Stellung der empirischen Sozialforschung in Deutschland', in *Gesammelte Schriften*, vol. 8, Soziologischen Schriften I (Frankfurt am Main: Suhrkamp, 1972): 478–93; Uta Gerhardt, *Denken der Demokratie. Die Soziologie im atlantischen Transfer des Besatzungsregimes* (Stuttgart: Franz Steiner Verlag, 2007).
132 Hans B. Blumenberg, 'Ernst Cassirer gedenkend bei Entgegennahme des Kuno-Fischer-Preises der Universität Heidelberg 1974', in *Wirklichkeiten in denen wir leben: Aufsätze und eine Rede* (Stuttgart: P. Reclam, 1981), 170.
133 Blumenberg, 'Ernst Cassirer gedenkend bei Entgegennahme des Kuno-Fischer-Preises der Universität Heidelberg 1974', 170.
134 Bhaskar, *Scientific Realism;* George Steinmetz, 'Critical Realism and Historical Sociology', *Comparative Studies in Society and History* 40, no. 1 (1998): 170–86; Idem., 'Positivism and Its Others'; Douglas V. Porpora, *Reconstructing Sociology. The Critical Realist Approach* (Cambridge: Cambridge University Press, 2015).

Bibliography

Adler, Max. 'Mach und Marx. Ein Beitrag zur Kritik des modernen Positivismus'. *Archiv für Sozialwissenschaft und Sozialpolitik* 33 (1911): 348–400.
Adorno, Theodor W. 'Zur gegenwärtigen Stellung der empirischen Sozialforschung in Deutschland'. In *Gesammelte Schriften*, vol. 8 of 20, *Soziologischen Schriften I*, 478–93. Frankfurt am Main: Suhrkamp, 1972.
Adorno, Theodor W., Hans Albert, Ralf Dahrendorf, Jürgen Habermas, Harald Pilot and Karl R. Popper. *The Positivist Dispute in German Sociology*. New York: Harper & Row, 1976.
Albert, Hans. 'Entmythologisierung der Sozialwissenschaften: Die Bedeutung der analytischen Philosophie für die soziologische Erkenntnis'. *Kölner Zeitschrift für Soziologie und Sozialpsychologie* 8 (1956): 234–70.
Allen, Amy. *The End of Progress: Decolonizing the Normative Foundations of Critical Theory*. New York: Columbia University Press, 2016.
Althusser, Louis. *For Marx*. London: NLB, 1977.
Althusser, Louis. 'Marxism Is Not a Historicism'. Chap. 5 in *Reading Capital*, edited by Louis Althusser and Étienne Balibar. London: NLB, 1970.
Ankersmit, F. R. 'The Necessity of Historicism'. *Journal of the Philosophy of History* 4, no. 2 (2010): 226–40.

Antoni, Carlo. *From History to Sociology: The Transition in German Historical Thinking*. Detroit, CT: Wayne State University Press, 1959.

Aron, Raymond. *Introduction à la philosophie de l'histoire: Essai sur les limites de l'objectivité historique*. Paris: Gallimard, 1938.

Aron, Raymond. *La Sociologie allemande contemporaine*. Paris: Alcan, 1935.

Baverez, Nicolas. *Raymond Aron: un moraliste au temps des idéologies*. Paris: Flammarion, 1993.

Becker-Freyseng, Albrecht. *Die Vorgeschichte des philosophischen Terminus 'contingens': die Bedeutungen von 'contingere' bei Boethius und ihr Verhältnis zu den Aristotelischen Möglichkeitsbegriffen*. Heidelberg: F. Bilabel, 1938.

Beiser, Frederick C. *The German Historicist Tradition*. Oxford: Oxford University Press, 2011.

Bergson, Henri. *Durée et simultanéité, à propos de la théorie d'Einstein*. Paris: F. Alcan, 1922.

Bhaskar, Roy. *Scientific Realism and Human Emancipation*. London: Verso, 1986.

Blaikie, Norman. 'Positivism'. In *The SAGE Encyclopedia of Social Science Research Methods*, edited by Michael S. Lewis-Beck, Alan Bryman and Tim Futing Liao, 837–8. Thousand Oaks, CA: Sage, 2004.

Blumenberg, Hans B. 'Ernst Cassirer gedenkend bei Entgegennahme des Kuno-Fischer-Preises der Universität Heidelberg 1974'. In Blumenberg, *Wirklichkeiten in denen wir leben: Aufsätze und eine Rede*, 163–72. Stuttgart: P. Reclam, 1981.

Bock, Michael. 'Die "kritische Theorie" als Erbin der geisteswissenschaftlichen Soziologie der Zwischenkriegszeit'. In *Erkenntnisgewinne, Erkenntnisverluste Kontinuitaten und Diskontinuitäten in den Wirtschafts-, Rechts- und Sozialwissenschaften zwischen den 20er und 50er Jahren*, edited by Karl Acham, 223–49. Stuttgart: F. Steiner, 1998.

Bourdieu, Pierre. 'The Social Conditions of the International Circulation of Ideas'. In *Bourdieu. A Critical Reader*, edited by Richard Shusterman, 220–8. Oxford: Blackwell, 1999.

Bruun, Hans Henrik. *Science, Values and Politics in Max Weber's Methodology*. Aldershot: Ashgate, 2007.

Bubner, Rüdiger. 'Die Aristotelische Lehre vom Zufall: Bemerkungen in der Perspektive einer Annäherung der Philosophie an die Rhetorik'. In *Kontingenz*, edited by Rüdiger Bubner, Konrad Cramer and Riener Wiehl, 3–21. Göttingen: Vandenhoeck & Ruprecht, 1985.

Burger, Thomas. *Max Weber's Theory of Concept Formation: History, Laws, and Ideal Types*. Durham, NC: Duke University Press, 1976.

Calhoun, Craig. 'The Rise and Domestication of Historical Sociology'. In *The Historic Turn in the Human Sciences*, edited by Terrence J. McDonald, 305–38. Ann Arbor: University of Michigan Press, 1996.

Corradini, Antonella and Timothy O'Connor. 'Introduction'. In *Emergence in Science and Philosophy*, edited by Antonella Corradini and Timothy O'Connor, xi–xiii. New York: Routledge, 2010.

Dilly, Heinrich. 'Entstehung und Geschichte des Begriffs "Historismus" – Funktion und Struktur einer Begriffsgeschichte.' In *Geschichte allein ist zeitgemäss. Historismus in Deutschland*, edited by Michael Brix und Monika Steinhauser, 11–16. Lahn-Giessen: Anabas-Verlag Kämpf, 1978.

Engel-Jánosi, Friedrich. *The Growth of German Historicism*. Baltimore, MD: Johns Hopkins Press, 1944.

Eppstein, Paul. 'Die Fragestellung nach der Wirklichkeit im historischen Materialismus'. *Archiv für Sozialwissenschaft und Sozialpolitik* 60 (1928): 449–507.

Ermakoff, Ivan. *Ruling Oneself Out: A Theory of Collective Abdications*. Durham, NC: Duke University Press, 2008.

Festl, Michael G. *Scheitern an Kontingenz: politisches Denken in der Weimarer Republik*. Frankfurt am Main: Campus Verlag, 2019.

Freyer, Hans. 'Soziologie als Geisteswissenschaft'. *Archiv für Kulturgeschichte* 26 (1926): 113–26.

Freyer, Hans. *Soziologie als Wirklichkeitswissenschaft: Logische Grundlegung des Systems der Soziologie*. Leipzig: B. G. Teubner, 1930.

Frisby, David. *The Alienated Mind: The Sociology of Knowledge in Germany, 1918–33*. 2nd ed. London: Heineman, 1992.

Gallagher, Catherine and Stephen Greenblatt. *Practicing New Historicism*. Chicago: University of Chicago Press, 2000.

Gerhardt, Uta. *Denken der Demokratie. Die Soziologie im atlantischen Transfer des Besatzungsregimes*. Stuttgart: Franz Steiner Verlag, 2007.

Grimmer-Solem, Erik. *The Rise of Historical Economics and Social Reform in Germany, 1864–1894*. Oxford: Clarendon Press, 2003.

Gross, Matthias. '"Objective Culture" and the Development of Nonknowledge: Georg Simmel and the Reverse Side of Knowing'. *Cultural Sociology* 6, no. 4 (2012): 422–37.

Grünfeld, Ernst. *Die Peripheren: Ein Kapitel Soziologie*. Amsterdam: Noord-Hollandsche Uitgeversmij, 1939.

Halfpenny, Peter. *Positivism and Sociology: Explaining Social Life*. London: Allen & Unwin, 1982.

Hayek, F. A. von. 'Scientism and the Study of Society (Part 1)'. *Economica* 9 (1942): 267–91.

Healy, Kieran. 'Fuck Nuance'. *Sociological Theory* 35, no. 2 (2017): 118–27.

Hell, Julia. *The Conquest of Ruins: The Third Reich and the Fall of Rome*. Chicago: University of Chicago Press, 2019.

Heussi, Karl. *Die Krisis des Historismus*. Tübingen: J. C. B. Mohr, 1932.

Hoffmann, Arnd. *Zufall und Kontingenz in der Geschichtstheorie: mit zwei Studien zu Theorie und Praxis der Sozialgeschichte*. Frankfurt am Main: V. Klostermann, 2005.

Holzinger, Markus. *Der Raum des Politischen: politische Theorie im Zeichen der Kontingenz*. Munich: Wilhelm Fink, 2006.

Homann, Harald. 'Gesetz und Wirklichkeit in den Sozialwissenschaften: vom Methodenstreit zum Positivismusstreit'. PhD diss., Tübingen, 1989.

House, James S. 'The Culminating Crisis of American Sociology and Its Role in Social Science and Public Policy: An Autobiographical, Multimethod, Reflexive Perspective'. *Annual Review of Sociology* 45 (2019): 1–26.

Hözel, Emil. 'Das geographische Individuum bei Karl Ritter und seine Bedeutung für den Begriff des Naturgebietes und der Naturgrenze'. Pts. 1 and 2. *Geographische Zeitschrift* 2, no. 7 (1896): 378–96; no. 8 (1896): 433–44.

Iggers, Georg G. 'Historismus: Geschichte und Bedeutung eines Begriffs: eine kritische übersicht der neuesten Literatur'. In *Historismus am Ende des 20. Jahrhunderts: eine internationale Diskussion*, edited by Gunter Scholtz, 110–26. Berlin: Akademie-Verlag, 1997.

Jaffé, Edgar. Review of *Lehrbuch der Historischen Methode und der Geschichtsphilosophie*, by Ernst Bernheim. *Archiv für Sozialwissenschaft und Sozialpolitik* 27 (1908): 828–29.

Kettler, David and Colin Loader. 'Weimar Sociology'. In *Weimar Thought: A Contested Legacy*, edited by John P. McCormick and Peter E. Gordon, 15–34. Princeton: Princeton University Press, 2013.

Kiser, Edward and Michael Hechter. 'The Role of General Theory in Comparative-Historical Sociology'. *American Journal of Sociology* 97 (1991): 1–30.

Klingemann, Carsten. 2009. *Soziologie und Politik: Sozialwissenschaftliches Expertenwissen im Dritten Reich und in der frühen westdeutschen Nachkriegszeit*. Wiesbaden: VS Verlag für Sozialwissenschaften

König, René. 'Die deutsche Soziologie im Jahre 1955'. *Kölner Zeitschrift für Soziologie und Sozialpsychologie* 8 (1956): 1–11.

König, René. 'Soziologie in Berlin um 1930'. In *Soziologie in Deutschland: Begründer, Verfechter, Verächter*. Munich: Hanser, 1987.

Krohn, Claus-Dieter. 'Eppstein, Paul'. In *Biographisches Handbuch der deutschsprachigen wirtschaftswissenschaftlichen Emigration nach 1933*, edited by Harald Hagemann and Claus-Dieter Krohn, 142–3. München: K.G. Saur, 1999.

Kruse, Volker. *Historisch-soziologische Zeitdiagnose in Westdeutschland nach 1945. Eduard Heimann, Alfred von Martin, Hans Freyer*. Frankfurt am Main: Suhrkamp, 1994.

Kruse, Volker. 'Historische Soziologie als 'Geschichts- und Sozialphilosophie' – Zur Rezeption der Weimarer Soziologie in den fünfziger Jahren'. In *Erkenntnisgewinne, Erkenntnisverluste Kontinuitaten und Diskontinuitäten in den Wirtschafts-, Rechts- und Sozialwissenschaften zwischen den 20er und 50er Jahren*, edited by Karl Acham, 76–106. Stuttgart: F. Steiner, 1998.

Kühne, Eckehard. 'Historisches Bewusstsein in der deutschen Soziologie: Untersuchungen zur Geschichte der Soziologie von der Zeit der Reichsgründung bis zum Ersten Weltkrieg auf wissenssoziologischer Grundlage'. PhD diss., Marburg/Lahn, 1971.

Kuklick, Henrika. 'The Sociology of Knowledge: Retrospect and Prospect'. *Annual Review of Sociology* 9 (1983): 287–310.

Landshut, Siegfried. *Kritik der Soziologie: Freiheit und Gleichheit als Ursprungsproblem der Soziologie*. Munich: Duncker & Humblot, 1929.
Laube, Reinhard. *Karl Mannheim und die Krise des Historismus: Historismus als wissenssoziologischer Perspektivismus*. Göttingen: Vandenhoeck & Ruprecht, 2002.
Lukács, György. *The Destruction of Reason*. Atlantic Highlands, NJ: Humanities Press, 1980.
Mandelbaum, Maurice. *History, Man, and Reason: A Study in Nineteenth-Century Thought*. Baltimore, MD: Johns Hopkins Press, 1971.
Mannheim, Karl. *Conservatism: A Contribution to the Sociology of Knowledge*. London: Routledge & Kegan Paul, 1986.
Mannheim, Karl. 'Conservative Thought'. In *Essays on Sociology and Social Psychology*, edited by Paul Kecskemeti, 74–164. New York: Oxford University Press, 1953.
Mannheim, Karl. *Die Gegenwartsaufgaben der Soziologie: ihre Lehrgestalt*. Tübingen: J. C. B. Mohr, 1936.
Mannheim, Karl. 'German Sociology (1918-1933)'. *Politica* (February 1934): 12–33.
Mannheim, Karl. 'Historicism'. In *Essays on the Sociology of Knowledge*, edited by Paul Kecskemeti, 84–133. London: Routledge and Kegan Paul, 1952.
Mannheim, Karl. 'Historismus'. *Archiv für Sozialwissenschaft und Sozialpolitik* 52, no. 1 (1924): 1–60.
Mannheim, Karl. 'Zur Problematik der Soziologie in Deutschland'. *Neue Schweizer Rundschau* 36, no. 37 (1929): 820–9.
Marcuse, Ludwig. *Die Individualität als Wert und die Philosophie Friedrich Nietzsches*. Berlin: Schmitz & Bukofzer, 1917.
Maus, Heinz. 'Geschichte der Soziologie'. In *Handbuch der Soziologie*, 1–120, edited by Werner Ziegenfuss. Stuttgart: F. Enke, 1956.
Meinecke, Friedrich. *Historism: The Rise of a New Historical Outlook*. Translated by J. E. Anderson. London: Routledge and K. Paul, 1972.
Menger, Carl. *Die Irrthümer des Historismus in der deutschen Nationalökonomie*. Wien, A. Hölder, 1884.
Mises, Ludwig von. 'Soziologie und Geschichte'. *Archiv für Sozialwissenschaft und Sozialpolitik* 61 (1929): 465–512.
Muhlack, Ulrich. *Geschichtswissenschaft im Humanismus und in der Aufklärung: die Vorgeschichte des Historismus*. München: Beck, 1991.
Negri, Antonio. *Saggi sullo storicismo tedesco: Dilthey e Meinecke*. Milan: Feltrinelli, 1959.
Nipperdey, Thomas. 'Historismus und Historismuskritik heute'. In *Die Funktion der Geschichte in unserer Zeit*, edited by Eberhard Jäckel and Ernst Weymar, 82–95. Stuttgart: Klett, 1975.
Oakes, Guy. 'Introduction.' In Georg Simmel, *The Problems of the Philosophy of History: An Epistemological Essay*, 1–37. New York: Free Press, 1977.
Oakes, Guy. 'Weber and the Southwest German School: The Genesis of the Concept of the Historical Individual'. In *Max Weber and his Contemporaries*, edited by Theodor Mommsen and Jürgen Osterhammel, 434–46. London: Unwin Hyman, 1987.

Oexle, Otto Gerhard. *Geschichtswissenschaft im Zeichen des Historismus*. Göttingen: Vandenhoeck & Ruprecht, 1996.
Palonen, Kari. *Das 'Webersche Moment': zur Kontingenz des politischen*. Wiesbaden: Springer, 1998.
Plenge, Johann. 'Realistische Glossen zu einer Geschichte des Deutschen Idealismus'. *Archiv für Sozialwissenschaft und Sozialpolitik* 32 (1911): 1–35.
Popper, Karl R. *Logik der Forschung: zur Erkenntnistheorie der modernen Naturwissenschaft*. Vienna: J. Springer, 1935.
Popper, Karl R. *The Poverty of Historicism*. London: Routledge and Kegan Paul, 1957.
Porpora, Douglas V. *Reconstructing Sociology. The Critical Realist Approach*. Cambridge: Cambridge University Press, 2015.
Rauschning, Hermann. *Gespräche mit Hitler*. New York: Europa Verlag, 1940.
Rickert, Heinrich. *Die Philosophie des Lebens: Darstellung und Kritik der philosophischen Modeströmungen unserer Zeit*. 2nd ed. Mohr: Universitäts- und Landesbibliothek, 1922.
Rickert, Heinrich. *The Limits of Concept Formation in Natural Science: A Logical Introduction to the Historical Sciences*. Cambridge: Cambridge University Press, 1986.
Rickert, Heinrich. *Science and History: A Critique of Positivist Epistemology*. Princeton: Van Nostrand, 1962.
Riedel, Manfred. 'Positivismuskritik und Historismus. Über den Ursprung des Gegensatzes von Erklären und Verstehen im 19. Jahrhundert'. In *Positivismus im 19. Jahrhundert. Beiträge zu seiner geschichtlichen und systematischen Bedeutung*, edited by Jürgen Blühdorn und Joachim Ritter, 81–91. Frankfurt a. M.: V. Kostermann.
Rothacker, Erich. 'Das Wort Historismus'. *Zeitschrift für deutsche Wortforschung* 16 (1960): 3–6.
Rothacker, Erich. *Einleitung in die Geisteswissenschaften*. Tübingen: J. C. B. Mohr, 1920.
Rüsen, Jörn. *Konfigurationen des Historismus: Studien zur deutschen Wissenschaftskultur*. Frankfurt am Main: Suhrkamp, 1993.
Schams, Ewald. 'Der "zweite" Nationalökonomie: Bemerkungen zu Werner Sombarts Buch "Die drei Nationalökonomien"'. *Archiv für Sozialwissenschaft und Sozialpolitik* 64 (1930): 453–91.
Scheler, Max. *Nation und Weltanschauung*. Leipzig: Neue Geist-Verlag, 1923.
Schlott, Michael. 'Mythen, Mutationen und Lexeme. "Historismus als Kategorie der Geschichts- und Literaturwissenschaft". *Scientia poetica: Jahrbuch für Geschichte der Literatur und der Wissenschaften* 3 (1999): 158–204.
Schmoller, Gustav. *Grundriß der allgemeinen Volkswirtschaftslehre*. Leipzig: Duncker & Humblot, 1901
Schumpeter, Joseph A. *History of Economic Analysis*. New York: Oxford University Press, 1954.
Seifert, Friedrich. Review of *Der Mythus von Orient und Occident: eine Metaphysik der alten Welt*, by Johann Jakob Bachofen. In *Archiv für Sozialwissenschaft und Sozialpolitik* 56 (1926): 811–15.

Simmel, Georg. *Die Probleme der Geschichtsphilosophie*. 2nd ed. Leipzig: Duncker & Humbolt, 1905.

Söder, Joachim Roland. *Kontingenz und Wissen: die Lehre von den Futura contingentia bei Johannes Duns Scotus*. Munster: Aschendorff, 1999.

Spann, Othmar. 'Ein Wort an meine Gegner auf dem Wiener Soziologentage'. *Kölner Vierteljahrshefte für Soziologie* 6, no. 4 (1927): 311–36.

Stahl, Titus. *Immanente Kritik: Elemente einer Theorie sozialer Praktiken*. Frankfurt am Main: Campus, 2013.

Steinmetz, G. 'Positivism and Its Others in the Social Sciences'. In *The Politics of Method in the Human Sciences: Positivism and Its Epistemological Others*, edited by George Steinmetz, 1–56. Durham, NC: Duke University Press, 2005.

Steinmetz, George. 'American Sociology's Epistemological Unconscious and the Transition to Post-Fordism: The Case of Historical Sociology'. In *Remaking Modernity: Politics, Processes and History in Sociology*, edited by Julia Adams, Elisabeth Clemens and Ann Orloff, 109–57. Durham, NC: Duke University Press, 2005.

Steinmetz, George. 'Charles Tilly, Historicism, and the Critical Realist Philosophy of Science'. *American Sociologist* 41, no. 4 (2010): 312–36.

Steinmetz, George. 'Concept-Quake: Toward a Historical Sociology of Social Science'. In *The Social Sciences through the Looking-Glass: Studies in the Production of Knowledge*, edited by Didier Fassin and George Steinmetz. Forthcoming.

Steinmetz, George. 'Ideas in Exile: Refugees from Nazi Germany and the Failure to Transplant Historical Sociology into the United States'. *International Journal of Politics, Culture, and Society* 23, no. 1 (2020): 1–27.

Steinmetz, George. 'Inheriting Critical Theory: A Review of Amy Allen's *The End of Progress: Decolonizing the Normative Foundations of Critical Theory*'. *Current Perspectives in Social Theory* 36 (2019): 37–48.

Steinmetz, George. 'The Genealogy of a Positivist Haunting: Comparing Prewar and Postwar U.S. Sociology'. *boundary 2* 32, no. 2 (2005): 107–33.

Steinmetz, George. 'Field Theory and Interdisciplinary: Relations between History and Sociology in Germany and France during the Twentieth Century'. *Comparative Studies in Society and History* 59, no. 2 (April 2017): 477–514.

Steinmetz, George. 'La sociologie et l'empire: Richard Thurnwald et la question de l'autonomie scientifique'. *Actes de la recherche en sciences sociales*, no. 185 (2010): 12–29.

Steinmetz, George and Philip Gorski. 'Ideal Types vs Real Types'. Critical Realism Network, webinar series. Posted on 24 October 2017. YouTube video, 1:27:07. https://www.youtube.com/watch?v=OOr5jvUJtQk/.

Strubenhoff, Marius. 'The Positivism Dispute in German Sociology, 1954–1970'. *History of European Ideas* 44, no. 2 (2018): 260–76.

Tessitore, Fulvio. 'Die Frage des Historismus in Deutschland nach dem zweiten Weltkriege'. In Tessitore, *Kritischer Historismus: Gesammelte Aufsätze*, 104–18. Köln: Böhlau, 2005.

Thompson, E. P. 'The Poverty of Theory'. In *The Poverty of Theory and Other Essays*, 1–210. New York: Monthly Review Press.
Troeltsch, Ernst. *Christian Thought*. London: University of London Press, 1923.
Troeltsch, Ernst. *Der Historismus und seine Probleme*, vol. 1. Tübingen: J. C. B. Mohr, 1922.
Troeltsch, Ernst. 'Die Bedeutung des Begriffs der Kontingenz'. In *Gesammelte Schriften 2*, 769–78. Tubingen: J. C. B. Mohr, 1913.
Troeltsch, Ernst. 'Die Krise des Historismus'. *Die Neue Rundschau* 33 (1922): 572–90.
Troeltsch, Ernst. *Gesammelte Schriften 3: Der Historismus und seine Probleme*. Aalen: Scientia, 1961.
Vierkandt, Alfred. 'Die Überwindung des Positivismus in der deutschen Soziologie der Gegenwart'. *Jahrbuch für Soziologie* 2 (1926): 66–90.
Vogt, Peter. *Kontingenz und Zufall: eine Ideen- und Begriffsgeschichte*. Berlin: Akademie Verlag, 2011.
Von Wiese, Leopold. 'Der zweite Band des *Jahrbuchs für Soziologie*'. *Kölner Vierteljahrshefte für Soziologie* 5, no. 2 (1926): 153–67.
Warczok, Tomasz and Stephanie Beyer. 'Between the Global and the Local. The Field of American Sociology'. Manuscript, presented at the Annual Meeting of the American Sociological Association, 2019.
Weber, Alfred. *Alfred-Weber-Gesamtausgabe*, vol. 8 of 10, *Schriften zur Kultur- und Geschichtssoziologie (1906–1958)*. Marburg: Metropolis, 1997.
Weber, Alfred. *Ideen zur Staats- und Kultursoziologie*. Karlsruhe: G. Braun, 1927.
Weber, Max. *Collected Methodological Writings*, edited by Hans Henrik Bruun and Sam Whimster. London: Routledge, 2012.
Weber, Max. *Economy and Society*, vol. 1. Berkeley: University of California Press, 1978.
Weber, Max. 'Energetische Kulturtheorien'. *Archiv für Sozialwissenschaft und Sozialpolitik* 29 (1909): 575–98.
Weber, Max. *Roscher and Knies: The Logical Problems of Historical Economics*. New York: Free Press, 1975.
Weiß, Johannes. 'Negative Soziologie'. *Ethik und Sozialwissenschaften* 6, no. 2 (1995): 241–46.
Williams, Raymond. 'Positivist'. In *Keywords*, 238–9. New York: Oxford University Press, 1983.
Windelband, Wilhelm. *Die Lehren vom Zufall*. Berlin: F. Henschel, 1870.
Windelband, Wilhelm and Guy Oakes. 'History and Natural Science'. *History and Theory* 19, no. 2 (1980): 165–8.
Wittkau, Annette. *Historismus: Zur Geschichte des Begriffs und des Problems*. Göttingen: Vandenhoeck & Ruprecht, 1992.
Wulz, Monika. 'Vom Nutzen des Augenblicks für die Projekte der Wissenschaft'. *Berichte zur Wissenschaftsgeschichte* 35, no. 2 (2012): 131–46.

4

Historicism's arrival in the United States: Two routes from Germany

Adriaan van Veldhuizen

Abstract

By analysing two meanings attached to the concept of 'historicism' in a controversy on historical relativism among American historians in the 1930s, this chapter identifies two routes along which historicism had travelled from Germany to the United States. The focus of this chapter is on the works of Charles Beard and Maurice Mandelbaum. The latter's almost-forgotten PhD dissertation is discussed more thoroughly to contribute to a better understanding of his philosophy of history.

Introduction

In the early 1930s, prominent members of the American Historical Association notoriously disputed the possibility of 'objective historical knowledge'. Carl Becker and Charles Beard in particular argued that no historian was able to picture the past as it had actually been. This caused them to adopt a position that Beard would later describe as 'limited relativism', which might be summarized as the idea that all historical knowledge is relative to the social order from which it originates. Over the years the American philosopher Maurice Mandelbaum became a prominent voice opposing Becker and Beard. Mandelbaum's most elaborate contribution to the 1930s debate was a book entitled *The Problem of Historical Knowledge*, which culminated in the thesis that there are 'many reasons why history must often be rewritten, yet none of these reasons demands that we give up the ideal of objective historical knowledge'.[1]

Much has been written about this debate on historical relativism and its participants. A balanced overview of it can be found in Peter Novick's *That*

Noble Dream, and on a more detailed level, David Roberts has shown how all parties involved misinterpreted the important Italian 'relativist' Benedetto Croce.[2] Adding to these studies, my chapter focuses on the accusations of 'being a historicist' that went back and forth between participants in the debate. In a sense, it is remarkable that the role of historicism has not been studied before in this context, because Beard and Mandelbaum, while disagreeing about many things, shared a strong aversion of historicism. Confusingly, however, they consistently accused *each other* of being a historicist.

The first three sections of this chapter will reconstruct the different meanings associated with the term. After discussing Beard and Becker, I will examine Mandelbaum's work in somewhat greater detail. My analysis will not only draw on *The Problem of Historical Knowledge* (1938), but also on his almost-forgotten PhD thesis, 'Historical Relativism in the Recent Philosophy of History' (1936). By doing so, this chapter adds significantly to the existing literature on Mandelbaum. Although authors such as Ian Verstegen and Michael Ermarth have written about Mandelbaum and historicism, they have not examined what historicism meant to the young Mandelbaum or on what sources his understanding of historicism drew.[3] By filling gaps in his intellectual and personal history, this chapter offers a more finely textured account of the development of his ideas on historicism. In the final section, this chapter argues that the differences between Beard's and Mandelbaum's conceptions of historicism were rooted in different methodologies, different political views and different personal experiences.

Historicism and objectivism

The 1930s relativism debate was a lively one. In philosophy John Dewey took a position close to relativism, in law the 'legal realists' did, while in anthropology the cultural relativism of Franz Boaz was still quite topical. Moreover, relativism was not only a scholarly endeavour; especially in Europe the debate had been dramatically politicized. Back in 1924 Mussolini had embraced relativism as a part of his political doctrine, which later led Max Horkheimer to conclude that 'relativism which is without philosophical justification is an element of a social dynamic which moves toward authoritarian forms'.[4] In general, one could argue that both in Europe and in the United States the intellectual pros and cons of relativism were eagerly discussed in both academia and society at large.

In his 1931 presidential address to the American Historical Association, Carl Becker took the debate to the historians.[5] His famous 'Everyman His Own Historian' did not directly promote relativism, but Becker encouraged his audience to think of the role of the historian as an observer bound to his own time and place. 'It should be a relief to us,' Becker said, 'to renounce omniscience, to recognize that every generation, our own included, will, must inevitably, understand the past and anticipate the future in the light of its own restricted experience.'[6] Perhaps Becker proved to be a subjectivist rather than a relativist, but by presenting history in his speech as 'a convenient blend of truth and fancy, of what we commonly distinguish as "fact" and "interpretation"', he opened the doors for relativism.[7]

Two years later Charles Beard took all of this a step further. He highlighted the role of the historian in the 'construction' of history and called historical writing 'an act of faith'.[8] Beard was once a convinced positivist but had changed his mind after reading about relativity as introduced by the 'New Physics' of Einstein and Bohr, as well as works on history by the Italian philosopher Benedetto Croce. First and foremost, Beard turned against the idea, conventionally associated with Leopold von Ranke, that it is possible and desirable for historians to acquire impartial and objective knowledge about the past. Beard followed Croce's dictum that history is 'contemporary thought about the past', and therefore stressed that historiography is inevitably the product of a historian's time and place.[9] Of course, recognizing that historiography reflects the historian's epoch does not necessarily imply a rejection of the *aim* of objectivity, and indeed: Beard did not present himself as a full-blown relativist or an enemy of scientific methods as such. In fact, he considered the scientific method 'a precious and indispensable instrument of the human mind', adding that 'without it society would sink down into primitive animism and barbarism'. Concurrently, Beard proclaimed that 'the historian is bound by his craft to recognize the nature and limitations of the scientific method and to dispel the illusion that it can produce a science of history embracing the fullness of history, or of any large phase, as past actuality'.[10]

Although Becker and Beard's musings were broadly welcomed as a breath of intellectual fresh air, some people frowned upon their seemingly categorical rejection of Rankean epistemology.[11] The deepest frown might have appeared on the forehead of Theodor Clarke Smith, who replied that Beard irresponsibly contributed to 'the final extinction of a noble dream', after 'he summarily brushed aside the Ranke conception of impersonal search for truth'.[12]

Six months later, in October 1935, Beard replied to Smith in an article titled 'That Noble Dream'.[13] For the context of my chapter this article is of particular importance, as this is the piece in which Beard introduced historicism. It also represents the moment when Beard dropped the laconic tone of voice that he and Becker had applied so far. He now systematically refuted Smith's claim to objectivism:

> This theory of history and of human powers is one of the most sweeping dogmas in the recorded history of theories. It condemns philosophy and throws it out of doors. As practiced, it ignores problems of mind with which philosophers and theologians have wrestled for centuries and have not yet settled to everybody's satisfaction. As developed into Historicism (it may be well to Anglicize *Historismus*), it takes on all the implications of empiricism, positivism, and, if not materialism, at least that rationalism which limits history to its purely experiential aspects.[14]

Beard aimed to add some philosophical considerations to the epistemological claims of positivism. He stressed that he did not reject the scientific method as such, but rejected *scientism*, in which the outcome of historical research was considered an objective truth. Neither did he refute objectivity as a practical ambition, but he did remind his colleagues that their personal contexts would always follow them into their texts.

When Beard wrote about 'historicism', the concept was not very well defined or canonized by other American scholars. Although it had been mentioned in some philosophy, theology and sociology journals in the 1920s, the concept was not used systematically. When in 1954 Dwight Lee and Robert Beck reflected on how '[o]ver the past twenty years, the word "historicism" appears to have been definitely established in the vocabulary of history and philosophy', they added that 'its meaning has varied greatly and has often been obscure'.[15]

So, what *could* Beard have meant? One of the first Americans who had mentioned historicism in a historical context was philosopher Sidney Hook. Using the term in at least four articles and book reviews from 1929 onwards, Hook labelled Hegel and Marx as historicists, though without specification of what he exactly meant by this.[16] In the early 1930s, several historians introduced their own versions of the concept. Possibly the most notable one came from the Russian American historian Vladimir Simkhovitch, who in six long and learned articles on 'Approaches to History' in the works of Hegel, Schelling and Fichte described historicism as an 'intellectual mass movement', propagating a historicizing mindset and a 'struggle against the Rationalism of Enlightenment and Revolution'.[17]

In this context it was no surprise that Beard also introduced his own understanding of historicism. He described Ranke as a 'historicist', and used 'historicism' and what he called the 'Ranke formula' of 'wie es eigentlich gewesen ist [sic]' as mutually exchangeable.[18] For Beard, historicism was 'an all-embracing philosophy of historiography, even though it denies philosophy'.[19] It stood for impartiality, positivism and objectivism. By emphasizing, however, that this so-called '"impartial" historian proved to be a bulwark for Prussian authoritarianism', Beard in fact strongly criticized Ranke and his historicism for politicizing historical studies.[20] Consequently, Beard urged his colleagues, whom he considered to be Rankean in the majority, to drop their so-called 'impartial' positivism.[21]

Beard's interpretation of historicism emerged as the product of a dialogue with a number of German authors. Beard had visited Germany, had German scholars as friends and was one of the few American authors to contribute to the Frankfurt *Zeitschrift für Sozialforschung*.[22] It annoyed Beard that most of his American colleagues were not interested in engaging with German intellectual life. He rhetorically asked: 'How many watched carefully the development of the critical attitude toward Historicism in Europe at the turn of the century, and especially after 1914?'[23]

To understand what was at stake for Beard, it is helpful to look at Karl Heussi's *Die Krise des Historismus*. Beard read this German-language book shortly after its publication in 1932 and it struck him as alarming.[24] Heussi distinguished four 'moments' or defining features of historicism: (1) Historicism focused on methodological objectivity, (2) it expressed the idea that all historical developments are related to each other, (3) it approached history as a process of development and (4) it acknowledged that historians are not concerned with the profound but merely with what is observable and recordable. Heussi at one point 'summarized' these theses with the statement that historicism is 'the historical method by which history was written around 1900'.[25] Beard reproduced this rather brief definition and subsequently equated historicism with what he understood as Rankean scientism.[26]

In 1937 Beard again reflected on historicism, now together with the German historian Alfred Vagts, who happened to be his son-in-law as well. This time, 'historicism' was rendered as 'historism', which gave it an even more German ring. The article proposed a non-historicist scientific method, which could be 'the chief safeguard against the tyranny of authority, bureaucracy, and brute power'.[27] Once again the political urgency of non-historicist research was emphasized. Beard and Vagts wondered whether there was 'any philological historian or archivist so engrossed in his labours that the headlines of the morning newspapers, the sound of marching men, and the throbbing of sectarian drums pass unheeded, leaving no traces on his sense of values and his selection of themes for exploration'.[28] And again a rhetorical question was posed: 'Did that outbreak of war have anything to do with the positivism and materialistic conceptions which had long prevailed in historical thought? That was a neat question for the historian himself'.[29] There was one thing they knew, and that was that 'German historians were literally forced to think about the relation of the craft of history writing to history as actuality'.[30] Moreover, they connected historicism to the false expectations of positivism and scientism. Ellen Nore, Charles Beard's biographer, summarized his position as follows:

> Beard's purpose in calling the attention of historians in the United States to the revision of historicism taking place in Europe was not to urge others to adopt his own eclectic relativism, but rather to focus on the great fallacy of [Rankean] historicism: the idea that the historian stood outside the *Zeitgeist*, a scholar without politics, a neutral mind at work reflecting the connections in a mass of facts.[31]

Despite their warning words, it is questionable whether Beard and Vagts grasped the German intellectual scene as thoroughly as some of their colleagues thought they did. Doubts rise especially when we see Beard and Vagts' critical review of Friedrich Meinecke's newly published book on the crisis of historicism. As Lloyd Sorensen later concluded, their 'examination was so biased and confused that nothing of profit resulted from it for him or for the historical profession generally'.[32] Meinecke, after all, emphasized that historicism was a worldview and, as such, much more than the methodology that Beard, following Heussi, associated with the term. Beard and Vagts hardly seem to have realized how different Meinecke's interpretation was. Indeed, by dismissing Meinecke as an eccentric new contributor to the debate on historicism, they most of all showed how unaware they were of Meinecke's central position in prewar German historiography.

Historicism in Mandelbaum's PhD thesis

In 1936 Maurice Mandelbaum defended his PhD thesis 'Historical Relativism in the Recent Philosophy of History', written under the supervision of philosopher Wilbur Marshall Urban at Yale University. Although Mandelbaum realized that, at least in English, the phrase 'philosophy of history' had often been used to denote speculations about the course of the historical process, he deliberately sought to recalibrate the concept. He suggested that philosophy of history should address the philosophical implications of historians' practice. Therefore, his thesis – although mainly a philosophical endeavour – could not avoid touching upon the debates that were going on in the American historical discipline at that time. Although the thesis was finished by 1936, it should not be read as a direct response to Beard and Becker. In fact, Mandelbaum had started his research in 1930, if not earlier, so at least a year before Becker's 'Everyman' speech.[33] Nevertheless, Beard and Becker each play their role in the dissertation. The thesis is a long fulmination against historical relativism as represented, among others, by two 'eminent American historiographers' who are, as Mandelbaum did not fail to mention, not 'professional philosophers': Carl Becker and Charles Beard.[34]

The dissertation, however, starts with an analysis of the relation between historiography and the past, in the context of which he also introduces the problem of historical relativism. The central theme in this section is what Mandelbaum calls the 'historiographical standpoint'. He states that there is always an element of selection involved in the work of the historian and that every historical account needs a beginning and an end. This implies the historian is outside the series of the events, looking to the past 'from across a gap'.[35] This 'historiographical standpoint' is inherent to the nature of historiography. According to Mandelbaum, it is 'the omnipresence of the historiographical standpoint that has given rise to that relativism'. And then, with a quote from Ernst Troeltsch, he equals this kind of relativism with 'vielberufener schlecter [sic] Historismus'.[36]

This equation of historicism and relativism gains more depth when Mandelbaum reveals some 'Relativistic Views on Historiography'. He finds them in the works of authors he considers to be key advocates of historical relativism: Benedetto Croce, Wilhelm Dilthey, Erich Rothacker and Karl Mannheim. For Mandelbaum, historical relativism is 'the belief that in every historiographical judgment there is involved a valuational standpoint on the part of the historiographer such as to make valid knowledge of the past impossible'.[37] While exposing the 'sources' of this historical relativism, he touches upon the notion of historicism:

> To find the sources of historical relativism one need merely look to the development of the notions of knowledge as valuational and knowledge as dependent on socially accepted value-structures. These two notions need not to be traced back in their detail, but we can see how the first source (knowledge

as valuational) has been fed by Schopenhauer, Nietzsche, Kant, Pragmatism, Bergson, Pareto, Freud, and others; while the second is a result of our modern 'Historismus' for which the Hegelian Dialectic, the growth of sociology, and Marx, are perhaps most largely responsible.[38]

So, to be precise: for Mandelbaum, historicism is one of the two sources of the modern-day historical relativism he investigates.

If Mandelbaum subsequently distinguishes three 'aspect[s] of the historiographical judgement which [have] fostered historical relativism', the term 'historicism' disappears, even though the author discusses concepts often closely related to it. Firstly, there is the idea that history is written over and over again: historians, each with their own 'value-charged historiographical standpoint', make new selections of historical facts all the time.[39] Secondly, there is the idea that not only the historian, but also the past is value-charged. Relativists consider knowledge to be dependent on value structures as a 'hidden stratum under the thought of a time'. According to these relativists, Mandelbaum writes, the value structure – or, in German, the *Zeitgeist* – has a formative role in the course of events. Because it can never be fully known, the true nature of the past cannot be known either, relativists argue.[40] The third cause leading to historical relativism is 'the fact that the past stretches through the present into the future, and that this historical continuity makes it impossible to divorce our knowledge of the past from our expectations of the future'.[41] All of these ideas are discussed without any reference to historicism.

Mandelbaum then tests his ideas on many authors whom he regards as relativists and concludes that all relativists share some features:

> This common denominator, as will be recognized from our discussion, is to be found in the insistence of these theorists on the activistic (and therefore valuational) character of knowledge. To this view there is joined, in each of their systems, an espousal of that doctrine which is best termed Lebensphilosophie, a doctrine which we may be permitted to delineate as the attempt to understand all forms of human activity through the emphasis on the dynamic aspects of reality construed in terms of an immanent, 'vital' process.[42]

So, while all authors emphasize the valuational character of historical knowledge for different reasons and in different manners, they all accept the valuational element in historical knowledge as well. Mandelbaum even encounters this phenomenon in authors who explicitly distanced themselves from relativism, such as Georg Simmel, Heinrich Rickert, Max Scheler and Ernst Troeltsch. Although all of them, in one way or another, tried to overcome relativism, they were unable to get rid of the idea that all historical knowledge is value-bound.[43]

To Mandelbaum, finding an 'answer to relativism' therefore requires rejection of the idea that historical knowledge is value-bound. He tries to show, more precisely, how 'judgements of fact are related to values without being value-bound'.[44] He argues that true historiographical statements are desirable and therefore valuable, although this does not imply that these statements themselves are value-bound.[45] Mandelbaum finds an answer in the idea that 'no conditions attaching to the historiographical judgement, nor to the material of that judgement ... throws doubt on its validity'.[46] What remains is a deep trust in the historiographical method, which can lead to different views that are nevertheless objective.

One could doubt whether this 'Historical Pluralism', as Mandelbaum calls it, is really an answer to relativism, but that is a question my chapter does not address. More interesting for now is that Mandelbaum concludes his thesis with a suggestion for practising historians. Arguing that 'the contemporary historiographer need no longer be ashamed at agreeing with the Rankean ideal', he evokes Ranke's dictum that encourages historians to show 'wie es eigentlich gewesen'.[47] As a reviewer once described Mandelbaum's later position: '[T]he historian can "grasp" or "find" or "give a picture of" the self-contained order and structure of events, not by imposing his understanding upon his materials or effecting a selection of them in terms of his own values, but by "following where the materials lead"'.[48]

Historicism, albeit in a specific interpretation of the word, is central to how Mandelbaum develops this argument in his dissertation. While Mandelbaum adheres to Ranke, he does not call him a historicist. Neither does historicism, for him, refer to 'Romanticist' historiography, judging by the fact that the term is absent even from Mandelbaum's discussion of 'a completely organic view of development'.[49] For Mandelbaum, historicism almost exclusively referred to relativism,[50] or more precisely, to a particular kind of relativism: the argument that knowledge depends on socially accepted value structures.[51] I will come back to this in the section 'Two Meanings of Historicism', after discussing the better-known book version of Mandelbaum's thesis.

Historicism in *The Problem of Historical Knowledge*

Like the dissertation, *The Problem of Historical Knowledge* aims to overcome the position of 'current scepticism with which historical knowledge is regarded'.[52] The conceptualization of historical relativism, however, is slightly different than in the dissertation. Whereas the thesis defined historical relativism as 'the belief that in every historiographical judgment there is involved a valuational standpoint on the part of the historiographer such as to make valid knowledge of the past impossible', *The Problem of Historical Knowledge* describes it as the belief that 'no historical work grasps the nature of the past (or present) immediately, [and] that whatever "truth" a historical work contains is relative to the conditioning processes under which it arose and can only be understood with reference to those processes'.[53]

Mandelbaum distinguishes three key presuppositions of historical relativism as he sees it developing from the late nineteenth-century onwards. First, there is the view that no historical text can ever do justice to what happened in the past: the past is far richer than its representation can ever be.[54] Second, there is the idea that the past has a different structure than historical representations. In fact, a historical text can never do justice to what happened in the past, because structures in historiography never match the ones in the past.[55] The third and, according to Mandelbaum, most characteristic element of historical relativism is the idea that there is always a 'value-charged' judgement in writing about the past. Because historians impose their values on the historical material, their accounts of the past are determined by their personal and present positions.[56]

As in the dissertation, Mandelbaum examines to what extent these three 'presuppositions of historical relativism' can be detected in the work of Dilthey, Croce and Mannheim, whom he considers the most important advocates of historical relativism.[57] He finds that the first is employed by none of them. The second and the third arguments, however, are used by all three authors. In his analysis of the second presupposition – the idea that the past has a different structure than historical representations – historicism is mentioned for the first time, as a 'doctrine' which holds 'that historical knowledge is to be understood and estimated with reference to its setting in the historical process'.[58] According to Mandelbaum, '[h]istoricism consists in the attempt to take seriously (in a philosophic sense) the fact of change. It sees behind every particular fact the one ultimate fact of change: every particular [fact] is treated with relation to the process of change out of which it arises, and this process is seen as immanent in it.'[59]

Mandelbaum distinguishes two forms of historicism: 'historicism of knowledge' and 'historicism of values'. Historicism of values 'holds every set of cultural values ... relative to the age in which it is dominant', whereas historicism of knowledge 'claims that no statement can be considered true or false without reference to the time at which it was formulated'.[60] This is important, since historicism is 'basic to the argument that the structure and continuity of the historian's work do not reflect the structure and continuity of the historical process itself' and it therefore is the root of historical relativism.[61] Mandelbaum's criticism is not only targeted at Dilthey, Croce and Mannheim. According to Mandelbaum, Charles Beard's relativism also springs from 'specific metaphysical doctrines which demand that every work should be estimated with respect to its position in the historical process', which is obviously in line with the 'doctrine' of historicism.[62]

The second part of the book, devoted to 'Historical Knowledge', examines 'the two philosophic presuppositions which we have found to be basic in the arguments of the historical relativists'.[63] These two are the same as the three presuppositions of historical relativism he discerned earlier, minus the first one that nobody actually uses. Historicism emerges here when Mandelbaum elaborates on the first presupposition: 'the relativistic assumption that the validity of knowledge is to be understood and estimated with reference to the conditions under which it was formed'.[64] Beard and Vagts are again presented as key representatives of relativism. Mandelbaum underlines that their 'limited relativity' will eventually fall prey to 'absolute scepticism'.[65] For as long as one states that the validity of knowledge must be understood with reference to the conditions under which it was formed, this position, even in its most moderate form, inevitably leads to '"the chaos" of unlimited relativism'.[66] In a conventional reading of Leopold von Ranke, Mandelbaum then claims that 'the truth of a historical work consists in the truth of its statements, not in the fact that the author judged as he did on such-and-such grounds. To consider historical truth, therefore, as a function of the conditions on which the historian judged the statements which he made to be true, is a totally irrelevant procedure.'[67]

Subsequently, Mandelbaum presents Beard and Vagts as exponents of what he calls 'historicism of knowledge'.[68] Scholars adhering to this doctrine believe that every era has its own unique knowledge structure, and that therefore 'no statement can be considered true or false without reference to the time at which it was formulated'.[69] Because of this presupposition, historicists mix up judgement and statement and cannot believe in a correspondence theory of truth – which turns them into relativists. The second, more important philosophical presupposition that Mandelbaum distinguishes is 'the view that valuational factors [enter] into and [determine] the content of historical knowledge'.[70] So although *The Problem of Historical Knowledge* is a different book than 'Historical Relativism in the Recent Philosophy of History', it shares with the thesis a strong focus on the valuational aspects of historical understanding, while closely associating historicism with the 'philosophic presuppositions' held by historical relativists.

Two Meanings of Historicism

The Problem of Historical Knowledge received serious attention from reviewers in both philosophical and historical journals.[71] The book's reception, however, was not overwhelmingly positive. Especially two practising historians wrote critical reviews of the book: Charles Beard and Carl Becker. Most noteworthy was their declaration that Mandelbaum had represented their positions incorrectly.[72] Neither Beard nor Becker considered himself a relativist in Mandelbaum's definition of the word, and both defended their 'limited relativism'. Beard, the harshest of the two, stated unequivocally: 'Mr. Mandelbaum does not cite any lines from my writings to prove this statement, and if I have ever printed anything like that, then I cannot write the English language.'[73]

Peter Novick has discovered that Beard and Becker even ridiculed the book in their private correspondence. They criticized Mandelbaum for being 'clumsy' and 'simply preposterous'.[74] Although Beard and Becker might have been correct about Mandelbaum misrepresenting their positions, they should have recognized that *The Problem of Historical Knowledge* was not primarily about them. As an adaptation of his PhD thesis, the book focused on European philosophical debates. The names of Beard and Becker only appeared in sections on 'historicism of knowledge'.[75] In these sections, Mandelbaum might have been a bit too eager to debate Beard and Becker – which made him complicit in the unbalanced reception of his own book – but they did not represent the main aim of the book.

A few years after the reviews, Mandelbaum wrote an article in which he came back to the topic. He argued that, as a theoretician, Beard did not take the same position as the historian Beard: his historical work was full of objectivity claims.[76] However, Mandelbaum did not use the occasion to reflect on what, from the perspective of this chapter, is the most pressing issue at stake in the exchange: What exactly does 'historicism' mean?

So, what is historicism? As we saw above, for Mandelbaum, historicism comes close to being synonymous to relativism. In a section on Rothacker, Mandelbaum praises Rothacker's attempts for 'the salvation of logical validity from the inroads of Historismus'. Also, he claims that Rickert (the author who is mentioned most often in the dissertation) is 'influenced by the far-flung "Historismus"'.[77] But what does this mean? In a footnote Mandelbaum acknowledges: 'The meaning of "Historismus" is by no means unambiguous. It may best be characterized as a view of reality which feels itself forced to take seriously (in a metaphysical sense) the constant becoming of new forms of life and thought.' Mandelbaum refers to Mannheim, Litt and Troeltsch and describes *Historismus* as 'a deep stream in the thought of our time: Vico, Hamann, Herder, the whole "Historical School" (Ranke, Savigny et al.) may be considered, along with Hegel, Marx and the sociologists, as confluent sources of its growth'.[78]

Although reluctant to give a fixed meaning to the concept, Mandelbaum focuses on concepts such as development, individuality and, most of all, relativism. His description of historicism as 'a view of reality' reveals that it was closer to a *Weltanschauung* than to a methodology. This conception matches best with the ideas on historicism developed by Ernst Troeltsch, the author also mentioned often in the context of historicism. Mandelbaum advises readers interested in historicism to consult Troeltsch's article 'Der Historische Entwicklungsprozess' in the *Historische Zeitschrift*. And quoting Ernst Troeltsch, Mandelbaum equals the kind of relativism he investigates with 'vielberufener schlecter [sic] Historismus'.[79] It should be noted here that Troeltsch was an important source of inspiration for Mandelbaum in general, for instance in his (important) thoughts on *Lebensphilosophie*.[80] When we examine the teachers who exerted formative influences on Mandelbaum, a similar Troeltschean orientation becomes visible.

Mandelbaum's supervisor at Yale, Wilbur Marshall Urban, is not often mentioned in the dissertation – his name is even absent from the bibliography. Mandelbaum only evokes the name of his *Doktorvater* in arguing that judgements concerning the presence of valuations are not themselves valuational. Here he thanks Urban for introducing the idea of 'comparative value judgement', though without any bibliographic reference.[81] It is likely that Mandelbaum's ideas on historicism were more substantially formed during a visit to Berlin in 1930– 1931. Here Mandelbaum attended classes from two professors whom he said he was 'indebted to': Kurt Breysig and Helmut Kuhn.[82] Breysig had been a student of Johann Gustav Droysen and Heinrich von Treitschke, and a friend of Karl Lamprecht. He was well acquainted with the latest debates on historicism and had tried to move beyond them. Although his belief in historical laws would make him an outcast among Berlin historians, Breysig was a famous professor at the time when Mandelbaum arrived in Berlin.[83] Together with Otto Hintze he was seen as one of the most dedicated advocates of a social scientific approach to history, which eventually should lead to universal history. It was in the year Mandelbaum arrived that Breysig decided to focus fully on his history of humanity.[84] Yet Breysig could never fully detach himself from historicist principles: he developed an evolutionary theory of history in which he stated that every society in the world develops through a fixed number of stages.[85] Breysig's negotiations between historicism and the social sciences may well have been a source of inspiration for Mandelbaum.

In these years, Helmut Kuhn was a young academic finishing his *Habilitationsschrift* in Berlin. When Mandelbaum attended both a series of lectures and a seminar by him, Kuhn had just published an article titled 'Das Problem des Standpunkts und die geschichtliche Erkenntnis', in which he wrote that 'the question of standpoint in philosophy of history raises the question of personal factors determining all historical knowledge'.[86] It is not difficult to recognize that Kuhn addressed here the very same questions that Mandelbaum tried to answer in the first chapter of his dissertation, on the 'historiographical standpoint'. Mandelbaum did not agree with everything Kuhn wrote, but his footnotes directly refer to Kuhn's seminar.[87] Since the seminar was called 'Uebungen zur Geschichtsphilosophie' (exercises in philosophy of history) and Kuhn had published on historicism before, it is likely that this was one of the earlier moments for Mandelbaum to get acquainted with historicism. What ideas Kuhn held exactly at the time are difficult to retrace, but later he wrote about historicism in a way that is comparable to Mandelbaum's treatment of the subject: 'In making truth a function of historical change, historicism denies all universals. So it can become a [universally valid] theory only by sinning against its own principle.'[88]

In addition to meeting German critics of historicism in Berlin, Mandelbaum got acquainted with German émigré historians who had fled their country in the 1930s. Especially Hajo Holborn, a former student of Friedrich Meinecke, became an important interlocutor for Mandelbaum.[89] However, the author did not credit all of his German sources. While Breysig and Kuhn had figured prominently in the dissertation, their names were absent from *The Problem of Historical Knowledge*. In many respects, the book was, or looked, less German than the dissertation; however, it was not as American as it was read by historians in the United States. As the foregoing makes clear, Mandelbaum's work on historicism cannot be understood apart from his German connections.

Conclusion

Let us by way of conclusion return to the historicism of which Beard and Becker were afraid. Beard wrote: 'Seekers after truth in particular and general have less reason to fear [his kind of history writing] than they have to fear any history that comes under the guise of the Ranke formula or Historicism.'[90] Later he added: 'Slowly it dawns in contemporary consciousness that historiography so conceived furnishes such guides to grand public policy as are vouchsafed to the human mind.'[91] This was also German historicism, at least in Heussi's version of it (not Troeltsch's). Beard, whose main goal was to attack scientism in the American historical discipline, equated historicism with Ranke's methodological approach, thereby showing his indebtedness to a typical late nineteenth-century American interpretation of Ranke.[92]

Whereas Becker, Beard and Vagts associated historicism with scientism and positivism in the historical profession, Mandelbaum regarded historicism as a philosophical position. In line with his German interlocutors, Mandelbaum considered historical relativism the product of the disillusionment with universalism and positivism. These two interpretations of historicism witness to the different routes along which the concept had arrived in the United States. While Mandelbaum drew on Troeltsch, Breysig and Kuhn, Beard based himself primarily on Heussi.

These different sources of inspiration help explain some of the confusion between Mandelbaum and his critics in the American historical profession. An additional layer of complexity may have been the fact that Mandelbaum's book appeared in 1938, six years after Heussi's one, although Mandelbaum's ideas were formed no later than 1931, when Heussi's book was not yet published. What made the situation even less comprehensible was that the American debate on historicism lacked much of the political urgency that the debate had for European thinkers like Troeltsch. Still, only against this European background, it becomes clear why historicism mattered to Mandelbaum and why neither Beard nor Becker even remotely grasped what was at stake for him.

Notes

1   Maurice Mandelbaum, *The Problem of Historical Knowledge: An Answer to Historical Relativism* (1938; repr., New York, NY: Harper & Row, 1967), 304.

2   Peter Novick, *That Noble Dream: The 'Objectivity Question' and the American Historical Profession* (Cambridge: Cambridge University Press, 1988); David D. Roberts, 'Croce in America: Influence, Misunderstanding, and Neglect', *Humanitas* 8, no. 2 (1995): 3–34.
3   Michael Ermarth, 'Mandelbaum on History, Historicism, and Critical Reason: Answering the Destructive Gestalt of the Twentieth Century's Intellectual Crisis with the Constructive Gestalt of Critical-Realist Reason', in *Maurice Mandelbaum and American Critical Realism*, ed. Ian F. Verstegen (London: Routledge, 2010), 19–46.
4   This is mentioned in a fascinating footnote on the concept of relativism in Max Horkheimer, *Critical Theory: Selected Essays* (New York, NY: Continuum, 1972), 165.
5   Carl Becker, 'Everyman His Own Historian', *The American Historical Review* 37, no. 2 (1932): 221–36.
6   Ibid., 235.
7   Ibid., 231.
8   Charles A. Beard, 'Written History as an Act of Faith', *The American Historical Review* 39, no. 2 (1934): 219–31, at 220, 226, 229.
9   Ibid., 219–20.
10 Ibid., 227.
11 On the positive reception of Becker and Beard: Novick, *That Noble Dream*, 258–60.
12 Theodore Clarke Smith, 'The Writing of American History in America, from 1884 to 1934', *The American Historical Review* 40, no. 3 (1935): 439–49, at 448–9.
13 Charles A. Beard, 'That Noble Dream', *The American Historical Review* 41, no. 1 (1935): 74–87.
14 Ibid., 76–7.
15 Dwight E. Lee and Robert N. Beck, 'The Meaning of "Historicism"', *The American Historical Review* 59, no. 3 (1954): 568–77, at 568.
16 Sidney Hook, review of *Hegels Staatsidee, ihr Doppelgesicht und ihr Einfluss im 19. Jahrhundert* by Julius Löwenstein, *The Journal of Philosophy* 26, no. 19 (1929): 526–30; Sidney Hook, 'A Critique of Ethical Realism', *International Journal of Ethics* 40, no. 2 (1930): 179–210; Sidney Hook, 'A Personal Impression of Contemporary German Philosophy', *The Journal of Philosophy* 27, no. 6 (1930): 141–60; Sidney Hook, 'Hegel and Marx', in *Studies in the History of Ideas*, vol. 3 (New York, NY: Columbia University Press, 1935), 331–404.
17 Vladimir G. Simkhovitch, 'Approaches to History III', *Political Science Quarterly* 47, no. 3 (1932): 410–39, at 417, 438; Vladimir G. Simkhovitch, 'Approaches to History IV', *Political Science Quarterly* 48, no. 1 (1933): 23–61, at 23.
18 Beard, 'That Noble Dream', 81, 86.
19 Ibid., 77.
20 Ibid., 78.

21 For a deeper analysis of the (partly failed) reception of Leopold von Ranke in the United States, and of Beard's ideas on Ranke in particular, see Novick, *That Noble Dream*; Georg G. Iggers, 'The Image of Ranke in American and German Historical Thought', *History and Theory* 2, no. 1 (1962): 17–40.
22 Ellen Nore, 'Charles A. Beard's Act of Faith: Context and Content', *The Journal of American History* 66, no. 4 (1980): 850–66, 862.
23 Beard, 'That Noble Dream', 81.
24 Arthur Lloyd Skop, 'The Primacy of Domestic Politics: Eckart Kehr and the Intellectual Development of Charles A. Beard', *History and Theory* 13, no. 2 (1974): 119–31, at 123–4.
25 Lloyd R. Sorensen, 'Charles A. Beard and German Historiographical Thought', *The Mississippi Valley Historical Review* 42, no. 2 (1955): 274–87, at 278. Beard followed Heussi by defining four assumptions: 'a definite position with respect to the age-long objective-subjective problem, the conviction that a thoroughgoing organization of great historical events in an all-embracing coherence was possible, the idea of continuous evolution, and the limitation of history to the world of the recorded and observable'. This quotation is from the article by Charles Beard and Alfred Vagts, however they state explicitly that it is the same idea as used in *That Noble Dream*. See Charles Beard and Alfred Vagts, 'Currents of Thought in Historiography', *The American Historical Review* 42, no. 3 (1937): 460–83, at 462.
26 Beard's reliance on Heussi was also discussed by Sorenson, 'Charles A. Beard', 277–8.
27 Beard, 'Written History', 227.
28 Beard and Vagts, 'Currents of Thought', 460.
29 Ibid., 462.
30 Ibid., 463.
31 Nore, 'Charles A. Beard's Act of Faith', 865–6.
32 Sorenson, 'Charles A. Beard', 286.
33 Already in 1930, Mandelbaum had visited Germany for research on this topic. See Maurice Mandelbaum, 'Historical Relativism in the Recent Philosophy of History' (PhD thesis Yale University, 1936), bibliography x.
34 Ibid., 102–3.
35 Ibid., 8–9.
36 Ibid., 13.
37 Ibid., 102.
38 Ibid., 103.
39 Ibid., 104–5.
40 Ibid., 105.
41 Ibid.
42 Ibid., 137.
43 Ibid., 205.

44   Ibid., 206.
45   Ibid., 211.
46   Ibid., 261.
47   Ibid., 284.
48   E. McClung Fleming, review of *The Problem of Historical Knowledge: An Answer to Relativism* by Maurice Mandelbaum, *Political Science Quarterly* 55, no. 2 (1940): 262–4, at 263.
49   Mandelbaum, 'Historical Relativism', 29.
50   Ibid., 13, 88.
51   Ibid., 103.
52   Mandelbaum, *Problem of Historical Knowledge*, x.
53   Mandelbaum, 'Historical Relativism', 102; Mandelbaum, *Problem of Historical Knowledge*, 19.
54   Ibid., 21.
55   Ibid., 24.
56   Ibid., 31.
57   Ibid., 83.
58   Ibid., 88.
59   Ibid., 88–9.
60   Ibid., 89.
61   Ibid.
62   Ibid., 91.
63   Ibid., 177.
64   Ibid.
65   Ibid., 178. Mandelbaum refers to Beard and Vagts, 'Currents of Thought in Historiography', 481.
66   Mandelbaum, *Problem of Historical Knowledge*, 180.
67   Ibid., 183.
68   Interestingly Mandelbaum does not mention the term here, but does describe this presupposition as 'historicism with respect to knowledge' (ibid., 99). According to the index of the book, however, exactly the ten pages of this chapter that deal with Beard and Vagts are about 'historicism'.
69   Ibid., 89.
70   Ibid., 190.
71   T. E. Jessop wrote a lyrical review in *Philosophy*: T. E. Jessop, review of *The Problem of Historical Knowledge: An Answer to Relativism* by Maurice Mandelbaum, *Philosophy* 14, no. 54 (1939): 217–19. The Norwegian historian Andreas Elviken wrote: 'On what grounds, may it be asked, can it be ascertained that "some insight" and "the context" are objective and not in themselves value-impregnated thought-forms? In short, it appears to the reviewer that the author takes for granted points which most evidently need establishment in an escape from the relativity of values.'

Andreas Elviken, review of *The Problem of Historical Knowledge: An Answer to Relativism* by Maurice Mandelbaum, *The Journal of Modern History* 11, no. 4 (1939): 567–8, at 568.

72 Charles A. Beard, review of *The Problem of Historical Knowledge: An Answer to Relativism* by Maurice Mandelbaum, *The American Historical Review* 44, no. 3 (1939): 571–2; Carl Becker, review of *The Problem of Historical Knowledge* by Maurice Mandelbaum, *The Philosophical Review* 49, no. 3 (1940): 361–4.

73 Beard, review, 571.

74 Novick, *That Noble Dream*, 263.

75 Mandelbaum, *Problem of Historical Knowledge*, 17–9, 178–80.

76 Maurice Mandelbaum, 'Causal Analysis in History', *Journal of the History of Ideas* 3, no. 1 (1942): 30–50, at 37–39.

77 Mandelbaum, 'Historical Relativism', 123, 178.

78 Ibid., 140 n. 12.

79 Ibid., 13.

80 Ibid., 147. Some of his ideas on the concept of *Lebensphilosophie* might well have been inspired by Richard Kroner, whose seminar Mandelbaum attended in December 1935 at the thirty-fifth annual meeting of the Eastern Division of the American Philosophical Association. Mandelbaum also attended seminars by Harrold A. Larrabee, James Burnham and Sterling P. Lamprecht. He seems to have been particularly interested in the concept of historical causation (Mandelbaum, 'Historical Relativism', bibliography x). The talk by Kroner be found here; other talks are available in the same volume: Richard Kroner, 'Philosophy of Life and Philosophy of History', *The Journal of Philosophy* 33, no. 8 (1936): 204–12.

81 Mandelbaum, 'Historical Relativism', 220–1, 224, 264 n. 44.

82 Ibid., bibliography x.

83 Eckhardt Fuchs, 'The Alternatives to German Historicism', in *The Oxford History of Historical Writing*, vol. 4, ed. Stuart Macintyre, Juan Maiguashca and Attila Pók (Oxford: Oxford University Press, 2011), 59–78, at 71–2.

84 Bernhard vom Brocke, *Kurt Breysig: Geschichtswissenschaft zwischen Historismus und Soziologie* (Lübeck: Matthiesen Verlag, 1971), 120.

85 This struggle has been noted by others, too. Vom Brocke's biography of Breysig is titled *Geschichtswissenschaft zwischen Historismus und Soziologie*. In response, Hayden White wrote that Breysig 'remained a dualist to the end'. See Hayden White, review of *Kurt Breysig: Geschichtswissenschaft zwischen Historismus und Soziologie* by Bernhard vom Brocke, *The Journal of Modern History* 45, no. 1 (1973): 161–3, at 163.

86 Helmut Kuhn, 'Das Problem des Standpunkts und die geschichtliche Erkenntnis', *Kant-Studien* 35 (1930): 496–510, at 497.

87 Mandelbaum, 'Historical Relativism', 33–4, n. 44, 45, 50. In note 45, Mandelbaum explicitly refers to the seminar he did with Kuhn. Mandelbaum's teachers in

Berlin were never recognized as being an inspiration for him. Ian Verstegen does mention Meinecke as a possible contact in Berlin but Mandelbaum does not mention him in his dissertation. Ian F. Verstegen, 'Mandelbaum's Noble Dream: Historical Objectivism through a Century of Historical Debates', in *Maurice Mandelbaum and American Critical Realism*, ed. Ian F. Verstegen (London: Routledge, 2010), 65–84, at 68.
88   Helmut Kuhn, *Der Staat: Eine philosophische Darstellung* (Munich: Kösel, 1967), 42–3.
89   Mandelbaum thanked Holborn 'for his friendly aid and advise' in the introduction of *The Problem of Historical Knowledge*, x.
90   Beard, 'That Noble Dream', 84.
91   Beard and Vagts, 'Currents of Thought', 483.
92   Peter Novick stated about this interpretation that there has been an 'almost total misunderstanding' of Ranke in the American historical discipline (Novick, *That Noble Dream*, 26).

Bibliography

Beard, Charles A. 'Written History as an Act of Faith'. *The American Historical Review* 39, no. 2 (1934): 219–31.

Beard, Charles A. 'That Noble Dream'. *The American Historical Review* 41 (1935): 74–87.

Beard, Charles A. and Alfred Vagts. 'Currents of Thought in Historiography'. *The American Historical Review* 42, no. 3 (1937): 460–83.

Beard, Charles A. 'Review of Maurice Mandelbaum, The Problem of Historical Knowledge: An Answer to Relativism'. *The American Historical Review* 14, no. 3 (1939): 571–2.

Becker, Carl. 'Everyman His Own Historian'. *The American Historical Review* 37, no. 2 (1932): 221–36.

Becker, Carl. 'The Problem of Historical Knowledge by Maurice Mandelbaum'. *The Philosophical Review* 49, no. 3 (1940): 361–4.

Elviken, Andreas. 'The Problem of Historical Knowledge: An Answer to Relativism. Maurice Mandelbaum'. *The Journal of Modern History* 11, no. 4 (1939): 567–8.

Ermarth, Michael. 'Mandelbaum on History, Historicism, and Critical Reason: Answering the Destructive Gestalt of the Twentieth Century's Intellectual Crisis with the Constructive Gestalt of Critical-Realist Reason'. In *Maurice Mandelbaum and American Critical Realism*, edited by Ian F. Verstegen, 19–46. London: Routledge, 2010.

Fuchs, Eckhardt. 'The Alternatives to German Historicism'. In *The Oxford History of Historical Writing*, vol. 4, edited by Stuart Macintyre, Juan Maiguashca and Attila Pok, 59–78. Oxford: Oxford University Press, 2011.

Hook, Sidney. 'Hegels Staatsidee, Ihr Doppelgesicht Und Ihr Einfluss Im. 19. Jahrhundert'. *The Journal of Philosophy* 26, no. 19 (1929): 526–30.
Hook, Sidney. 'A Critique of Ethical Realism'. *International Journal of Ethics* 40, no. 2 (1930): 179–210.
Hook, Sidney. 'A Personal Impression of Contemporary German Philosophy'. *The Journal of Philosophy* 27, no. 6 (1930): 141–60.
Hook, Sidney. 'Hegel and Marx'. In *Studies in the History of Ideas, Vol. 3*, edited by the Department of Philosophy of Columbia University, 331–404. New York: Columbia University Press, 1935.
Iggers, Georg G. 'The Image of Ranke in American and German Historical Thought'. *History and Theory* 2, no. 1 (1962): 17–40.
Jessop, T. E. 'The Problem of Historical Knowledge: An Answer to Relativism. By Maurice Mandelbaum'. *Philosophy* 14, no. 54 (1939): 217–19.
Kroner, Richard. 'Philosophy of Life and Philosophy of History'. *The Journal of Philosophy* 33, no. 8 (1936): 204–12.
Kuhn, Helmut. 'Das Problem des Standpunkts und die geschichtliche Erkenntnis'. *Kant-Studien* 35 (1930): 496–510.
Kuhn, Helmut. *Der Staat: Eine philosophische Darstellung*. Munich: Kösel, 1967.
Lee, Dwight E. and Robert N. Beck. 'The Meaning of "Historicism"'. *The American Historical Review* 59, no. 3 (1954): 568–77.
Mandelbaum, Maurice. 'Historical Relativism in the Recent Philosophy of History'. PhD diss., Yale University, New Haven, 1936.
Mandelbaum, Maurice. 'Causal Analysis in History'. *Journal of the History of Ideas* 3, no. 1 (1942): 30–50.
Mandelbaum, Maurice. *The Problem of Historical Knowledge: An Answer to Historical Relativism*. 1938. Reprinted Torchbook edition. New York, NY: Harper & Row, 1967.
McClung Fleming, E. 'The Problem of Historical Knowledge: An Answer to Relativism. By Maurice Mandelbaum'. *Political Science Quarterly* 55, no. 2 (1940): 262–4.
Nore, Ellen. 'Charles A. Beard's Act of Faith: Context and Content'. *The Journal of American History* 66, no. 4 (1980): 850–66.
Novick, Peter. *That Noble Dream: The 'Objectivity Question' and the American Historical Profession*. Cambridge: Cambridge University Press, 1988.
Roberts, David D. 'Croce in America: Influence, Misunderstanding, and Neglect'. *Humanitas* 8, no. 2 (1995): 3–34.
Simkhovitch, Vladimir. 'Approaches to History III'. *Political Science Quarterly* 47, no. 3 (1932): 410–39.
Simkhovitch, Vladimir. 'Approaches to History IV'. *Political Science Quarterly* 48, no. 1 (1933): 23–61.
Skop, Arthur Lloyd. 'The Primacy of Domestic Politics: Eckart Kehr and the Intellectual Development of Charles A. Beard'. *History and Theory* 13, no. 2 (1974): 119–31.
Smith, Theodore Clarke. 'The Writing of American History in America, from 1884 to 1934'. *The American Historical Review* 40, no. 3 (1935): 439–49.

Sorenson, Lloyd R. 'Charles A. Beard and German Historiographical Thought'. *The Mississippi Valley Historical Review* 42, no. 2 (1955): 274–87.

Verstegen, Ian F. 'Mandelbaum's Noble Dream: Historical Objectivism through a Century of Historical Debates'. In *Maurice Mandelbaum and American Critical Realism*, edited by Ian F. Verstegen, 65–84. London: Routledge, 2010.

Vom Brocke, Bernhard. *Kurt Breysig: Geschichtswissenschaft zwischen Historismus und Soziologie*. Lübeck: Matthiesen Verlag, 1971.

White, Hayden. Review of *Kurt Breysig: Geschichtswissenschaft zwischen Historismus und Soziologie* by Bernhard vom Brocke. *The Journal of Modern History* 45, no. 1 (1973): 161–3.

Part Three

Travel companions

5

The spectre of historicism: A discourse of fear

Herman Paul

Abstract

Historians of historicism have done a lot to uncover the various *meanings* associated with the term. By contrast, the *rhetorical uses* of this emotionally charged term, especially in contexts of controversy, have never received systematic attention. This chapter argues that such a rhetorical approach can bring to light patterns that have so far remained invisible. Drawing on the case of Dutch intellectuals between the 1870s and the 1970s, it examines how people used 'historicism' to frame perceived dangers, appeal to anxieties broadly shared among their audiences and depict the intellectual landscape as a battlefield with dangerous worldviews roaming around. This chapter thereby shows the fruitfulness of extending conventional history of ideas approaches with a rhetorical perspective sensitive to the emotional aspects of polemical language.

Introduction

On a Tuesday in November 1952, the old St Peter's Church in Utrecht resounded with Psalm singing.[1] A large audience of mostly Protestant pastors, social workers, journalists and academics had gathered, partly to celebrate the half-centenary of the Christian Social Congress – a conference in 1891 that had given a major impetus to the social movement in the Netherlands – but partly also to explore how the movement's concern for social justice could take on new forms in postwar society. The conference programme spoke boldly about the Kingdom of God and the needs of the world. Yet the tone of most speakers was not nearly as resolute and self-confident as had been the case in 1891. Back then, poverty and hardship had been condemned as contrary to a God-given social order.

'In general, aberration from these laws and ordinances, decreed by God to his creatures, is the cause of all social abuses.'[2] But in the early 1950s, at a time when social life was beset with unrest because of experienced and anticipated societal changes, such firm language no longer seemed appropriate.

Henk Berkhof, most notably, a leading figure in the country's largest Protestant church, used his keynote lecture for a critical retrospective on the 'ordinances' and 'principles' beloved by late nineteenth Reformed (*gereformeerde*) theologians such as Abraham Kuyper. It is one thing, he said, to try to develop a Christian view on social issues like labour and poverty, but another to think that such a Christian view can be formulated once and for all. Christian social ethics cannot be timeless. Precisely because it deals with changing social realities, it is 'dependent on place, time, people, and situations'. Berkhof's lecture therefore resulted in a plea for humility. Every generation, he said, has to read the Bible anew, trying to discern what is important 'here and now'. To which the speaker added, in a self-reflective moment, that this cautious stance itself was a product of historical circumstances, too. 'We feel,' said Berkhof, 'that we belong to a different age, not the age of development, but the age of eradication [*ontworteling*] ... '[3]

This was not a feeling shared by all attendees. The discussion following Berkhof's lecture had hardly begun when Herman Dooyeweerd, a neo-Calvinist philosopher at the Free University, accused the speaker of 'dangerous historicism'. Under influence of 'the historicist zeitgeist', Berkhof was conveying a 'relativist and historicist' message, which would undermine the very ordinances and principles that the founding fathers of the Free University, in the closing decades of the nineteenth century, had identified as footholds against historical relativism. In the second round of the debate, the next day, another neo-Calvinist philosopher, Sytse Ulbe Zuidema, joined Dooyeweerd in criticizing the speaker for defending a historicism 'that only knows situations'. This situationalism amounted, 'if not to nihilism, then at least to relativism and historicism', or so an angry Zuidema asserted.[4]

The sources do not reveal how Berkhof, the irenic rector of the theological seminary of the Netherlands Reformed Church, responded to these neo-Calvinist objections. Berkhof's publications, however, show that he himself also had strong reservations about historicism. Historicism, Berkhof wrote in 1958, is a 'weary scepticism', unable to detect any meaning in the historical process. 'For all ideals, norms, and attributions of meaning are products of their own time; they do not stand above history, but are results of and elements in the historical process. Who would be able to find stability in this endless process?'

As late as 1971, Berkhof would argue that such relativizing of norms and values is a deadlock. 'We need to be liberated ... from such absolutized historicism.'[5]

The history of historicism

I start with this vignette because it illustrates in nice detail to what extent historicism in the 1950s served as a polemical term, charged with pejorative connotations and emotional power. If historicism could be perceived as breeding nihilism, an 'unstable signifier' of which historian Nitzan Lebovic has argued that 'it carries the semantic structure of an accusation',[6] then historicism might be interpreted similarly, not as a position that people claimed themselves, but as an accusation. For the Christian Social Congress attendees under the vaults of Utrecht's St Peter's Church at least, historicism was a word of warning, referring to a threat for which Dutch Protestants had reasons to be frightened. Although others were less fearful of historicism – some historians in the 1970s even proudly identified as historicists[7] – it is fair to say that Berkhof, Dooyeweerd and Zuidema were representative of large segments of Dutch intelligentsia insofar as they used historicism as a derogative term imbued with emotional subtexts.

Although the history of historicism is not exactly an understudied topic, these emotional subtexts – fear, anger, worry – have never been taken very seriously. Arguably, this is largely because scholars tend to approach historicism *conceptually*, with a dominant interest in the *meanings* associated with the term. This is most evident among scholars who try to turn historicism into a useful analytical concept. Friedrich Jaeger and Jörn Rüsen, for instance, define historicism as a nineteenth-century tradition of treating historical scholarship as a *verstehende Geisteswissenschaft*.[8] Similarly, Frederick Beiser equates it with an epistemological tradition of legitimizing history as a science.[9] Precisely to the extent that such definitions try to turn a derogatory term into a more descriptive label, they evade the question why historicism for most twentieth-century users of the term was so emotionally charged. More promising, in this respect, is a line of research advocated by Otto Gerhard Oexle and his students. Building on earlier work by Georg G. Iggers and others,[10] Oexle *cum suis* have meticulously examined what the word 'historicism' meant to early and mid-twentieth-century German intellectuals.[11] But although this second approach has much more to say about dangers and threats than the first one, it still focuses predominantly on what historicism *meant* to those who warned against it. Historicism, in other words, has been studied almost consistently through conceptual prisms.

What would be the benefit of broadening the scope of enquiry by drawing attention to *rhetorical* uses of a term charged with emotional connotations? Judging by how Dutch intellectuals from the 1870s to the 1970s spoke, wrote, argued, quarrelled and sermonized about historicism, such an approach might bring to light patterns that have so far remained invisible. As I will argue in this chapter, it can reveal similarities in how people framed their perceived dangers, rhetorically appealed to anxieties shared by their audiences and drew on language of 'isms' in depicting the intellectual landscape as a battlefield with dangerous worldviews roaming around, eager to make victims. So, while the beginning of all wisdom may be that historicism meant different things to different people, this should not be the end: the intellectual life did not exist of meaning alone.

In what follows I will address three questions bearing upon the rhetoric of historicism, thereby focusing on the twentieth-century Netherlands (a country intellectually oriented on Germany, but distinct enough to add a fresh perspective to the largely Germany-focused secondary literature). First, if Dutch authors used historicism as a word of warning, what were their objects of fear? What were they afraid of? Secondly, what do these fears reveal about the authors' preferred attitudes towards history? What, in other words, was the *logos* behind their *pathos*, or the argument behind their rhetoric? Finally, in what language did Dutch critics of historicism articulate their worries? Where did historicism come from and to what broader discourses did it belong?

Sources and methods

Before turning to these questions, however, I will say a few words about sources and methods. My sources are printed texts (books, journals, newspapers), occasionally supplemented with unpublished archival material (letters, notes). The first selection of relevant material has been made with digital search techniques. This selection has subsequently been expanded through close reading of other publications by authors identified as critics of historicism. This double strategy has yielded hundreds of texts – lectures, newspaper articles, book reviews and so on – in fields as diverse as musicology, architecture, sociology, theology and philosophy, from the 1870s until well into the 1970s. My analysis of this material has been published in 2012 as *Het moeras van de geschiedenis* – a book that examines in considerable detail what historicism meant to various groups of Dutch commentators.[12]

Although the current chapter draws on research done for the book, it expands on this earlier publication in trying to move beyond the question what historicism *meant*. In revisiting Dutch perceptions of historicism through a *rhetorical* prism, my aim is to enrich the history of historicism with insights drawn from rhetorical history – a branch of research that focuses on how 'symbols and systems of symbols' express and shape people's 'beliefs, values, attitudes and action[s]'.[13] In this line of research, emotions are never far away. As Kathleen Turner emphasizes: 'the fears, the anxieties, the frustrations, the aggressive impulses of a society are the very stuff of rhetorical studies'.[14] Obviously, emotions *as such* are not accessible to historical enquiry: we cannot possibly know what Berkhof felt when Dooyeweerd and Zuidema attacked him after his lecture in Utrecht. So what rhetorical historians study is not emotional states of mind, but what William Reddy calls *emotives*: textual expressions like 'I fear' and 'I am worried' that are, on the one hand, descriptions of emotional states, but also, on the other, speech acts that seek to persuade an audience by using an emotional register.[15] The rhetorical perspective adopted in this chapter will focus on such emotives – on fears and worries that were explicitly brought up in Dutch reflections on historicism – beginning with the question what objects of fear these emotives denoted.

Objects of fear

Ernst Troeltsch's 1922 lecture at Leiden University – a preview of his soon-to-appear book, *Der Historismus und seine Probleme* – is a good place to start, as it elicited extensive responses from various corners. In a packed lecture hall, Troeltsch told his audience that historicism amounted to a 'fundamental historicization of intellectual life'.[16] Was this a promise, a threat, a *fait accompli* or an ideological agenda? Dutch commentators did not agree. In the liberal Protestant bulwark that was Leiden's faculty of theology, the view took hold that 'historicization of intellectual life' in Troeltsch's sense of the word was a stance cultivated by all branches of modern historical scholarship, the history of religion included. While insisting on the need to interpret the past in its own terms, it cultivated virtues of accuracy, carefulness and impartiality. This was the very air that Leiden students breathed: the university was well-known for its critical historical ethos, in Biblical studies and history of religions just as in church history and national history.[17] If this historicism posed a threat, it consisted in forgetting that the historian's perspective can never claim monopoly: a preacher in Leiden's St Peter's Church could and had to say more than a professor of Old Testament studies in the Academy Building.

Thus, when Troeltsch's host in Leiden, the young theologian Karel Roessingh, spoke about historicism, the term referred to sceptical questions of the kind: Why would Christianity as preached from Dutch Protestant pulpits be truer than other religions from other cultures? Students only need to take a course in the history of religion, said Roessingh, to be infused with 'a substantial dose of doubt about the superiority of one's own twentieth-century Christianity over the religiousness of the Torajas discussed [in class] or that of Egyptians in the Eighteenth Dynasty'.[18] Historicism, for Roessingh, denoted an overdose of such scepticism – a relativist stance that nobody actively encouraged, but could easily develop during students' courses of study, gnawing at their moral and religious beliefs. Similarly, Roessingh's students Willem Banning and Heije Faber associated historicism with the stance of a passive observer who engages in historical studies without daring to stake a position or issue a judgement. Both insisted on the need to make personal choices and develop what Faber called an 'active attitude' – that is, vigorous commitment to a moral-religious cause.[19] So, for these Leiden theologians, historicism represented the danger of losing oneself in reflection – a perhaps not altogether imaginary danger in Leiden's academic context, but still a danger that most students managed to avoid.

Rhetorical framings of historicism as a danger looming at the horizon, visible but not yet actual, were even more explicitly offered at another faculty of theology, in Groningen, where so-called 'ethical' theologians sought to steer a constructive middle course between liberalism and orthodoxy or, more concretely, between Troeltsch and Karl Barth – two names that were on everyone's lips during much of the 1920s and 1930s. Groningen theologians like Willem Jan Aalders and Theo Haitjema followed Barth in portraying Troeltsch as an incarnation of dangerous historicism – theology reduced to historical study of religion – but hesitated about Barth's explicitly anti-historicist alternative, in which divine revelation seemed entirely disconnected from human history. Both their own publications and the PhD dissertations they supervised testify to Aalders's and Haitjema's reluctance about historicism and anti-historicism alike (though Haitjema, the youngest of the two, was slightly more 'Barthian' than Aalders). In this context, historicism again appeared as a danger on the horizon. 'If Ernst Troeltsch is your man,' wrote Haitjema in 1931 to a younger colleague, 'then imitate him, that is, examine carefully where Troeltsch's historicism had to end up, and did end up, even though he preferably obscured this end for himself and others alike.'[20] Similarly, in response to a Leiden theologian, Haitjema wrote: 'I cannot see it otherwise than that a theologian who has noddingly walked one mile with Troeltsch will have to go on two miles under his guidance and even to continue in his footsteps until the bitter end.'[21]

Here we encounter the rhetoric figure of the slippery slope as it pops up in many of the sources consulted for this chapter ('If you take a first step in this direction, you'll end up in dangerous historicism'). It takes the form, more specifically, of a logical slippery slope argument, neatly corresponding to what Alfred Sidgwick, more than a century ago, called the 'objection to a thin end of a wedge' ('If we once begin to take a certain course there is no knowing where we shall be able to stop with any show of consistency; there would be no reason for stopping anywhere in particular, and we should be led on, step by step, into action or opinions that we all agree to call undesirable or untrue').[22]

Recognizing that charges of historicism were typically premised on a logic of slippery slopes subsequently allows us to see why this derogative term was used especially in exchanges between relatively kindred spirits. When Dooyeweerd polemicized against historicism, he preferably attacked fellow-Protestants like Berkhof and the more progressive wings of his Reformed Churches in the Netherlands (*Gereformeerde Kerken in Nederland*).[23] Likewise, Haitjema brought the charge against fellow 'ethical' theologians, just as the neo-Kantian philosopher and theologian Jacob Leonard Snethlage struck out against perceived historicist tendencies in liberal and ethical circles – not in the orthodox camp that was largely beyond his radar.[24] Even Arnold de Hartog, a gifted debater known for his rallies against the 'atheist' freethinkers movement, directed his combative energy on enemies close to home. When in 1908 De Hartog founded a journal with the rather unique mission of combatting historicism and empiricism, the first of these 'isms' turned out to refer primarily to orthodox Protestants who used terms like 'facts of salvation' in speaking about the birth, death and resurrection of Jesus, thereby capturing divine action in the factual language of historical scholarship. Consistent with the logic of slippery slopes, De Hartog's criticism was not that orthodox believers speaking about 'facts of salvation' had ceased to believe in a supernatural God; the point was that he perceived them as making an impermissible step in the direction of such a dangerous position.

This allows for a twofold answer to the question what critics of historicism actually feared. While their *objects* of fear were often far away, looming at some distant horizon, the *triggers* of those worries were usually much closer to home, among fellow theologians, sometimes even members of the same church branch. Typically, the distant and the near-by were connected through slippery slope arguments of the sort we already encountered in the introduction, in Zuidema's criticism of Berkhof: 'If you say that each generation has to read the Bible for themselves, then you will end up in nihilist historicism.'

Underlying arguments

To examine this rhetorical figure in greater depth, I turn to my second question: What was the *logos* behind the *pathos*, or the argument behind the rhetoric of slippery slopes? Let's return to Troeltsch's 1922 lecture at Leiden University, which was attended not only by theologians, but also by Johan Huizinga, the soon-to-be-famous author of *The Waning of the Middle Ages*. In response to Troeltsch's talk, the historian made some brief notes – never published, tucked away in his personal papers – that took the form of a series of questions:

1. Does your attitude towards life and spirit correspond to what Troeltsch calls historicism?
2. Do you in your historical thinking regard historical humanity as one large individual?
3. Do you search in history for solid points for the present?
4. Does history make you relativistic? (nothing absolute, nothing independent)
5. Does the epistemology of history make you sceptical?[25]

Huizinga's answer to these questions can be found elsewhere, in his lecture notes: 'Whoever knows [one's] life to be limited by [one's] own personality and context, and bound to the past as well as the future, has no reason to be anxious about history. He tries to understand in time something [that lies] behind the time. The eternal imperfection, the eternal aspiration.'[26]

These words, enigmatic as they may seem, do not only show that Troeltsch's lecture elicited different responses (though Huizinga's musings were as peppered with emotives as were Roessingh's). More importantly, they convey that Huizinga believed that anxiety about a Troeltschean 'historicization of intellectual life' was not unavoidable. Whether or not there were reasons to be anxious depended on metaphysical assumptions about history, the self and the human moral condition. Huizinga seemed to imply that a hermeneutic awareness of one's being situated in time and place is a problem only on the assumption that such situatedness amounts to a limitation or, more precisely, a failure to anchor one's ideas, beliefs or practices in transhistorical certainties.

If we survey the broad variety of complaints about historicism put forward by Dutch authors in the late nineteenth and twentieth centuries, such longing for transhistorical certainties turns out to be quite rare. Despite secondary literature suggesting that interwar critics of historicism desperately tried to defend what they believed to be timeless truths,[27] not even theologians conform to this picture. Among Dutch theologians, Pierre Daniel Chantepie de la Saussaye was one of only few who reported something close to what Richard J. Bernstein calls the 'Cartesian anxiety' ('Either there is some support for our being, a fixed foundation for our knowledge, or we cannot escape the forces of darkness that envelop us with madness, with intellectual and moral chaos').[28]

Instead of contrasting timeless truths with historical contingencies, most Dutch commentators thought in terms of *balances* – balances between historical knowledge and religious belief, balances between historical accuracy and aesthetic achievement, or balances between historical development and moral-political order. Crucial is that these balances were perceived as getting distorted if too much emphasis was laid upon historical change, historical facts or historical accuracy. Gerardus van der Leeuw, another Groningen theologian, offers a case in point. His 1919 book *Historical Christianity* warned at length against a historicist reading of the Bible, characterized by an overdose of sensitivity to questions of historical factuality (Was Jesus really born in Bethlehem?). With equal force, however, Van der Leeuw distanced himself from the 'anti-historicism' that he encountered in rationalist thinkers like Lessing, for whom Jesus' birth in Bethlehem had no significance at all. Theology suffered, not only when its practitioners emphasized the historical too much, but also when they paid it too little respect.[29]

Such efforts at balancing can be found also among non-theologians. For instance, in his 1941 reflections on the state of Dutch literary studies, the Nijmegen professor Gerard Brom declared to have no objections against colleagues adopting historical methods and using archival sources in writing the history of Dutch literature. But if they reduced the enterprise to collecting historical data, at the expense of aesthetic evaluation, the result was nothing more than 'meagre historicism'.[30] Similarly, Brom's spouse, Willemien Brom-Struick, a gifted musician, argued that it was no 'dead historicism' to perform sixteenth-century music on period instruments like the lute.[31] Historical accuracy did not need to compromise on aesthetic beauty – even though it would take a couple of decades before the early music movement could convince its critics that a balance between the two was feasible.

The rhetorical trope of balancing was even more prominent in a 1946 debate on the decolonization of the Netherlands Indies. Sieuwert Bruins Slot, chief editor of a Protestant newspaper, criticized supporters of an independent Indonesia for undermining a God-given political order with historicist appeals to 'the demands of the time' or even, in biblical language, 'the signs of the times'. This led Gerard van Walsum, another prominent Protestant journalist, to argue that Bruins Slot himself was advocating a historicist political theology by identifying moral-political standards with a nineteenth-century colonial order. But if you accuse me of 'static historicism', responded Bruins Slot to Van Walsum, I accuse you of 'dynamic historicism'.[32] This situation was not unlike the one in Utrecht's St Peter's Church, a couple of years later. All quarrelling parties dissociated themselves from historicism, but did so in different ways, simply because they had different views on how a balance between historical sensitivity and moral-political reasoning would look like.

What these examples show, apart from illustrating once again that Protestant authors were rather prominent voices in Dutch debates about historicism, is that arguments behind charges of historicism did not necessarily draw on a logic of timeless truths versus historical contingencies. More prominent, in the Dutch case, was a thinking in terms of balances, with ongoing debate on what the balance precisely entailed, in terms of both *what* had to be balanced and *how* this could be done. It was these balances that served as frames of reference for accusations of 'going too far' in emphasizing historical change, accuracy or factuality. This is to say that historicism served as a *deictic* term – a term that assesses a situation in relation to a deictic centre that embodies the norm. Although the authors discussed in this chapter defined this deictic centre in different ways, they all explicitly or implicitly identified it with a balance, distortion of which they denounced in terms of historicism. So, whereas a traditional history of ideas approach faces a plethora of meanings attached to the term 'historicism', the rhetorical perspective adopted in this chapter allows us to discern behind these manifold meanings a pattern of deictic reasoning.

Language of 'isms'

So far, we have seen that historicism was mostly perceived as a danger, still far away, but threatening everyone who moved a step too far in its direction. The image of a step too far fits the logic of slippery slopes popular among critics of historicism, but also points to the deictic character of historicism.

Like its negative counterpart, anti-historicism, the term denoted disturbance of a precarious balance. However, not everyone who cared about balanced historical thinking employed language of historicism. Catholic philosophers, most notably, hardly spoke about historicism, despite the fact that balancing historical distance and philosophical proximity to Thomas Aquinas was a key challenge for all neo-Thomist thinkers. A rhetorical examination of historicism is therefore not complete without an attempt to answer the question: Where did historicism come from and to what discourses did it belong? Did Catholic philosophers draw on other languages than their Protestant colleagues?

In an academic culture that was largely oriented on Germany, especially before the Second World War, it almost goes without saying that historicism was a German loanword. Early users of the term said as much when they referred to 'the disease that the Germans ... call by the appropriate name of *"historicism"'* or to 'what the Germans call the period of historicism'.[33] Although these are generic references, closer examination of intellectual origins reveals that, among academics at least, language of historicism travelled to no small degree through discipline-specific channels. Whereas Protestant theologians in the interwar years heavily quoted Troeltsch and Barth, philosophers like Dooyeweerd and Snethlage mainly drew on neo-Kantian thinkers. Historians in their turn often referred to Friedrich Meinecke's *Die Entstehung des Historismus*. Insofar as these are representative examples, they suggest that Dutch academics borrowed the term, not primarily from each other, but from discipline-specific German sources. The term did travel, however, from Dutch academic jargon to the vocabulary of politicians and journalists – or even novelists, in the case of Pieter Hendrik van Moerkerken, the author of a novel featuring two friends who sit down in an orchard to discuss 'the historicism that our culture suffers from'.[34] The politicians who disagreed about the Netherlands Indies most likely picked up the term from Dooyeweerd, just as museum director Adriaan Pit drew on historians of art and architecture in warning against 'historicism pushed too far' (i.e. staying as closely as possible to the original in rebuilding the Leiden city hall after its destruction by fire in 1929).[35]

Why, then, did Dutch neo-Thomists, with one notable exception, refrain from using language of historicism? Briefly put, their intellectual orientation was southward, not eastward. Most of them had close connections to the Higher Institute of Philosophy in Leuven, which until the early 1930s was entirely French-speaking. Neither the Leuven neo-Scholastics, as they preferred to call themselves, nor their Dutch admirers did refer more than in passing to historicism – not because they were unfamiliar with the intellectual and existential dilemmas of their Protestant colleagues, but because they largely discussed these in terms of 'tradition', 'traditionalism', 'breach of tradition' and 'lack of respect for tradition'.[36] Also, since the so-called modernist crisis, modernism instead of historicism had been the preferred Catholic invective for those found guilty of overemphasizing historical change or development. (The exception that proves the rule was Karel Bellon, a Leuven-trained philosophy professor at Nijmegen, who more than any of his Dutch or Flemish colleagues engaged with German Protestant theologians and philosophers, thereby bridging discourses that existed largely separate from each other.[37])

However, the confessional divide loses much of its significance when we realize that historicism was seldom used alone. Zuidema was one among many who connected historicism to relativism, existentialism, atheism and nihilism,[38] just as De Hartog was far from alone in simultaneously attacking historicism and empiricism. For many of the authors discussed in this chapter, historicism was part of a larger vocabulary of 'isms'. Bellon and Dooyeweerd warned against psychologism and sociologism, too. When Philip Kohnstamm assumed his Amsterdam lectureship in 1907 with a talk on the dangers besieging philosophy, he discussed not only historicism, but also the threats embodied by materialism, naturalism and positivism. Historicism, in other words, belonged to a broader collection of 'isms', which helps explain the occurrence of combinations like 'relativist historicism' and 'the historicist-empiricist orientation of the last half a century'.[39] Especially in the interwar *Weltanschauungskämpfe* – polemics between competing 'worldviews', with all the Idealist baggage of that term – historicism was one of many 'isms' that were used as words of warning, especially to kindred spirits, fellow-believers or members of the same tradition who seemed to take a step too far in dangerous directions.[40]

Conclusion

These last words touch upon issues far beyond the focus of this chapter: the military rhetoric that was used in mapping the intellectual landscape, the aggressive styles of polemicizing that were customary especially among philosophers and theologians, and the emotions of fear or anger that were fuelled by such rhetorical conventions. By way of conclusion, I can only say that the rhetorical perspective adopted in this chapter seems a promising one for researchers interested in broadening the range of questions typically raised with regard to intellectual life in the period under discussion. How could it be that merciless polemicists like Zuidema were held in high regard, at least among kindred spirits? What sort of intellectual culture allowed for a former prime minister demanding Free University students to swear an oath of loyalty to 'Reformed principles' in the Amsterdam Vondel Park?[41] What was the appeal of polemics revolving around 'isms' that, in 1936, even working-class people from The Hague showed up in great numbers to hear Dooyeweerd address the dangers of historicism?[42]

A couple of years ago, Elías Palti suggested that historicism should be treated, not as an idea or concept, but as a language in John Pocock's and Quentin Skinner's sense of the word: 'the intellectual soil and the set of assumptions underlying a given order of discourse' that help explain, not only what an author said, but also 'how it was possible for him or her to say what he or she said'.[43] In a sense, this chapter ties in with Palti's proposal by drawing attention to rhetorical conventions and discursive repertoires that travelled across geographical and disciplinary borders, most notably from the German *Geisteswissenschaften* to Dutch philosophy and theology. However, the rhetorical perspective that this chapter has adopted is even richer than Palti's history of languages perspective. By treating historicism as a derogative term charged with emotional baggage, a rhetorical perspective is able to explain why historicism came to serve as what one German historian called 'a struggle-concept, attacked, asserted, discarded, befogged in the tumult of countless discussions and polemics'.[44] Also, by examining emotives like 'I fear' and 'I am worried', this chapter has been able to identify a rhetoric of slippery slopes popular among Dutch critics of historicism. Closer analysis of this rhetoric has revealed that 'historicism' was a deictic term, used in relation to the deictic centre of a precarious balance between historical knowledge and religious belief, historical accuracy and aesthetic achievement, or historical development and moral-political order.

If this makes sense, then a search for patterns in or beneath the variety of meanings associated with historicism does not have to focus on the *langue* underlying the *parole*. Even in its actual rhetorical usage, historicism was often used in similar ways, to frame a danger, to appeal to anxieties shared by the audience and to advocate 'a step back' to restore a balance endangered by overemphasis on historical facts, change or accuracy. From a rhetorical point of view, the musicians who quarrelled about the early music movement and its commitment to using period instruments were engaged in similar controversies as Berkhof, Dooyeweerd and Zuidema at the 1952 Christian Social Conference in Utrecht.

Notes

1. A draft of this chapter was presented at the 'Relativism: Historical, Philosophical, and Sociological Perspectives' conference at the University of Vienna on 24 May 2019. I would like to thank Martin Kusch and Katherina Kinzel for their kind invitation and the audience for a lively discussion afterwards. Funding was provided by the Netherlands Organization for Scientific Research (NWO). Unless otherwise noted, all translations are mine.
2. J. A. Wormser, *Proces-verbaal van het sociaal congres, gehouden te Amsterdam den 9, 10, 11 en 12 november 1891* (Amsterdam: Höveker & Zoon, 1892), 361.
3. *Proces verbaal christelijk sociale conferentie 1952 gehouden te Utrecht op 4, 5, 6 en 7 november 1952* (Utrecht: Libertas, [1953?]), 51, 53.
4. Ibid., 83, 82, 94, 95.
5. H. Berkhof, *Christus, de zin der geschiedenis* (Nijkerk: Callenbach, 1958), 25; N. N., 'Historisme en neo-marxisme bedreiging Schriftgezag: Prof. dr. H. Berkhof voor predikanten', *Reformatorisch Dagblad*, 22 April 1971.
6. James Chappel, 'Nihilism and the Cold War: The Catholic Reception of Nihilism between Nietzsche and Adenauer', *Rethinking History* 19, no. 1 (2015): 95; Nitzan Lebovic, 'Introduction: The History of Nihilism and the Limits of Political Critique', *Rethinking History* 19, no. 1 (2015): 3.
7. E.g., C. Offringa, 'Plaatsbepaling in de strijd', *Bijdragen en Mededelingen betreffende de Geschiedenis der Nederlanden* 89, no. 1 (1974): 67–8.
8. Friedrich Jaeger and Jörn Rüsen, *Geschichte des Historismus: Eine Einführung* (Munich: C. H. Beck, 1992), 1.
9. Frederick C. Beiser, *The German Historicist Tradition* (Oxford: Oxford University Press, 2011), 6, 8.
10. Georg G. Iggers, 'Historicism: The History and Meaning of the Term', *Journal of the History of Ideas* 56, no. 1 (1995): 129–52.
11. Reinhard Laube, *Karl Mannheim und die Krise des Historismus: Historismus als wissenssoziologischer Perspektivismus* (Göttingen: Vandenhoeck & Ruprecht, 2004), 87–197; *Krise des Historismus, Krise der Wirklichkeit: Wissenschaft, Kunst und Literatur 1880–1932*, ed. Otto Gerhard Oexle (Göttingen: Vandenhoeck & Ruprecht, 2007). See also Annette Wittkau, *Historismus: Zur Geschichte des Begriffs und des Problems* (Göttingen: Vandenhoeck & Ruprecht, 1992).
12. Herman Paul, *Het moeras van de geschiedenis: Nederlandse debatten over historisme* (Amsterdam: Bert Bakker, 2012).
13. Kathleen J. Turner, 'Introduction: Rhetorical History as Social Construction', in *Doing Rhetorical History: Concepts and Cases*, ed. Kathleen J. Turner (Tuscaloosa: University of Alabama Press, 1998), 2.
14. Ibid., 6.

15 William M. Reddy, 'Against Constructionism: The Historical Ethnography of Emotions', *Current Anthropology* 38, no. 3 (1997): 327–51.
16 N. N., 'Der moderne Historismus', *Het Vaderland,* 1 April 1922. See also A. L. Molendijk, 'Ernst Troeltschs holländische Reisen: Eine Skizze – Im Anhang: Drei Briefe Troeltschs an Karel Hendrik Roessingh', *Mitteilungen der Ernst-Troeltsch-Gesellschaft* 6 (1991): 24–39.
17 Herman Paul, 'The Scholarly Self: Ideals of Intellectual Virtue in Nineteenth-Century Leiden', in *The Making of the Humanities*, ed. Rens Bod, Jaap Maat and Thijs Weststeijn, vol. 2 (Amsterdam: Amsterdam University Press, 2012), 397–411.
18 K. H. Roessingh, 'De Leidsche theologische faculteit 1875–1925', in A. R. Zimmerman et al., *Pallas Leidensis MCMXXV* (Leiden: S. C. van Doesburgh, 1925), 149.
19 W. Banning, 'Historisme', in *Encyclopaedisch handboek van het moderne denken*, ed. A. C. Elsbach et al., vol. 1 (Arnhem: Van Loghum Slaterus, 1931), 393–6; H. Faber, *De geschiedenis als theologisch probleem: een studie naar aanleiding van Ernst Troeltsch 'Der Historismus und seine Probleme'* (Arnhem: Van Loghum Slaterus, 1933), 8.
20 Th. L. Haitjema, 'Evangelische katholiciteit?', *Onder Eigen Vaandel* 6 (1931): 291.
21 Th. L. Haitjema, 'Ethisch cultuurbewustzijn', *Nieuwe Theologische Studiën* 15 (1932): 139–40.
22 Alfred Sidgwick, *The Application of Logic* (London: Macmillan, 1910), 40.
23 H. Dooyeweerd, *Vernieuwing en bezinning: om het reformatorisch grondmotief*, ed. J. A. Oosterhoff (Zutphen: J. B. van den Brink, 1957).
24 J. L. Snethlage, *Openbaring en het debat Kohnstamm-Snethlage: met aanteekeningen* (Arnhem: Van Loghum Slaterus, 1926).
25 Notes on 'historicism', n.d., inv. no. 12/2.4, Johan Huizinga papers, Leiden University Library.
26 Lecture notes 'Inleiding geschiedwetenschap', [1920s], inv. no. 5/1, Johan Huizinga papers, Leiden University Library, 33.
27 Kurt Nowak, 'Die "antihistoristische Revolution": Symptome und Folgen der Krise historischer Weltorientierung nach dem Ersten Weltkrieg in Deutschland', in *Umstrittene Moderne: Die Zukunft der Neuzeit im Urteil der Epoche Ernst Troeltschs*, ed. Horst Renz and Friedrich Wilhelm Graf (Gütersloh: Gerd Mohn, 1987), 133–71; Friedrich Wilhelm Graf, 'Die "antihistoristische Revolution" in der protestantischen Theologie der zwanziger Jahre', in *Vernunft des Glaubens: Wissenschaftliche Theologie und kirchliche Lehre: Festschrift zum 60. Geburtstag von Wolfhart Pannenberg*, ed. Jan Rohls and Gunther Wenz (Göttingen: Vandenhoeck & Ruprecht, 1988), 377–405; Friedrich Wilhelm Graf, 'Geschichte durch Übergeschichte überwinden: Antihistoristisches Geschichtsdenken in der protestantischen Theologie der 1920er Jahre', in *Geschichtsdiskurs*, ed. Wolfgang

Küttler, Jörn Rüsen and Ernst Schulin, vol. 4 (Frankfurt am Main: Fischer, 1997), 217–44.

28 P. D. Chantepie de la Saussaye, 'Geestelijke machten: indrukken, denkbeelden, vragen: het absolute', *Onze Eeuw* 5, no. 4 (1905): 375–416; Richard J. Bernstein, *Beyond Objectivism and Relativism: Science, Hermeneutics, and Practice* (Philadelphia: University of Pennsylvania Press, 1983), 18.

29 G. van der Leeuw, *Historisch christendom* (Utrecht: A. Oosthoek, 1919), 49, 83–4.

30 Gerard Brom, *Geschiedschrijvers van onze letterkunde* (Amsterdam: Elsevier, [1944?]), 102.

31 Willemien Brom-Struick, 'Ons oude Nederlandse lied', *Tijdschrift der Vereeniging voor Nederlandsche Muziekgeschiedenis* 13, no. 2 (1929): 125.

32 [J. A. H. J. S. Bruins Slot], 'Schrift en geschiedenis', *Trouw*, 24 September 1946, responding to [Gerard van Walsum], 'Zoo gaat het goed', *De Nieuwe Nederlander*, 18 September 1946. The latter was a rejoinder to three earlier articles by Bruins Slot: [J. A. H. J. S. Bruins Slot], 'Onjuist gewaardeerd', *Trouw*, 12 September 1946; [J. A. H. J. S. Bruins Slot], 'Gezag en revolutie', *Trouw*, 13 September 1946; [J. A. H. J. S. Bruins Slot], 'Verontrustend', *Trouw*, 14 September 1946.

33 Is. van Dijk, 'Boekaankondiging', *Theologische Studiën* 19 (1901): 383; N. N., 'De theologische faculteit', *De Heraut*, March 5, 1905.

34 Peter Dumaar [P. H. van Moerkerken], 'Gijsbert en Ada', *Elsevier's Geïllustreerd Maandschrift* 39 (1910): 411.

35 J. A. G. van der Steur and [J.] Kalf, 'Advies van de afdeeling B der Rijkscommissie voor Monumentenzorg over den herbouw van het Leidsche stadhuis', *Bouwkundig Weekblad Architectura* 50 (1929): 222.

36 Herman Paul, 'Vetera Novis Augere: Neo-Scholastic Philosophers and Their Concepts of Tradition', in *So What's New about Scholasticism? How Neo-Thomism Helped Shape the Twentieth Century*, ed. Rajesh Heynickx and Stéphane Symons (Berlin: Walter de Gruyter, 2018), 255–80. See also Herman Paul, 'Religion and the Crisis of Historicism: Protestant and Catholic Perspectives', *Journal of the Philosophy of History* 4, no. 2 (2010): 172–94.

37 K. L. Bellon, *Wijsbegeerte der geschiedenis* (Antwerpen: Standaard, 1953), 164–232.

38 S. U. Zuidema, *Nacht zonder dageraad: naar aanleiding van het atheïstisch en nihilistisch existentialisme van Jean-Paul Sartre* (Franeker: T. Wever, 1948).

39 [A. H.] d[e] H[artog], 'Plicht en wet', *Nieuwe Banen* 8 (1915): 62.

40 Cf. Martin Kusch's insightful study on 'psychologism' as a derogatory term in European philosophy around 1900: Martin Kusch, *Psychologism: A Case Study in the Sociology of Philosophical Knowledge* (London: Routledge, 1995), esp. 95–121.

41 J. V., 'Lustrumverslag', in *Almanak van het Studentencorps aan de Vrije Universiteit 1931* (Amsterdam: Herdes, [1931]), 111.

42 Herman Paul, 'Who Suffered from the Crisis of Historicism? A Dutch Example', *History and Theory* 49, no. 2 (2010): 169–93.

43   Elías J. Palti, 'Historicism as an Idea and as a Language', *History and Theory* 44, no. 3 (2005): 433.
44   Walther Hofer, *Geschichtschreibung und Weltanschauung: Betrachtungen zum Werk Friedrich Meineckes* (Munich: R. Oldenbourg, 1950), 322, quoted in English translation from Dwight E. Lee and Robert N. Beck, 'The Meaning of "Historicism"', *The American Historical Review* 59, no. 3 (1953–1954): 570.

Bibliography

Banning, W. 'Historisme'. In *Encyclopaedisch handboek van het moderne denken*, edited by A. C. Elsbach et al., vol. 1, 393–6. Arnhem: Van Loghum Slaterus, 1931.
Beiser, Frederick C. *The German Historicist Tradition*. Oxford: Oxford University Press, 2011.
Bellon, K. L. *Wijsbegeerte der geschiedenis*. Antwerpen: Standaard, 1953.
Berkhof, H. *Christus, de zin der geschiedenis*. Nijkerk: Callenbach, 1958.
Bernstein, Richard J. *Beyond Objectivism and Relativism: Science, Hermeneutics, and Practice*. Philadelphia: University of Pennsylvania Press, 1983.
Brom, Gerard. *Geschiedschrijvers van onze letterkunde*. Amsterdam: Elsevier, [1944?].
Brom-Struick, Willemien. 'Ons oude Nederlandse lied'. *Tijdschrift der Vereeniging voor Nederlandsche Muziekgeschiedenis* 13, no. 2 (1929): 105–25.
[Bruins Slot, J. A. H. J. S.]. 'Onjuist gewaardeerd'. *Trouw*, 12 September 1946.
[Bruins Slot, J. A. H. J. S.]. 'Gezag en revolutie'. *Trouw*, 13 September 1946.
[Bruins Slot, J. A. H. J. S.]. 'Verontrustend'. *Trouw*, 14 September 1946.
[Bruins Slot, J. A. H. J. S.]. 'Schrift en geschiedenis'. *Trouw*, 24 September 1946.
Chantepie de la Saussaye, P. D. 'Geestelijke machten: indrukken, denkbeelden, vragen: het absolute'. *Onze Eeuw* 5, no. 4 (1905): 375–416.
Chappel, James. 'Nihilism and the Cold War: The Catholic Reception of Nihilism between Nietzsche and Adenauer'. *Rethinking History* 19, no. 1 (2015): 95–110.
Dijk, Is. van. 'Boekaankondiging'. *Theologische Studiën* 19 (1901): 378–84.
Dooyeweerd, H. *Vernieuwing en bezinning: om het reformatorisch grondmotief*, edited by J. A. Oosterhoff. Zutphen: J. B. van den Brink, 1957.
Dumaar, Peter [P. H. van Moerkerken]. 'Gijsbert en Ada'. *Elsevier's Geïllustreerd Maandschrift* 39 (1910): 116–26, 181–201, 257–73, 332–44, 406–17.
Faber, H. *De geschiedenis als theologisch probleem: een studie naar aanleiding van Ernst Troeltsch 'Der Historismus und seine Probleme'*. Arnhem: Van Loghum Slaterus, 1933.
Graf, Friedrich Wilhelm. 'Die "antihistoristische Revolution" in der protestantischen Theologie der zwanziger Jahre'. In *Vernunft des Glaubens: Wissenschaftliche Theologie und kirchliche Lehre: Festschrift zum 60. Geburtstag von Wolfhart Pannenberg*, edited by Jan Rohls and Gunther Wenz, 377–405. Göttingen: Vandenhoeck & Ruprecht, 1988.

Graf, Friedrich Wilhelm. 'Geschichte durch Übergeschichte überwinden: Antihistoristisches Geschichtsdenken in der protestantischen Theologie der 1920er Jahre'. In *Geschichtsdiskurs*, edited by Wolfgang Küttler, Jörn Rüsen and Ernst Schulin, vol. 4, 217–44. Frankfurt am Main: Fischer, 1997.

Haitjema, Th. L. 'Evangelische katholiciteit?' *Onder Eigen Vaandel* 6 (1931): 290–308.

Haitjema, Th. L. 'Ethisch cultuurbewustzijn'. *Nieuwe Theologische Studiën* 15 (1932), 133–40.

H[artog], [A. H.] d[e]. 'Plicht en wet'. *Nieuwe Banen* 8 (1915): 56–64.

Hofer, Walther. *Geschichtschreibung und Weltanschauung: Betrachtungen zum Werk Friedrich Meineckes*. Munich: R. Oldenbourg, 1950.

Iggers, Georg G. 'Historicism: The History and Meaning of the Term'. *Journal of the History of Ideas* 56, no. 1 (1995): 129–52.

Jaeger, Friedrich and Jörn Rüsen. *Geschichte des Historismus: Eine Einführung*. Munich: C. H. Beck, 1992.

Kusch, Martin. *Psychologism: A Case Study in the Sociology of Philosophical Knowledge*. London: Routledge, 1995.

Laube, Reinhard. *Karl Mannheim und die Krise des Historismus: Historismus als wissenssoziologischer Perspektivismus*. Göttingen: Vandenhoeck & Ruprecht, 2004.

Lebovic, Nitzan. 'Introduction: The History of Nihilism and the Limits of Political Critique'. *Rethinking History* 19, no. 1 (2015): 1–17.

Lee, Dwight E. and Robert N. Beck. 'The Meaning of "Historicism"'. *The American Historical Review* 59, no. 3 (1953–1954): 568–77.

Leeuw, G. van der. *Historisch christendom*. Utrecht: A. Oosthoek, 1919.

Molendijk, A. L. 'Ernst Troeltschs holländische Reisen: Eine Skizze—Im Anhang: Drei Briefe Troeltschs an Karel Hendrik Roessingh'. *Mitteilungen der Ernst-Troeltsch-Gesellschaft* 6 (1991): 24–39.

N. N. 'De theologische faculteit'. *De Heraut*, 5 March 1905.

N. N. 'Der moderne Historismus', *Het Vaderland*, 1 April 1922.

N. N. 'Historisme en neo-marxisme bedreiging Schriftgezag: Prof. dr. H. Berkhof voor predikanten', *Reformatorisch Dagblad*, 22 April 1971.

Nowak, Kurt. 'Die "antihistoristische Revolution": Symptome und Folgen der Krise historischer Weltorientierung nach dem Ersten Weltkrieg in Deutschland'. In *Umstrittene Moderne: Die Zukunft der Neuzeit im Urteil der Epoche Ernst Troeltschs*, edited by Horst Renz and Friedrich Wilhelm Graf, 133–71. Gütersloh: Gerd Mohn, 1987.

Oexle, Otto Gerhard, ed. *Krise des Historismus, Krise der Wirklichkeit: Wissenschaft, Kunst und Literatur 1880–1932*. Göttingen: Vandenhoeck & Ruprecht, 2007.

Offringa, C. 'Plaatsbepaling in de strijd'. *Bijdragen en Mededelingen betreffende de Geschiedenis der Nederlanden* 89, no. 1 (1974): 62–80.

Palti, Elías J. 'Historicism as an Idea and as a Language'. *History and Theory* 44, no. 3 (2005): 431–40.

Paul, Herman. 'Religion and the Crisis of Historicism: Protestant and Catholic Perspectives'. *Journal of the Philosophy of History* 4, no. 2 (2010): 172–94.
Paul, Herman. 'Who Suffered from the Crisis of Historicism? A Dutch Example'. *History and Theory* 49, no. 2 (2010): 169–93.
Paul, Herman. *Het moeras van de geschiedenis: Nederlandse debatten over historisme.* Amsterdam: Bert Bakker, 2012.
Paul, Herman. 'The Scholarly Self: Ideals of Intellectual Virtue in Nineteenth-Century Leiden'. In *The Making of the Humanities*, edited by Rens Bod, Jaap Maat and Thijs Weststeijn, vol. 2, 397–411. Amsterdam: Amsterdam University Press, 2012.
Paul, Herman. 'Vetera Novis Augere: Neo-Scholastic Philosophers and Their Concepts of Tradition'. In *So What's New about Scholasticism? How Neo-Thomism Helped Shape the Twentieth Century*, edited by Rajesh Heynickx and Stéphane Symons, 255–80. Berlin: Walter de Gruyter, 2018.
Proces verbaal christelijk sociale conferentie 1952 gehouden te Utrecht op 4, 5, 6 en 7 november 1952. Utrecht: Libertas, [1953?].
Reddy, William M. 'Against Constructionism: The Historical Ethnography of Emotions'. *Current Anthropology* 38, no. 3 (1997): 327–51.
Roessingh, K. H. 'De Leidsche theologische faculteit 1875-1925'. In A. R. Zimmerman et al., *Pallas Leidensis MCMXXV*, 139–52. Leiden: S. C. van Doesburgh, 1925.
Sidgwick, Alfred. *The Application of Logic.* London: Macmillan, 1910.
Snethlage, J. L. *Openbaring en het debat Kohnstamm-Snethlage: met aanteekeningen.* Arnhem: Van Loghum Slaterus, 1926.
Steur, J. A. G. van der and [J.] Kalf. 'Advies van de afdeeling B der Rijkscommissie voor Monumentenzorg over den herbouw van het Leidsche stadhuis'. *Bouwkundig Weekblad Architectura* 50 (1929): 217–24.
Turner, Kathleen J. 'Introduction: Rhetorical History as Social Construction'. In *Doing Rhetorical History: Concepts and Cases*, edited by Kathleen J. Turner, 1–15. Tuscaloosa: University of Alabama Press, 1998.
V., J. 'Lustrumverslag'. In *Almanak van het Studentencorps aan de Vrije Universiteit 1931*, 99–128. Amsterdam: Herdes, [1931?].
[Walsum, Gerard van]. 'Zoo gaat het goed'. *De Nieuwe Nederlander*, 18 September 1946.
Wittkau, Annette. *Historismus: Zur Geschichte des Begriffs und des Problems.* Göttingen: Vandenhoeck & Ruprecht, 1992.
Wormser, J. A. *Proces-verbaal van het sociaal congres, gehouden te Amsterdam den 9, 10, 11 en 12 november 1891.* Amsterdam: Höveker & Zoon, 1892.
Zuidema, S. U. *Nacht zonder dageraad: naar aanleiding van het atheïstisch en nihilistisch existentialisme van Jean-Paul Sartre.* Franeker: T. Wever, 1948.

6

Thinking in uncertain times: Raymond Aron and the politics of historicism

Sophie Marcotte-Chenard

Abstract

During the interwar period, the 'essentially contested' concept of historicism became a *Schlagwort* associated not only with historical relativism, but with moral and political disarray. A whole generation of political thinkers in Europe inherited this problem and confronted the practical implications of the crisis, such as Leo Strauss and Karl Löwith in Germany and Raymond Aron in France. Focusing on Aron in particular, this chapter argues that the 'crisis of historicism' is best understood as a catalyst for a renewed reflection on reason and judgement in history.

Introduction

'May you live in interesting times': the origins of this 'old curse' can actually be traced back to the 1930s in Europe. It appears for the first time in a newspaper report in 1936. The article reports Chamberlain's words in reaction to Germany's recent violation of the Locarno Treaty:

> It is not so long ago that a member of the Diplomatic Body in London … told me that there was a Chinese curse which took the form of saying, 'May you live in interesting times.' There is no doubt that the curse has fallen on us. We move from one crisis to another. We suffer one disturbance and shock after another.[1]

The reference to the notion of crisis expresses the general and pervasive feeling in Europe in the interwar period: that things are on the verge of a radical change, and not necessarily for the better. During that period, the raging debates among theologians, historians, philosophers and political thinkers around the problem or crisis of historicism become but one symptom or indicator of that anxiety and uncertainty. The 'crisis of historicism', which began around 1870, reached its peak during the interwar period in Germany (as evidenced by the publication of Ernst Troeltsch's *Der Historismus und seine Probleme* (1922), as well as Meinecke's *Die Entstehung des Historismus* (1936) and Karl Mannheim's essay on historicism (1933)).[2] It expresses a crisis in the foundations of knowledge in view of historical diversity and the relativity of values. Many political philosophers of that generation inherited this theoretical and practical problem, including thinkers such as Leo Strauss, Karl Löwith and Hannah Arendt.

The question is thus: What are the implications, for political philosophy, of thinking about historicism in these uncertain times? This chapter proposes to examine this question by focusing on a French political thinker whose contribution to the understanding of the problem of historicism is often neglected: Raymond Aron. Aron's confrontation with the 'crisis of historicism' in the 1930s uncovers a vision of historicism as a *political and practical concept*. While the literature on historicism and its development in the nineteenth and twentieth centuries focuses primarily on Germany – the country *par excellence* of historicism – the concept's peregrinations in other parts of Europe deserve our attention. If Raymond Aron is mostly known for his work in international relations and political sociology as well as his journalistic involvement, he also left a significant contribution in the field of philosophy of history and epistemology of social sciences. In his later work he reaffirmed that the fundamental preoccupations that the historicist *Fragestellung* raised – about the objectivity of knowledge in the social sciences, the possibility of a justification of social and political norms, the perils of historical and moral relativism – remained a constant throughout his life. He is as a matter of fact one of the first thinkers to introduce the questions and problems of German philosophy of history in France in the 1930s. As he travelled from France to Germany and back, the 'crisis of historicism' also travelled across countries, philosophical traditions and disciplines. As we will see, it is with a heavy baggage that Aron comes back to France in 1933, accompanied by the uncertainty and instability of the future.

Historism or historicism (*Historismus*) suffers a fate worse than many other modern neologisms: an obscure meaning, polemical from its first use by Schlegel in 1797,[3] meant to be a *Kampfbegriff*, that is, an evaluative concept rather than a descriptive one. In a late essay on historicism, Aron writes: 'The quest for the true meaning of words in -ism, historicism or historism, only leads to arbitrary conclusions.'[4] The same goes for the 'crisis of historicism': Is historicism itself in crisis? Or is it rather the cause of one? Aron never sought to provide one unequivocal definition of the term, but rather accepted its various meanings as part of our intellectual, moral and political configuration. In a way, Aron grasped what seemed to be the essence of the crisis of historicism in the 1920s and 1930s in Germany: not merely a theoretical debate about the epistemology of knowledge, but a problem of moral and political judgement with practical implications. In that sense, the concept of historicism represents a dynamic force rather than a descriptive term; it becomes, as I will show, a 'site of debate'.[5]

Aron's confrontation with the problem of historicism thus leads us to focus on one specific dimension of the polemical history of the term: the politics of historicism or, to be more precise, historicism as a vehicle for a political *malaise*. Understood as an awareness of the historicity and relativity of values, it expresses, in the context of the 1930s in Europe, a crisis in the foundations of moral and political judgement.[6] To anticipate on my thesis, while Aron sees the perils of historicism brought to its limits (in the form of historical relativism, a loss of a moral standpoint, a crisis of rationalism, or as a celebration of irrationalism, scepticism and even nihilism), he nonetheless considers the crisis of historicism as an invitation to rethink the foundations of political philosophy as a *practical pursuit*. The confrontation between political philosophy and historicism, as this chapter will demonstrate, alters the former; and as Aron argues, a genuine practice of political philosophy should be historical,[7] that is to say, based on the recognition of historical diversity as a fundamental fact and attention to the particular character of events as a necessary condition of a proper understanding of political affairs.

To make my case, I will not proceed with the exposition of the philosophical arguments in favour or against historical relativism. Aron himself rightly notes that the opposition between both camps – the 'relativists' and the 'non-relativists' – is often overplayed.[8] Rather, I wish to propose a narrative of two successive biographical moments that will each shed a light on the practical implications of the debates about historicism and on Aron's specific contribution to these discussions. The first section will expose the context of Aron's encounter with philosophy of history in Germany in the early 1930s in order to demonstrate how historicism took on a practical and even existential meaning during that period. I will then turn in the second section to the analysis of one specific intellectual event, which has been significant in the reception of historicist themes in France (or lack thereof): Raymond Aron's thesis defence in 1938. The defence, which has been described as the moment of the introduction of

'German philosophy of history in the history of French philosophy,'[9] constitutes an event that showcases the political tensions surrounding the accusations of historicism in the confrontation between Aron and the older generation of French intellectuals. I will conclude by assessing Aron's position towards historicist themes (in particular the notions of historical individuality and contingency) to demonstrate the way in which his 'moderate' historicism impacts his own practice as a political philosopher. Aron's 'diluted' historicism inspired from critical philosophy of history serves as a tool to criticize potentially dangerous consequences of historical determinism and leads him to develop a political 'praxeology' more attuned to the ambiguity, contingency and unpredictability of 'history in the making'.[10]

The aim of this chapter is twofold: to shed light on Aron's contribution to the understanding of historicism as a concept, especially in France where these debates remained at the margins of academic life, and more importantly to demonstrate the way in which there could be a productive retrieval of 'historicist' insights in political philosophy.

Raymond Aron's 'German period' (1930–1933)

Aron's first encounter with philosophy of history took place in Germany in the early 1930s. At the time, many French intellectuals considered a stay in Germany as a *passage obligé*; Aron was no exception to the rule.[11] He moved to Germany in 1930 to take a position as an assistant lecturer at the University of Köln.[12] In 1931, he obtained a position at the *Französisches Akademiker Haus* in Berlin, where he spent most of his time at the *Staatsbibliothek* discovering German neo-Kantianism and phenomenology through the reading of Dilthey, Rickert, Simmel, Weber, Husserl, Heidegger, Mannheim, Troeltsch, Meinecke, to name a few.[13]

Aron's 'German period' is of great significance in the development of his thought. It is on the banks of the Rhine that he discovered the intuitions that would constitute the foundations of his philosophy as a whole.[14] As he was searching for the proper topic for his doctoral thesis – something that would interest 'the mind and the heart'[15] – he came to the 'historicist' realization that the most fundamental fact from which one ought to start was the historical condition of man. The deepening of his understanding of thinkers such as Dilthey, Rickert and Simmel reinforced his conviction that human thought and action are shaped by historical circumstances, and that the exercise of understanding oneself and the world takes place within a specific horizon. In short, one should start with the fact that human beings are both the makers and products of history. This insight, which he gained from 'critical philosophy of history' (to be distinguished from speculative philosophy of history), could be summarized in one expression: the primacy of historical consciousness. Historical consciousness, in Aron's view, is synonymous with political consciousness.[16] We are not simply pure spirits or abstract beings, but first and foremost citizens, individuals engaged in practical pursuits.[17] Aron will remain faithful to that initial insight and will later argue that to possess a 'historical consciousness' is to have the ability to interpret the present and apprehend the future in light of what has occurred in the past; and this capacity, in his eyes, is inherently political.

If Aron had first encountered these thinkers in France, the result would not have been the same. The confrontation with the problem of historicism in particular only acquired its decisive importance through the *German experience* of 'history in the making'.[18] From 1930 to 1933, Aron attended several of Hitler's speeches; he was with his friend Golo Mann – Thomas Mann's son – when they witnessed the Nazi books burning in Berlin in 1933. Aron was, so to speak, in the front row seat of history as it was unfolding. In the context of the rise of Nazism, coupled with the increasing fragility of the international order and the looming collapse of the Weimar Republic, Aron's encounter with theory of history and historicism took on a very concrete meaning. For instance, he recalls in his *Memoirs*: 'Reading Max Weber, I heard the rumours, the creaking of our civilizations, the voice of the Jewish prophets and, as a sardonic echo, the ravings of the Führer.'[19] Pierre Manent rightly notes that Aron's writings always make explicit 'the co-dependence of political events and the adventures of thought'.[20] In the 1930s in Europe, one could not help but recognize that historical events and political thought were indeed completely intertwined.[21]

In the context of the collapse of the Weimar Republic in 1933, which Aron later described as the 'paroxysm of a rivalry between different worldviews', the 'crisis' of historicism took on a tragic and existential meaning, one that will shape Aron's views of history and politics. He writes:

> At the end of the Weimar Republic, after the catastrophe of 1918, the historical diversity of values – one of the several meanings of the term *Historismus* – sparked not only an epistemological interrogation, but also a moral crisis. How should one live if what is considered good here is bad over there? « Vérité en deçà des Pyrénées, erreur au-delà »: the theme predates the 19th century. Why did the Germans, after the First World War, take the arguments of historicism seriously, or even tragically ... The German crisis, or rather historicism *experienced as a*

crisis, was the result of an unleashing of political passions, of political parties' claim to represent, defend or illustrate a specific view of the world.[22]

Aron did not escape this intellectual and political configuration: He shared the concern of many prominent philosophers, historians and theologians at the time, for which the term *Historismus* was closely associated with *Verwirrung*, with disarray and pessimism.[23] Debates about historicism thus convey something about the political *Zeitgeist*. For Aron historicism appears to be both a tragic and a productive concept. It is a symptom and indicator of a crisis (it is thus not a coincidence that the two notions of 'crisis' and 'historicism' continually appear side by side), but one that forces political philosophers to think anew about the foundations of political judgement and action.

Historicism, because it focuses on the 'changing and local' rather than the 'eternal and universal',[24] is often defined as a doctrine of historical relativism or, as Strauss would describe it later on, as a doctrine according to which all thought, actions, norms and beliefs are relative, bound to and determined by a specific time and place in history.[25] The relativity of values entails practical consequences, namely, a 'fundamental uneasiness ... in all questions of practical conduct'[26] that stems from the critique of rationalism and universalism as elements of an outdated worldview. One of the main questions to which we are confronted is: How are we to evaluate what counts as a valid political judgement or what is the most desirable outcome in the absence of any objective or universal criteria? How to live in a world where the validity of our beliefs solely depends upon circumstances?[27]

Aron is well aware of these difficulties and of the political risks of such a position, which could lead either to decisionism (what matters if the ultimate, unilateral decision of the sovereign power) or to a form of nihilism (the radical absence of any belief, which could be accompanied by a desire to destroy the moral principles of our civilization). In his *Introduction to Philosophy of History*, he dedicates a whole section to this problem and addresses some of the misunderstandings that fuel both the camps of the historicists and anti-historicists.[28] Aron's position in that debate is nuanced. He insists on the fact that, on a philosophical level, one should distinguish between *historical relativity* – an inescapable element of the moral and political fabric of our world – and the *doctrine of historical relativism*. Briefly stated, his argument is that the latter proceeds to an illegitimate leap from the factual observation that there are diversity and heterogeneity of values and norms, to the *normative thesis* that this heterogeneity is the final truth about the human condition. Factual relativity, which is unavoidable and constitutes the truth of historicism, is not necessarily synonymous with relativism. According to Aron, the problem arises when the observation of the heterogeneity of forms of life is transformed into a philosophical postulate.

Despite these difficulties, Aron contends that there are valid historicist insights and that one should not reduce historicism to the doctrine of historical relativism. He thus finds in the philosophers of the 'historicist tradition' a fertile ground. He even writes a first doctoral dissertation – which will become his secondary thesis – on the problem of objectivity in the thought of Rickert, Dilthey, Simmel and Weber.[29] While he argues in this work that all these thinkers fail in part to ensure an objective foundation for the *Geisteswissenschaften*, he nonetheless remains profoundly indebted to their work in the working of his own philosophical enterprise. Following the intuitions of neo-Kantian critical philosophy of history, Aron's starting point is what Dilthey calls a 'critique of historical reason'. Simply stated, it means to side with a Hegelian critique of Kantian formalism and to partially historicize reason.[30] More concretely, this means that rationality as it was previously understood could not fully grasp the complexity of the human political experience and should therefore be redefined.

Thus understood, the crisis of historicism expresses one great tension, not only in Weimar thought, but among a whole generation of intellectuals: a growing gap between *Wissenschaft* and *Erfahrung*, between scientific knowledge and our experience of the world. In the writings of Dilthey, Simmel and Weber among others, one can grasp this feeling that the traditional categories of thought and practice of academic philosophy did not succeed in expressing the very texture of political and social life. For Aron, this gap between theory and practice had a practical impact, namely, the inability of intellectuals – especially in France – to recognize the signs of the looming crisis.

The return to France: Aron's thesis defence (1938)

As the political situation in Germany deteriorated and anti-Semitism grew stronger, Aron, as was the case for many Jewish thinkers, feared for his life and had to return to Paris in August 1933, a few months after Hitler's appointment as Chancellor. He came back to France and he was not travelling alone; he was accompanied by this new thinking about historicity, *Verstehen* and the plurality of interpretation in the social sciences. The French intellectuals from the previous generation – most of his professors – were far from delighted by this change of heart. As a matter of fact, many of the German themes that became the cornerstone of Aron's conception of history and politics stood in direct opposition to the French intellectual tradition, then dominated by Kantianism in philosophy and positivism in sociology. To add to the general uneasiness, most of these authors – Troeltsch, Meinecke, Mannheim, Weber – were virtually unknown figures in France at the time.

Upon his return, Aron wrote his first doctoral thesis; his advisor Léon Brunschvicg deemed it insufficient – a work on obscure *and* contemporary German thinkers was far from the norm at the Sorbonne at the time. Aron thus went on to write a second and more substantial and ambitious work entitled *Introduction à la philosophie de l'histoire. Essai sur les limites de l'objectivité historique.*[31] He presented both these works to a jury of French philosophers and sociologists on 26 March 1938. This biographical precision is far from anecdotal; as we will see, the timing of the defence is revealing of the politically charged atmosphere in the discussions surrounding the problem of historicism.

The reactions to Aron's two theses were mixed, to say the least. Many reasons explain this lack of enthusiasm, and, to a certain extent, the open hostility towards his work. First of all, there was a relative ignorance of these authors and themes in France. Aron began his secondary thesis with the following claim: 'Traditional philosophy of history reaches its peak in Hegel's system. Modern philosophy of history *begins with a rejection* of Hegelianism.'[32] As George Canguilhem rightly notes: to reject Hegel, one had first to know about it, and this was not the case in France. There were some exceptions, the most famous being Alexandre Kojève's seminar on Hegel's philosophy of history at the *Ecole pratique des hautes études* from 1933 to 1939. Aron attended the seminar assiduously during its last years and it played quite an important role in his thought (although on the mode of rejection more than assent). In a note written a few days before his death, Aron affirms: 'I never endorsed Kojeve's Hegelian thought, which exerted a tremendous influence on several French thinkers (Lacan, Queneau, perhaps Merleau-Ponty) ... But I preserved a form of diluted Hegelianism – historicity of man, historical condition of human beings, philosophical meaning of events and regimes.'[33] While speculative philosophy of history was well known in certain circles, thinkers such as Dilthey, Simmel and Weber remained unknown, which made Aron's work even more daring (and for some, downright horrifying).

And yet Aron was after all a product of the French system.[34] This raises the question: Why did the German historicist tradition resonate with him so much? Why did he feel the need to import these problems into the French academic scene? His interest and for the problem of historicism stemmed from two sources: a rejection of French positivism and ahistorical rationalism on the one hand, and a criticism of speculative philosophies of history on the other. Both dominant trends had in common to postulate a rational 'happy ending' of the historical process, which made Aron grow wary.

Aron's stay in Germany – and his increasing awareness and attention to politics – provided him with a more thorough understanding of the impending European tragedy. Part of the academic philosophy in France (the Kantian rationalists and sociological positivists) offered very limited resources to engage with politics, whereas German phenomenology and theory of history appeared much closer to the lived experience of the world, with all its ambiguities and imperfections.[35] Historicism understood as a conception of human history based on a fundamental diversity of epochs and societies left more room for the understanding of the particular and the individual than an Enlightenment rationalism based on universal values.[36] That being said, Aron always considered himself a rationalist. A disciple of Weber, he believed in achieving a certain level of objectivity in the social sciences, and he always preserved throughout his life some vague Kantian notion of a regulatory 'Idea of Reason' with a capital 'R'.[37] However, interestingly enough, he passed for a radical historicist in the 1930s in the French intellectual milieu.

This can be explained by the existentialist tones of his doctoral theses. Very early on Aron adopted the fundamental premise of what he later calls 'hermeneutic historicism' (to be distinguished from political or existential historicism), namely, the recognition of the specific character of human or historical knowledge in contrast with the knowledge of the natural world.[38] In a Diltheyian manner, he believes that we know ourselves only through the institutions we create and through the traces of our past.[39] In short, he sides with *Verstehen* against *Erklären* (understanding through interpretation rather than explanation through universal regularities or laws).[40] What characterizes our enquiry into historical reality are the plurality of interpretation and diversity of worldviews. The clash with French Kantians and positivist sociologists thus proved inevitable.

The thesis defence became – as they were in France – an intellectual and philosophical event, but it also became, through the debate about historicism, the illustration of a generational confrontation. Multiple accounts of the event were published. In the official transcript, Paul Fauconnet, a proponent of positivism, ended his long critical intervention with the claim that Aron's thesis threatened the whole work of the previous generation and led to relativism against universal science. He concluded by saying that he could not decide whether this was the work of someone 'Satanic or desperate' and hoped that the youth would not follow him down that dangerous path.[41] This dangerous path is the one opened by German historicism. Looking back at Aron's work, it is not difficult to see what had made his professors react so strongly. In the first pages of his *Introduction to Philosophy of History*, he writes:

> At a higher level, this book leads to a historical philosophy opposed to scientist rationalism as well as to positivism. This historical philosophy would allow to understand concrete consciousness, the passions and conflicts which move the human world, the historical ideas of which the moralists only have an abstract representation … Such a philosophy would overcome the opposition between the philosophies of the moralists or novelists, which express a singular existence, and those of theorists or scholars, which appear to be completely foreign to the practical concerns of life.[42]

We can observe here the phenomenological dimension of his enterprise, the insistence on concrete singularity rather than universal norms. Moreover, the last part of Aron's *Introduction to Philosophy of History* focuses on historicity and political decision. There he presents the subject of knowledge and action as a living, historical self, faced with decisions that are in part dictated by contingent factors. By historicity Aron means the realization that human beings can never transcend their historical situation; they are bound to think and act within a specific horizon.[43] Aron's position was thus antipositivist, and the members of the jury interpreted his criticism of abstract rationality as a defence of historical relativism.

But this is to miss Aron's point. We have to remember that his thesis defence took place on 26 March 1938, exactly thirteen days after the *Anschluss* of Austria proclaimed by Hitler. His work was meant not only as an epistemological contribution to the foundations of social sciences, but also as a political warning. His insistence on contingency, the singularity of historical situations, the plurality of interpretations and the gap between political actions and outcomes was not a defence of historicism understood as historical relativism. Rather, it was a cautionary tale about the fact that things could always take another turn than the one expected.[44] Aron believed that the German historicist tradition offered resources to understand that fundamental truth.

Witnesses to the defence recalled that the tone of the whole exchange was politically charged. In that context, the theme of historicism was discussed not as a theoretical issue, but as a practical one. Aron's ultimate aim was not solely to shed light on problems in epistemology of history; it was to understand *history in the making*.⁴⁵ To do that, Aron had to liberate himself from the categories of thought in which he first evolved, including abstract moral universality, Kantian *a priori* principles and so on. The 'critical philosophy of history' of Dilthey, Rickert, Simmel and Weber offered a starting point, an imperfect one, but nonetheless one that allowed to consider the complexity and ambiguity of our experience of history. To be sure, the awareness of human diversity and historical singularity is not specific to historicism as such,⁴⁶ but historicist thinking makes it its focal point. Aron's professors – all prominent French intellectuals – were oblivious to the looming tragedy in part because their positivist-rationalist premises blinded them. The thesis defence thus became a striking illustration of a political gap between a generation that did not want to admit that Europe was on the verge of an unprecedented catastrophe, and a new generation more attuned to the reality of crisis.⁴⁷

Accused of defending a historical and moral relativism that would lead to nihilism, Aron answered during his defence that there are degrees of relativity, and that while *excessive* historicism indeed ends in scepticism, a historical critique (or critique of historical reason) should constitute the foundation of political philosophy. Relativity (and not relativism) is the defining feature of historical and political reality.⁴⁸ One can preserve a belief in the objectivity of social sciences, but not a belief in the completely rational or progressive character of the historical process. In a section of his *Introduction to Philosophy of History* entitled 'The Overcoming of Historicism',⁴⁹ Aron argues that the benefit of historicist thinking is the sobering realization that the development of history does not obey any preconceived progressive plan. Historicism thus reminds us that 'the future will be different, neither better nor worse'. Aron adds: 'Freeing ourselves from historicism means overcoming fatalism.'⁵⁰ How do we proceed to achieve that, according to him? The position of the young Aron here is closer to his existentialist comrades at the time: through the radical exercise of our freedom. In that sense, the positive dimension of the crisis of historicism is that it reveals the contradictions of modernity that we have to face and discloses the margin of human liberty opened by an undecided future.⁵¹

The members of Aron's jury could not imagine how one could be antipositivist without embracing nihilism. An older French Catholic thinker and friend of Aron, Gaston Fessard, published a summary of the defence and proposed what is probably the most accurate metaphor to describe the event: it was as if the audience was witnessing 'hens who brooded a duck and watched it with horror rush toward the pond and move effortlessly in an element than was completely foreign to them'.⁵² Despite these criticisms and the obvious distance between

Aron and his professors, they still recognized in the end his contribution in importing German thought in France. Edmond Vermeil, who was perhaps the most sympathetic to Aron's enterprise, underlined the candidate's role as a philosophical translator and welcomed the bridge he created between German and French philosophy.[53] Canguilhem later went on to declare the moment of the thesis defence as the day philosophy of history was finally introduced in the history of French philosophy.[54]

Ultimately, this second biographical episode points to two main elements: first, France's very limited reception of historicism and philosophy of history as well as Aron's role in introducing these themes and problems. Second, this episode reveals the practical and even existential nature of the problem of historicism for Aron, which cannot be detached from the lived experience of history. The crisis of historicism unveils, his in view, the limits of a universalist model of reason that would be oblivious to the uncertainty that is the essential feature the political realm.

The plea for contingency: Aron's 'moderate' historicism

We could argue that Aron remained throughout his life truthful to the philosophical and practical lessons learned during his 'German period'. Through his journalistic work and weekly editorials at the *Figaro*, he pursued after the war his quest to understand 'history in the making'. As a scholar of international relations and as a political philosopher, his work on war and peace, industrial societies, democracy and totalitarianism all constitute applications – or attempts of applications – of the ideas he developed in his *Introduction à la philosophie de l'histoire*.[55] The insights he found in the historicist tradition, such as the importance of historical knowledge, the primacy of *Verstehen* as the proper method of understanding political and social reality, the immanent meaning of lived experiences (*Erlebnisse*), the limits of objectivity in the realm of the social sciences, but also the rejection of grand historical narratives and the idea of progress in history, all those elements contributed to form Aron's 'moderate' historicism. For him, there is no doubt that the peak of the crisis of historicism sparked a reflection on plurality in history, which in turn led many philosophers and historians to conclude to the existence of an inescapable relativism of values that would entail practical consequences. However, Aron insists on the fact that this conception of the essential diversity of 'ways of thinking, feeling, willing and judging' is only one aspect – and perhaps a 'relatively superficial' aspect – of historical thinking.[56]

The historicist tradition provides in fact many essential elements to the development of a genuine philosophy of politics. Since the realm of social and political affairs is by essence complex, ambiguous and subject to contingency, a theory of politics (or 'praxeology,' as Aron will later call it) should mirror these uncertainties. The insistence on historical singularity, plurality of interpretation, the historicity of human action and the role of contingency in human affairs that we find at the core of the historicist tradition are all key features of a genuine understanding of the mechanisms of human action. Human beings belong to a specific horizon from which they apprehend the past and the future. Their specific place in history and their status as historical beings should be the starting point of a reflection on politics.

In that sense, one of the fundamental reasons that explain Aron's 'moderate' historicism or inclination towards critical philosophy of history is his scepticism towards speculative philosophies of history and historical determinism. Marxism and communism progressively became the dominant ideology in France, especially after the war. While Aron was a rigorous reader of Marx, he had a problem with what he called 'idolatry of History'.[57] Aron's encounter with the writings of Dilthey, Troeltsch, Weber, Heidegger and others served to reinforce his criticism of totalizing visions of history. Loyal to his neo-Kantian roots, he thus rejected all types of grand historical narratives that could, on a political level, lead to the justification of atrocious behaviours in the name of a radically new future. One important lesson of historicism is the realization that singular historical events cannot be subsumed into a general, singular and meaningful path towards an end of History. There is no History with a capital 'H': There are only multiple histories. The insistence in the historicist tradition on the plurality of interpretations of historical events, coupled with the attention to contingent factors in the unfolding of history, served as an antidote to the overly ambitious and potentially dangerous visions of History.

Aron's insistence on the role of contingency in politics is thus a reaction to the idea of historical determinism in all its forms. On a philosophical level, it should be rejected on the following ground: narratives of progress (as well as narratives of decline, for that matter) are both dogmatic in the Kantian sense insofar as they exclude the ever-present possibility of a new, unforeseen political experience.[58] Both progressive and pessimistic philosophies of history can be refuted or negated by the irruption of an unexpected course of action or, to put it simply, by the existence of contingency. Transposed into politics, totalizing narratives are dangerous insofar as they can serve to justify, under an authoritarian regime, any type of measure in the name of a future ideal to be achieved historically.[59]

In that regard, Aron is a 'historicist' thinker (or in political terms, a liberal one), if by that we mean that he is suspicious of any metaphysics of History, as did the neo-Kantian philosophers and the German historical school who were critical of Hegel's philosophy of history. Aron's position also reveals his tragic disposition: history, in his view, is more often than not ironic. He often writes that 'men make history, but they do not know the history they are making'.[60] In other terms, while we have the power to act in history, we can never completely master the historical process. In that regard, awareness of contingency and historicity would lead to a more prudent and responsible attitude towards political events. Hermeneutic historicism's insistence on historical singularity is thus salutary: attending to the particular means knowing about the 'servitudes of thought and action' rather than acting in view of an ideal society that will emerge at the end of the historical process. For Aron, a more historically oriented view calls for tolerance, whereas philosophy of history (in speculative sense) encourages fanatism.[61]

Against the positivist tendencies of the previous generation and the dogmatist inclination of his own, Aron saw in German theory of history the basis of a praxeology or philosophy of politics based on the insight that we can only conceptualize politics by paying attention to the particular set of circumstances in which political action takes place. We have to recognize that politics is intertwined with contingency and that the future of the human adventure remains an open one. Aron, in the 1930s, was looking for a political philosophy grounded in history, not in *a priori* moral principles or universalist values, and the German 'historicist tradition' offered the foundations to do just that.

Conclusion. Historicity, pluralism and political philosophy

This chapter did not seek to present a systematic view of the multiple meanings of historicism in Aron's work. Rather, the aim was to demonstrate how the politics of historicism in Aron's early years shaped the subsequent development of his thought.

Aron owes a lot to German philosophy of history and more specifically to the neo-Kantian critical philosophy of history. But he also owes it to the experience of history, to the political, social and moral crisis and the tragedy that was the Second World War. If there is one defining element that stands at the core of Aron's vision of politics, it is the notion of contingency. Aron's political philosophy includes crisis as a permanent possibility, and this awareness, in turn, precludes one from grandiose claims or beliefs. It leads, in other terms, to an attitude of prudence, or as Aron would say, in Weberian terms, an ethics of responsibility.[62] One could argue that this moderate stance is reformist rather than revolutionary and that it could encourage *status quo* rather than change. However, Aron, having seen the excesses and mistakes of French communism after the war as well as the tragic consequences of the millenarist ideal of the Nazi Party, preferred this accusation to that of embracing an ideological discourse. As Sylvie Mesure rightly points out, Aron sought to overcome the excesses of historicism through a practical project that, similar to Dilthey's critique of historical reason, would amount to a critique of *political* reason.[63]

Although Aron recognized in his *Memoirs* that his books published before the war – in particular his *Introduction à la philosphie de l'histoire* – were in certain aspects too 'historicist',[64] he still stands by his conclusion: His aim is not to relativize knowledge, values or norms, but to set the limits – in a very Kantian way – to what we can possibly know (in his case, in the domain of political affairs). As he writes in *L'Opium des Intellectuels*, 'the plurality of dimensions open to understanding [characteristic of historicist thought] does not reflect the failing of knowledge, but rather the infinite resources of reality'.[65] In this case, historicism can be considered as a 'productive' concept insofar as it opens a space of interrogation about the foundations of knowledge of politics and about the degree of certainty one can achieve in knowing about the historical world.

Did Aron succeed in tracing a third way between a Kantian moral system of norms and complete historicization? His final position can be unsatisfactory for the philosopher in quest of a clear, definitive answer. Faithful in that regard to Weber's position, Aron contends that there is no overcoming the tension between universality and relativity. Rather, the work of political philosophy precisely *lies in* this tension; it happens in this 'in-between'. Understanding political affairs means being a bit of a 'historicist': one has to accept the essential variability, contradictions, *zones d'ombre* and antinomies of political life rather than attempt to refute or overcome them.

Notes

1   *The Yorkshire Post*, 'Lesson of the Crisis: Sir A. Chamberlain's Review of Events', 21 March 1936, page 11, Column 7, Leeds, West Yorkshire, England (British Newspaper Archive).

2   One could even count the earlier publication of Edmund Husserl's *Philosophy als strenge Wissenschaft* (1910).
3   See Georg G. Iggers, 'Historicism: The History and Meaning of a Term', *The Journal of History of Ideas* 56, no. 1 (1995): 129–30.
4   Raymond Aron, 'Remarques sur l'historisme-herméneutique', in *Culture, science et développement: contribution à une histoire de l'homme; mélanges en l'honneur de Charles Morazé* (Toulouse: Privat, 1979), 185. My translation.
5   On concepts as 'sites of debates', see Mieke Bal, *Travelling Concepts in the Humanities: A Rough Guide* (Toronto: University of Toronto Press, 2002), 11.
6   Aron associates the crisis of historicism with a crisis of European consciousness (Aron, 'Remarques sur l'historisme-herméneutique', 191).
7   Raymond Aron, *Introduction à la philosophie de l'histoire: Essai sur les limites de l'objectivité historique*, rev. ed. by Sylvie Mesure (1938; repr., Paris: Gallimard, 1986), 13.
8   Raymond Aron, *De l'existence historique* (Inédit, 1979), 158. ('Le tournoi des relativistes et des non-relativistes m'a toujours paru caricatural.')
9   Georges Canguilhem, 'Raymond Aron et la philosophie critique de l'histoire: De Hegel à Weber', *Enquête* 7 (2005): 8.
10 Aron often uses this expression ('l'histoire en train de se faire').
11 Gwendal Châton, *Introduction à Raymond Aron* (Paris: La Découverte, 2017), 10. On that note, Aron was the one who encouraged his comrade Jean-Paul Sartre to follow in his footsteps and to take the same position he held in Germany a few years after his return.
12 See Raymond Aron, 'La découverte de l'Allemagne', chap. 3 in *Mémoires* (1983; repr., Paris: Robert Laffont, 2010).
13 Aron, *Mémoires*, 82–103.
14 Aron, *Mémoires*, 84; Raymond Aron, 'Lettres à Pierre Bertaux', in *Raymond Aron 1905-1983: Histoire et politique; Textes et témoignages* (Paris: Julliard, 1985), 281.
15 Ibid.
16 Raymond Aron, 'La notion du sens de l'histoire', in *Dimensions de la conscience historique* (Paris: Plon, 1961), 32.
17 For Aron, this passage from philosophy to political reality was drastic: 'I was not confronted with the mystery of time in Kant's philosophy anymore, but with German students and professors who cursed the Versailles Treaty, the French and the economic crisis' (Raymond Aron, *De l'existence historique* (Inédit, 1979)).
18 Canguilhem, 'Raymond Aron', 7.
19 Aron, *Mémoires*, 102–3. My translation.
20 Pierre Manent, 'Raymond Aron éducateur', in *Enquête sur la démocratie: études de philosophie politique* (Paris: Gallimard, 2007), 218.
21 We can also observe Aron's concerns with the rise of Nazism while he was working on his thesis through his letters to Pierre Bertaux from 1930 to 1933 ('Lettres

d'Allemagne à Pierre Bertaux (1930–1933)', in *Raymond Aron 1905–1983: Histoire et politique; Textes et témoignages* (Paris: Julliard, 1985).
22 Aron, 'Remarques sur l'historisme-herméneutique', 202.
23 See, for instance, the work of Troetlsch, Mannheim and Husserl among others.
24 See Frederick C. Beiser, 'Weimar Philosophy and the Fate of Neo-Kantianism', in *Weimar Thought: A Contested Legacy*, ed. Gordon and McCormick (Princeton, NJ: Princeton University Press, 2013), 117.
25 See Leo Strauss, 'Political Philosophy and History', *Journal of the History of Ideas* 10, no. 1 (1949): 42.
26 Annette Wittkau, *Historismus: Zur Geschichte des Begriffs und des Problems* (Göttingen: Vandenhoeck & Ruprecht, 1994), 15.
27 For a presentation of the challenge of historicism for morality and normativity, see Frederick C. Beiser, 'Normativity in Neo-Kantianism: Its Rise and Fall', *International Journal of Philosophical Studies* 17, no. 1 (2009): 9–27.
28 See the fourth section of Aron's *Introduction à la philosophie de l'histoire*, titled: 'Histoire et vérité'. The second part of that last section is devoted to historicism and historical relativism (Aron, *Introduction à la philosophie*, 335–437).
29 Raymond Aron, *La philosophie critique de l'histoire: Essai sur une théorie allemande de l'histoire* (1938; repr., Paris: Vrin, 1969).
30 Aron, *La philosophie critique de l'histoire*, 15–18; Wilhelm Dilthey, *Selected Works Volume 1: Introduction to the Human Sciences*, ed. with an introduction by Rudolf A. Makkreel and Frithjof Rodi (Princeton, NJ: Princeton University Press, 1989), 165; Wilhelm Dilthey, *Selected Works Volume 3: The Formation of the Historical World in the Human Sciences*, ed. with an introduction by Rudolf A. Makkreel and Frithjof Rodi (Princeton, NJ: Princeton University Press, 2002), 139–40.
31 It has been translated into English and published under the title: *Introduction to Philosophy of History. Essay on the Limits of Objectivity in the Social Sciences*.
32 Aron, *La philosophie critique de l'histoire*, 15.
33 Raymond Aron, 'Ma carrière. Note du 6 janvier 1983', in *Raymond Aron 1905–1983: Histoire et politique; Textes et témoignages* (Paris: Julliard, 1985), 518.
34 Not only that, but he was the proof of its success: He was received first at the Agrégation and was considered an outstanding student.
35 Wilhelm Dilthey and Max Weber in particular provided Aron with a more grounded view of social and political affairs. Dilthey's project of a 'critique of historical reason' precisely aimed to move away from the intellectualism of Kantian epistemology and to reduce the gap between lived experience and the *Geisteswissenschaften*.
36 On Aron's more thorough explanation of the different levels of meaning of historicism, see Raymond Aron, *Leçons sur l'histoire* (Paris: Éditions de Fallois, 1989), 14–15.

37 See, for instance, Raymond Aron, 'Note sur les rapports de l'histoire et de la politique', *Revue de métaphysique et de morale* 54, no. 3/4 (1949): 192.
38 Aron, as many commentators of the historicist tradition, traces back this distinction to Vico.
39 Aron, *Mémoires*, 161–2.
40 On that note, see Aron's analysis of the Hempel-Dray debate in Aron, *Leçons sur l'histoire*, 20–3, 175–91.
41 'Compte rendu de la soutenance de these de R. Aron dans la *Revue de métaphysique et de morale*', in Annexes to Aron, *Introduction à la philosphie*, 442.
42 Aron, *Introduction à la philosophie*, 13. My translation.
43 While Aron's use of the word 'historicity' comes from Dilthey, one can also see the influence of Heidegger's *Sein und Zeit*, which Aron had read during his German stay.
44 Aron insists on that Weberian insight according to which there is always an irremediable gap between the intentions of political actors and the outcome of their actions.
45 See Aron's introductory speech (Aron, *Introduction à la philosophie*, 443–4).
46 Aron recognizes that fact in later writings (see Aron, 'Remarques sur l'historisme-herméneutique', 191). One could argue that there were philosophers in France at the time who also offered a more phenomenological approach, such as Henri Bergson.
47 Aron reported in his *Mémoires* that he was 'living in advance the world war that [his] jury members in the Louis-Liard room did not see coming' (Aron, *Mémoires*, 180). My translation.
48 Aron affirms that explicitly in later writings: 'Le relativisme est l'expérience authentique du politique' (Aron, 'Note sur les rapports', 407).
49 'Les dépassements de l'historisme'.
50 Aron, *Introduction à la philosophie*, 377. My translation.
51 Aron does not cite Dilthey or Weber here, but this idea is found in both their work: that the fate of the human adventure remains open and that the effort of reflection must take that fundamental fact into account.
52 « Pour ma part, au sortir de ces cinq heures d'horloge, je retirai une impression d'ensemble restée très vivace: des poules qui ont couvé un canard et le voient avec terreur se précipiter vers la marae et se mouvoir avec aisance dans un élément qui leur est inconnu » ('Récit de la soutenance para le père G. Fessard', Annexe, Aron, *Introduction à la philosophie*, 457). My translation.
53 'Récit de la soutenance para le père G. Fessard', Annexe, Aron, *Introduction à la philosophie*, 451.
54 Canguilhem, 'Raymond Aron', 8.
55 Aron, 'Ma carrière. Note du 6 janvier 1983', 518.

56 See Aron, *Leçons sur l'histoire*, 14.
57 See Raymond Aron, 'Le sens de l'histoire', chap 5. in *L'Opium des Intellectuels* (Paris: Calmann-Lévy, 1955), 145–71.
58 See Philippe Raynaud, 'Introduction', in Kant, *Opuscules sur l'histoire* (Paris: Flammarion, 1990), 10.
59 This is in a nutshell, one of the main arguments that Aron presents in the *Opium des Intellectuels* ('The sublime end justifies the horrible means', 167).
60 'Les hommes font l'histoire, mais ne savent pas l'histoire qu'ils font': This expression comes back more than a dozen times in Aron's writings. It appears for the first time in his first book on contemporary German sociology (*La sociologie allemande contemporaine*) in 1935 and will become a recurrent formula.
61 Aron, *L'Opium des Intellectuels*, 170.
62 On that note, see Aron's preface to the French translation of Weber's *Wissenschaft als Beruf* and *Politik als Beruf* (Max Weber, *Le Savant et le Politique* (Paris: Plon, 1958).
63 Sylvie Mesure, 'Objectivité théorique et objectivité pratique chez Raymond Aron. De l'histoire à la politique', in *La politique historique de Raymond Aron*, ed. Alain Renaut and Sylvie Mesure, Cahiers de philosophie politique et juridique (Caen: Centre de Publications de l'Université de Caen, 1989), 15, 16.
64 Aron claims in his *Mémoires* that his work on philosophy of history was wrongly understood as a defence of relativism. He recognizes that some expressions (like 'the dissolution of the object') led readers to that conclusion, but he nonetheless maintains that his enquiry preserves an idea of truth and objectivity in the understanding of the historical world (see Aron, *Mémoires*, 172).
65 Aron, *L'Opium des Intellectuels*, 148.

Bibliography

Aron, Raymond. *De l'existence historique*. Inédit, 1979.
Aron, Raymond. *Études politiques*. Paris: Gallimard, 1972.
Aron, Raymond. *Introduction à la philosophie de l'histoire: Essai sur les limites de l'objectivité historique*. 1938. Revised edition by Sylvie Mesure. Paris: Gallimard, 1986.
Aron, Raymond. 'La notion du sens de l'histoire'. In Aron, *Dimensions de la conscience historique*, 32–45. Paris: Plon, 1961.
Aron, Raymond. *La philosophie critique de l'histoire: Essai sur une théorie allemande de l'histoire*. 1938. Paris: Vrin, 1969.
Aron, Raymond. *La sociologie allemande contemporaine*. 1935. Paris: Quadrige, 2007.
Aron, Raymond. *Leçons sur l'histoire*. Paris: Éditions de Fallois, 1989.

Aron, Raymond. *L'Opium des intellectuels*. Paris: Calmann-Lévy, 1955.
Aron, Raymond. *Mémoires*. 1983. Paris: Robert Laffont, 2010.
Aron, Raymond. 'Note sur les rapports de l'histoire et de la politique'. *Revue de métaphysique et de morale* 54, no. 3/4 (1949): 392–407.
Aron, Raymond. *Raymond Aron 1905–1983: Histoire et politique; Textes et témoignages*. Paris: Julliard, 1985.
Aron, Raymond. 'Remarques sur l'historisme-herméneutique'. In *Culture, science et développement: contribution à une histoire de l'homme; mélanges en l'honneur de Charles Morazé*, 185–205. Toulouse: Privat, 1979.
Bal, Mieke. *Travelling Concepts in the Humanities: A Rough Guide*. Toronto: University of Toronto Press, 2002.
Bambach, Charles R. 'Weimar Philosophy and the Crisis of Historical Thinking'. In *Weimar Thought: A Contested Legacy*, edited by Gordon and McCormick, 133–49. Princeton, NJ: Princeton University Press, 2013.
Beiser, Frederick C. 'Normativity in Neo-Kantianism: Its Rise and Fall'. *International Journal of Philosophical Studies* 17, no. 1 (2009): 9–27.
Beiser, Frederick C. 'Weimar Philosophy and the Fate of Neo-Kantianism'. In *Weimar Thought: A Contested Legacy*, edited by Gordon and McCormick, 115–32. Princeton, NJ: Princeton University Press, 2013.
Canguilhem, Geroges. 'Raymond Aron et la philosophie critique de l'histoire: De Hegel à Weber'. *Enquête* 7 (2005): 1–8.
Châton, Gwendal. *Introduction à Raymond Aron*. Paris: La Découverte, 2017.
Dilthey, Wilhelm. *Selected Works Volume 1: Introduction to the Human Sciences*. Edited with an introduction by Rudolf A. Makkreel and Frithjof Rodi. Princeton, NJ: Princeton University Press, 1989.
Dilthey, Wilhelm. *Selected Works Volume 3: The Formation of the Historical World in the Human Sciences*. Edited with an introduction by Rudolf A. Makkreel and Frithjof Rodi. Princeton, NJ: Princeton University Press, 2002.
Fessard, Gaston. *La philosophie historique de Raymond Aron*. Paris: Julliard, 1980.
Husserl, Edmund. *La philosophie comme science rigoureuse*. Paris: Presses universitaires de France, 1954. Translated from the German 'Philosophie als eine strenge Wissenschaft', *Logos* 1 (1911): 289–341.
Iggers, Georg G. 'Historicism: The History and Meaning of a Term'. *The Journal of History of Ideas* 56, no. 1 (1995): 129–52.
Manent, Pierre. 'Raymond Aron éducateur'. In Manent, *Enquête sur la démocratie: études de philosophie politique*, 217–48. Paris: Gallimard, 2007.
Mannheim, Karl. 'Historicism'. In Mannheim, *Essays on the Sociology of Knowledge*, 84–133. London: Routledge, 1952.
Meinecke, Friedrich. *Die Entstehung des Historismus*. Munich: Oldenbourg Verlag, 1936. Translated by J. E. Anderson as *Historism: The Rise of a New Historical Outlook* (New York, NY: Herder and Herder, 1972).

Raynaud, Philippe. 'Introduction'. In Immanuel Kant, *Opuscules sur l'histoire*, 7–36. Paris: Flammarion, 1990.

Renaut, Alain and Sylvie Mesure, ed. *La politique historique de Raymond Aron*. Cahiers de philosophie politique et juridique. Caen: Centre de Publications de l'Université de Caen, 1989.

Strauss, Leo. 'Political Philosophy and History'. *Journal of the History of Ideas* 10, no. 1 (1949): 30–50.

Troeltsch, Ernst. *Der Historismus und seine Probleme*. Tübingen: Mohr, 1922. Reprinted in *Gesammelte Schriften*, vol. 3 (Aalen: Scientia Verlag, 1977).

Weber, Max. *Le Savant et le Politique*. Paris: Plon, 1958.

Wittkau, Annette. *Historismus: Zur Geschichte des Begriffs und des Problems*. Göttingen: Vandenhoeck & Ruprecht, 1994.

Part Four

Travels beyond historicism

7

Friedrich Meinecke's *Historism* or the defeat of German historicism

Audrey Borowski

Abstract

This chapter offers a contextual reading of the works of Friedrich Meinecke. By discussing the importance of Goethe, Ranke and the political and methodological tensions in Meinecke's works on historicism, it shows, perhaps surprisingly, that the German historian actively (though unintentionally) contributed to the decline of the historicist tradition in twentieth-century Europe. He did so by making visible internal tensions within historicist thinking as well as its profound inability to relate the idealism of Johann Wolfgang von Goethe and Leopold von Ranke to the mundane realities of actual historical research. Instead of reinvigorating historicism, then, Meinecke illustrated the dead ends that historicism had reached by the mid-twentieth century.

Introduction

The concept of 'historicism' – a distinctly modern way of understanding the human world, as expressed in Ernst Troeltsch's definition of historicism as 'the fundamental historicization of all our thought about man, his culture, and his values'[1] – has always been in crisis. Criticism of the concept of historicism began as early as 1838, by Ludwig Feuerbach, and seems to have coincided with the term's entrance into common use, as its ability to bear multiple, even opposed, meanings, and hence be constantly re-appropriated, became manifest.[2] In this manner, historicism emerged as an essentially amorphous concept, the recipient of ever-changing meanings from which it was difficult to identify a stable 'core' or essence.[3]

The scientific and objectivistic claims of the early historicism practised by the nineteenth-century German historiographical and philosophical 'schools' (represented pre-eminently by the jurist Friedrich Karl von Savigny, the historian Leopold von Ranke, and before them philosophers Johann Martin Chaldenius, Johann Gottfried Herder and Justus Möser, the first advocates of a new science of human nature based on the natural sciences)[4] were soon criticized and rejected in favour of the hermeneutical programme promoted by the likes of Johann Gustav Droysen and Wilhelm Dilthey, and later Wilhelm Windelband and Heinrich Rickert.[5] By the early twentieth century historicism was said to be in crisis, or a cause of crisis, for reasons ranging from 'the confusion of the intellectual scene around 1920–30', to the self-doubt of the historical profession induced by 'the identity-crisis of the bourgeoisie after the First World War', to an increasing awareness 'of the limitations of human knowledge and the subjective character of all cognition in regard to human behaviour and social processes'.[6] These accounts shared a sense that the implications of historicizing thought and practices were profoundly disquieting both intellectually and morally. Among the most prominent expressions of discontent with historicism were Nietzsche's polemical essay 'On the Use and Disadvantage of History for Life' (1874), Windelband's critique of attempts to historicize reason, and Ernst Troeltsch's essay 'The Crisis of Historicism', which bemoaned the historicist relativization of human values.[7] This crisis, according to Troeltsch, could be overcome through a particular kind of ethical and moral 'synthesis', a 'decisionism' grounded in feeling, instinct or faith.[8] Published only fourteen years before Meinecke's landmark *Historismus*, Troeltsch's work seemed to mark the culmination of decades of controversy about a concept that had become all too polemical. While Meinecke agreed with Troeltsch about the problems brought about by relativism, he opted for a different solution.

Yet, it was perhaps Meinecke who most clearly articulated the inherent tension within historicism and even its self-contradictory nature, discerning how historicism's strength constituted at the same time its very weakness, and tracing within his own work, from its beginnings in the late nineteenth century to the landmark works of the 1930s, how historicism contained in itself the seeds of its own contestation. He eventually sought to salvage the concept from the implications of its premises by bypassing reason and rational enquiry altogether and relocating historicism away from the political realm[9] and firmly back within metaphysics,[10] in the process contributing to its marginalization around mid-century. This is the subject of this chapter.

Meinecke's historicism

The concept of historicism has proved enduring in its capacity to defy any clear-cut definition. Alternatively construed as pure, radical relativism paving the way towards a moral vacuum, as grasped by Leo Strauss, or as some sort of sinister historical determinism, as understood by Karl Popper, it initially came about as an attempt to derive meaning, no longer from the mechanical and repetitive world of Natural Law or abstract rationality of the Enlightenment, but from the individuality and spontaneity of historical events. Much more a *Weltanschauung* than a mere historiographical method, it set out to access a higher reality from within the multiplicity of various historical individualities, hoping to catch glimpses of the universal from within the particular.

Historicism thus emerged as the interplay between the objective and the subjective, the relative and the metaphysical, the concrete and the ideal, the time-bound and the timeless. Friedrich Meinecke's works, such as his *Cosmopolitanism and the National State (Weltbürgertum und Nationalstaat: Studien zur Genesis des deutschen Nationalstaates,* published in 1911) and *Machiavellism: The Doctrine of State Reason and Its Place in Modern History (Die Idee der Staatsräson,* published in 1924), have proved most enlightening in tracing his understanding of the emergence of a particular historical outlook and more broadly of history as a meaningful process. Building on the work of fellow historians Johann Gustav Bernhard Droysen, Wilhelm Dilthey and Ernst Troeltsch and referring back to such luminaries as Johann Wolfgang Goethe and Leopold von Ranke, Meinecke artfully set out to demonstrate how a new historical consciousness had come about, one rooted in a particular German spirit and which opposed the rationalizing outlook of Western European Enlightenment. Crucially, too, it had sought to embed itself anew within a metaphysical dimension which relocated the 'ideal' within the individual. As Meinecke himself recognized, this harmony between the ideal and the particular individual had, however, found itself being challenged throughout the nineteenth century by the realities of nationalism, the rise of power politics and the gradual weakening of the belief in an overarching metaphysical framework. This had opened the flood gates of pure relativism. In reaction to its attendant lack of ethical restraints and ontological anarchy, Meinecke, in his final work and after a lifetime of wrestling with the issue of historicity, sought to salvage this historical outlook and reassert the existence of a higher order and re-establish history as the marriage of the individual and the spiritual in his seminal *Historism, The Rise of a new Historical*

Outlook (*Die Entstehung des Historismus,* originally published in 1936). In order to achieve this and entertain the possibility of the continued viability of his concept of historicism, Meinecke chose to retreat towards the realm of ideals, thus isolating the latter from any complexity which would risk undermining it and reducing it to an aesthetic – and very much ahistorical – approach. The concept of historicism, one which was supposed to mark a 'revolution', thus appeared very much doomed from the start and was bound to be unmade by the premises it was built upon. Meinecke was never quite able to resolve this tension. Historicism's concept of individuality, divorced from early historicism's idealistic streak, threatened to reduce the world to one of chaos and struggle. On the other hand, apprehending history as the realization of ideals was equally untenable.

Meinecke's *Historism* culminates with an account of the German thinker, author and poet Goethe, whom Meinecke credits with the most significant contribution towards the emergence of historicism as a new historical consciousness. Considering Goethe's poor opinion of the historiographical practice of his time, Meinecke's unorthodox choice of the poet as sowing the seeds of what he considered a major intellectual revolution has often been met with bewilderment. Goethe however, according to Meinecke, had set the stage for a novel way of grasping reality, substituting the generalizing and rationalizing thought of the Enlightenment for an individualizing approach[11] which construed reality as an incessant whirlpool of creation of unique individualities whose essences themselves emanated from a higher metaphysical plane. Key to Goethe's – and Meinecke's – understanding had been the discovery of the principle of individuality[12] which enabled emancipation from a linear approach to time and historical progress predicated on Natural Law; reality was henceforth to be apprehended in its diversity and temporality.[13]

In keeping with Neo-Platonism,[14] those various individualities, according to Meinecke, originated from an eternal higher plane[15] with each one constituting 'a note, a single sound in a great harmony which must be studied as a whole'.[16] Goethe's understanding reconciled unity and multiplicity, the particular and the absolute in an 'ultimate permanence rising above all temporary restlessness'[17] in which the past and the present coincided.[18] His was thus a highly idealizing approach, always eager to uncover the divine in primal phenomena[19] and to catch glimpses of 'an ever-flowing ideal life at work behind the passing realities of the present, yet immanent in them'.[20] Goethe had therefore managed the feat, according to Meinecke, of formulating a worldview built on an apparent tension, between on the one hand individualities with their own spontaneous developments and on the other hand individualities tracing their inner essences back to an all-embracing spiritual whole, between freedom and inner necessity. This he had done by adopting a highly idealized and selective approach keen on uncovering the 'fulfilment of the fairest possibilities'[21] and rejecting 'the rest as chaff'.[22]

How did Meinecke reach the conclusion of advising his countrymen to recapture the spirit of Goethe's age and what was the process that led him to this conclusion? Already early on in his studies, Meinecke had been impressed by the German historian Johann Gustav Droysen's emphasis on the manner in which important dynamic forces worked themselves out in history.[23] This had led him before the evidence of the existence of an 'immeasurable force' rooted within history and the human spirit and which 'did not come under the jurisdiction of reason'.[24] Meinecke had also read the first volume of the German historian Wilhelm Dilthey's *Einleitung in die Geisteswissenschaften.* In it, Dilthey had further differentiated the human from the natural sciences and distinctness of the human spirit and 'the depth and totality of human self-consciousness'.[25]

Man, according to him, stood as an *imperium in imperio* in nature in his ability to create autonomous mental facts: 'Man, as yet unaffected by any examination of the origins of the world of thought, already finds in his self-consciousness the sovereignty of the will, responsibility for this actions, a power to subject everything to the process of thought and to offer spiritual resistance as lord of the free castle of his personality which distinguish him from nature as whole.' He 'separate[d] from the kingdom of nature a realm of history, where, in the midst of the network for objective necessity that constitutes nature, freedom flashes forth at innumerable places throughout the whole'.[26]

This freedom eluded strict logical processes and could not be reduced to 'ideal of historical progress worshipped by the idolaters of a purely mechanical development of intellect'.[27] In *Das Leben des Generalfeldmarschalls Hermann von Boyen,* Meinecke further refined his indictment of Enlightenment abstract rationalism and perhaps its foremost manifestation, Immanuel Kant's categorical imperative. Kant, in his 'anxiety to arrive at a unified and necessary principle for moral action', had 'looked down on this whole realm of the empirical as something random and unstable, and sacrificed the inner unity of man because he could not find the detailed link between the inclinations and feelings on the one hand and the formal moral law on the other'.[28] In striving to uncover 'rational principles of a strictly necessary kind' Kant had banished 'anything "given" in human experience from the moral law' in a movement that sought 'to force the wayward movements of the feelings and the imagination under the control of enlightened reason.'[29]

Meinecke had thus inherited from the early historicists the concept of History as a *Weltanschauung*. As he understood it, the interpretation of the historical process had gradually shifted from being grasped in terms of Natural Law to being understood as an individualizing historical outlook.[30] It was an essentially German movement of the mind[31] which had sought to counter Western European rationalism and value anew the forces of individuality, 'the unique quality of each … who [was] active at any and every point in the boundless cosmos of the mind'. Meinecke had welcomed

> the jubilant awakening of a new spirit that is also deeply rooted in the national soul as seen in the poems of Goethe and the thought of Herder. There was a fervent enthusiasm for all that was free and natural in what poured forth from his pen … Goethe, Herder and their fellow protagonists rediscovered the roots linking men to nature by seeing man as only the highest expression of a creative power that was active throughout the universe. There thus evolved the idea of a free organic development, passing on its fruitfulness from one generation to another, but requiring particularly at this present stage the unfettered growth of individuality.[32]

Drawing on Dilthey, Meinecke had probed further the kind of individuality at work in the world, taking on the problem of life itself, one which could no longer be remedied through the hitherto accepted 'transcendental solution'[33] especially in the wake of 'spectacle of the collapse of pure reason in France'.[34] Only a new understanding of life, in its psycho-physical and social dimensions, as continuous variability and evolution, would do:

> But we must also look upon every organism as a system in which the parts are subordinated to the whole by a corporate unity of purpose. This organic world shows a creative power in action in the plant and in the animal, in the growth of organisms from the germ-cell, and in the instincts by which nature taught us long before there was any conscious education. And so the recognizable unity that runs all through the machinery of nature is an indication of an indwelling creative power that works with consummate art.[35]

In *Weltburgertum und Nationalstaat*, Meinecke had already extended his analysis to the process of nation building and the particular type of 'voyage' undertaken by the German spirit 'in the realm of the individual' which 'ha[d] begun to reveal individuality in everything that unite[d] individuals to human beings'. In contradistinction to those European states built on Natural Law, those of the German movement were distinct in their 'aristocratic' nature and their impulse to liberate and increase 'all that is best in man'.[36]

> What is the general origin of our historical and political thought-forms, and our sense of individuality even in the supra-individual groupings? It is surely clear that it is essentially derived from an individualism that has in the course of centuries deepened its originally superficial view of the essence of an individual until it has got down to the root-levels, and so revealed the links that bind the specific single life to the specific life of the higher human groupings and orders. There is individuality, spontaneity, an urge towards self-determination and extension of power observable on every hand, and not least in the State and the nation.[37]

The state, like any other individuality, was an eminently historical structure which developed according to its specific character and through the mutual contacts with other nations.[38] Only by adopting the historicizing outlook could one hope to 'discern the true values in history'.[39]

In his next work, *Die Idee der Staatsräson,* Meinecke sought to trace the rise of the doctrine concerning the interests of states since Machiavelli. In his study, he paid particular attention to the historian Leopold von Ranke, whom he had hailed as the culmination of the German historicist tradition in his memorial address to the Prussian Academy (23 January 1936). Recent historians have scarcely paid justice to Ranke by portraying him merely as an empiricist and limiting his contribution to a methodological input, when the latter was merely the upshot of a novel, historically rooted worldview. As Meinecke recognized, Ranke had integrated much of Goethe's legacy and extended it to the historical realm per se, his principle of individuality underscored by a metaphysical – and in his case religious – dimension. His approach required not only a critical grasp of historical sources, but also an 'intuition' which could help sense the past and discern God's overarching hand in the various events, once more in a bid to derive some meaning from the masses of otherwise irrational elements.[40] Indeed, according to Ranke, God existed both above and within history and it fell to the historian to reveal his presence by means of meticulous historical investigation.[41] His was already a more complex, politicised world revolving around states related back to an all-embracing spiritual whole as 'ideas of God'.[42] Ranke relied on a highly idealistic grasp of reality and history in order to strike a balance between the idea of free individual development and metaphysical necessity, relativism and the absolute, immanent and transcendent. As Meinecke explained:

> His concept of God was enclosed by a very fine and subtle line. The concept was embracing enough in a strong, positive and fervent manner to be able to shed a radiance even on empirical history and to endow with a priestly sense those who investigated it; but at the same time, it was also prudently adjusted to the need

for carrying out an analysis that was completely free and not tied by any dogma or theory. The free movement of individual historical forces, which were 'just as good or as evil, as noble-minded or as animal, as cultured or as crude, aiming at eternity or subordinated to the moment' as their protagonists happened to be, now came into its full rights, but did not lose itself in an anarchy of values, because projected into it there was a great and absolute value which dominated and supported everything. Thus Ranke remained protected from the relativism to which his principle of individuality might have led. But it follows from this that a dualism which was logically irreconcilable was now capable of entering into his mode of viewing history and into his standards of value. It was certainly permissible that everything which happened in history should be interpreted freely and without presupposition as being the work of individual forces and circumstances; but it was not the case that everything could be granted and forgiven to it, because in the background there was present and absolute court of justice which did not allow contempt.[43]

Still, in spite of similarities, Ranke had rejected Hegel's transcendent idealism whose world-spirit acted out of deception to achieve its aims. The feeling for 'the eternal laws of the moral world-order' was firmly entrenched in Ranke and could not possibly admit any artificial harmonizing of the 'inevitable mire of history with its ultimate idealistic purpose'[44] for this would have refuted the divine essence of all concrete individualities and done away with the natural harmony which it presupposed. Indeed, Ranke's conception of history proved enduring in its optimism. Meinecke summed it up quite nicely:

> Ranke ... broke with all the methods of rationalization and abstraction, of deriving things from ideas that could be comprehended abstractly; and in order to do this he blended things and ideas together into a unity of 'the living' ... Individual life in history, incapable of being derived from universal ideas, but imbued with special ideas by which it is shaped, so that in the process idea and body, soul and flesh, become essentially one, and the whole enwreathed in the breath of original divine creativity – this was the particular synthesis of the ideas of individuality and identity which Ranke was able to provide. Thus even his philosophy of history was a kind of philosophy of identity.[45]

Ranke's dualism appeared in all its clarity in the increasingly important realm of power politics and did not fail to impress of ambiguity. Ranke was horrified by Machiavelli's allegedly universal precepts which clashed with his idea of each state developing according to its own terms and interest.[46] Amidst all the confusion and brute forces were 'creative spiritual forces ... moral energies'[47] being played out according to some mysterious design which would ultimately ensure the 'victory of true moral energy'. Therefore, *raison d'etat* was now acquired spiritual agency with a kind of 'necessity which has in it something inevitable, like a fate'.[48] Still, as much as Meinecke admired Ranke and credited him with attaining the 'marriage of Idea and Reality', he sensed a certain *naivete* on Ranke's part in regard to power. He felt that Ranke had limited himself to a simplistic and overly optimistic view of the state and its ability to synthesize power and spirit, thereby eluding the increasingly problematic nature of power.

The growing concern over political issues, the problem of good and evil and Ranke's own uneasy solution were bound to uncover the limits of this early idealistic Historicism. The latter was unable to come to grips with an increasingly socially and politically complex world; this was rendered all the more acute by the fact that the metaphysics of identity had gradually collapsed in favour of mere individuality. As it increasingly dawned on Meinecke, the new doctrine of individuality had certain clear implications for morality:

> It could easily act as a temptation to the morality of a single person if the right of individuality to express itself to the full was held to be unlimited, and was set up as a higher morality over against the general moral code. If applied to the supra-individual state, it could be used to legitimize all its excesses in the way of power politics as unavoidable by-products, organic to its essential being …
> In this way both the identity and the individuality concepts, two of the loftiest and most fruitful ideas of the German mind at that period, showed the tragically double-edged quality of all great historical ideas and forces.[49]

German historicism edged closer to an interpretation of the world merely in terms of volition, struggle and chaos.[50] Meinecke wrote his most important works in a context of growing militarism, nationalism and democracy, all of which he considered dangerous, prone to forcing upon *raison d'état* forces which it no longer was capable of controlling.[51] Passions and the drive for power consistently threatened the state's ability to develop its inner potential, thereby no longer warranting Ranke's unqualified optimism and confidence in an ultimate meaningful process.[52]

Indeed, as he wrote in his *Idee des Staatsräson*, in the course of the nineteenth century a dark cloud had descended over Europe in the shape of an unbridled principle of individuality which 'threatened in the end to run off into a relativism that would no longer recognize anything solid or absolute in history' ending up, in Dilthey's words, in an 'anarchy of convictions'.[53] The former organic dualism of the early historicism had surrendered to a pure individuality devoid of any metaphysical underpinning and which, as already noted by Ernst Troeltsch in *Der Historismus und seine Probleme* (1922), threatened an all-out relativism.[54]

But our desire to be different turned into a national tragedy. And whereas up till now our historism which individualised everything had lured us on with a happy outlook on the world, full indeed of struggle, but thoroughly creative struggle, we now began to sense profoundly tragic problems even in this prospect, and our picture of the world began to look much more sombre. This was not so much on account of the spiritual isolation in which we now found ourselves – for that was something we could bear, as long as historism continued to give us an inner feeling of superiority and a firm anchorage for facing all the basic problems of life. It has lavishly endowed us with intellectual treasure and taught us to understand the past and all its greatness, to love it and imitate its way of life, in a manner that produces a fabulous and fairylike atmosphere. But, to link up now with the observations we took up at the beginning, it is precisely this pluralism of individual values, which we discover on every hand, that may throw us into confusion and perplexity, particularly now in our state of clouded vision. Everything has individuality and is a law to itself, everything has its law of life, everything is relative and in a state of flux: then give me something, man cried out, on which can I stand firm. How can we emerge from this anarchy of values? How can one get back from a purely historical outlook to a doctrine of values.[55]

The crisis which had engulfed historism expressed itself all the more acutely in the political realm. The link between politics and morality had been dissolved, much to Meinecke's despair, giving way to a 'false idealization of power politics'[56] and clearing the way 'for the establishing of a crudely naturalistic and biological ethics of force'.[57] The material forces which had once enabled the actualization of historical 'ideas' were now responsible for their demise. What was needed, according to Meinecke, was the rediscovery of 'power politics and *raison d'etat* in the context of their duality and all their real problematic elements' in order to 'reach a doctrine that is not only *truer*, but also better and more *moral* in its effect'.[58]

The First World War and its attendant destruction had shattered Meinecke's former confidence in the character of political power. The state had become sheer power, and no longer as Meinecke had advanced in his earlier work on *Cosmopolitanism*, 'an individuality whose external form reflects an individualised but nevertheless real and timeless idea'.[59] Meinecke eventually failed to identify any morality and spirituality from within power politics, finally resolving on its inevitably 'daemonic' aspect.

Historicism had, mainly under the influence of political power, led to 'soulless specialization'[60] which it was now necessary to overcome by returning to a philosophy which strove after ultimate meaning and eternal ideals.[61] In the course of the nineteenth century, power politics and the historical brutality it had unleashed had undermined this perfect balance in loosening the bond between history and philosophy,[62] stripping historiography of its progressive unveiling of divinely inspired ideals. A need for some objectivity was making itself felt amidst pure relativism.[63] Goethe and Ranke, according to Meinecke, had been correct in trying to find the eternal within the historical and it is to them that Meinecke harked back to forge a solution and formulate historism's most accomplished incarnation.[64]

Unable to reconcile political power with spirit, Meinecke had finally resolved to retreat from the political realm into the realm of ideas. His *Der Enstehung des Historismus,* published in 1936, both marked the culmination of a lifelong reflexion on the nature of the historical process, the nature of historism and the crisis that had swept it, and constituted a call to renew this outlook, especially in its spiritual dimension. In it, Meinecke consecrated the return of the individual as ideal, one no longer threatening to drag the world into 'an abyss of relativism', but one that sought to re-locate the concept of individuality within a higher, metaphysical framework. In it, he described historism as

> perhaps the greatest revolution of thought the West had ever experienced. For it brought a shattering of hitherto prevailing belief in the comprehensible unity and uniformity of reason, and so of its universal validity and the pronouncements based upon it. This belief was dissolved by the recognition that reason could not provide general precepts for life, but only an infinite variety of forms of an evidently individual character ... [whose] ultimate unity was only to be found in an invisible, metaphysical and universal ground of being.

Germany had given birth to 'a new outlook on the world, which was now seen to be full of individuality', each of which 'was held to proceed from the one maternal bosom of a divine Nature', in each of which 'a specific and peculiar law of life was seen to be at work'.[65] Men 'were now confronted with an eternally new birth of the specific and unique. This more mature and deeper picture of the world created by the growing German historism required a certain pliability of thought and a language capable of handling ideas of a more complicated, imaginative and mystical kind.'[66]

Indeed, the formulation of a historical consciousness based on an individualizing approach had constituted an intellectual revolution; however, as the course of the nineteenth century had shown, it had also spelled its own degeneration by threatening to dissolve in a 'bottomless pit of relativism'. Once that metaphysical link had been loosened, the way had been cleared for pure historicity.[67] The concept of individuality as *Weltanschauung* – and not simply as mere historical methodology, as it is often mistakenly reduced to – had thus simultaneously made but also threatened the very historical outlook.

The only way Meinecke could attempt to salvage Historicism was by reasserting the spiritual content of history;[68] this implied restoring the idea at the heart of the historical individual, thereby renewing the fragile dualism of the early historicism which he located with Goethe and Ranke. According to him, only those two had proved able to escape the shallow relativism characteristic of later historicism by adopting a highly idealised, *sub specie aeternitas* approach which combined individual with absolute, objective with subjective.

> It belongs, however, to the inmost essence of an individualising historism that although it does not make any metaphysical presuppositions, it is nevertheless forced to arrive at metaphysical conclusions. An unprejudiced observation of individual living entities, and the conviction that they cannot be understood along purely causal lines, compels the historian to assume a metaphysical background. And he believes that this approach is a more scientific one than that of his positivist opponents. But just because historism must always remain within the bounds of the scientific and never leave the field of experience, the historian is reluctant to entrench himself in metaphysics and is content to put out suggestions and hints of a general kind. That which represents its scientific strength, however, is from the ethical and practical point of view a weakness. The historian is not in a position to say anything decisive and definite, and more particularly anything of general validity and attractiveness for the masses, on the subject of the highest values in life … his metaphysical words of comfort about the world as a whole are reserved for a highly cultured elite.[69]

The work of human consciousness would help reveal the presence of the absolute in the continuous flux made up by history and help reestablish a connection to a higher world; 'in the voice of conscience … all that is fluid and relative in form suddenly becomes firm and absolute', all that was temporal could be transmuted into 'eternal values' through 'the ethical decisions of men in action'.[70]

Human consciousness brought 'to birth and sustain[ed] all … higher values', reconciling the immanent with the transcendent, the eternal with the momentary,[71] in a largely mysterious process which Meinecke deliberately left ambiguous and open:

> The human conscience tells us about what is good and evil. It also plays a part (though not such a direct one) in bringing to birth and sustaining all the other higher values. And in conscience we see all at once a power which we can both immanent and transcendent. It is within us, and yet it can also tell us that there

is something there which is both outside us and above us, on the far side of the universal interplay of forces, which can never by themselves adequately explain it.[72]

Meinecke's solution therefore lay in effectively restricting historical study to the eternal verities of the world as these were embodied in historical individuals. History from now on was only to be perceived in terms of the actualization of 'ideals', *Kultur*-laden historical individuals through which the spirit could be traced. Departing from Ranke's transcendental system, Meinecke's history yielded meaning in entirely human terms no longer from above but from within; the human will was henceforth the only true catalyst in a labile universe.

Forces of naked causality, such as power, social or economic concerns, were to be implicitly precluded from the historian's purview or dismissed as 'accidental' (*Zufall*). This enabled Meinecke to reframe historicism and by doing so to transcend any of the earlier dilemmas incurred notably by power politics. Indeed, elemental forces were discounted as historical forces in favour of historical individuals even though they were themselves responsible for materially bringing about the latter. As Philip Wolfson has remarked, 'In such a context, the historian himself may become an epic hero, the seeker after the human soul and champion of humanity in its struggle toward fulfilment. For Meinecke, history could never be simply an intellectual fascination; it had to be above all an affirmation of the spirit and the will, a liberation from the "oppressive weight of physical law"'.[73]

Meinecke's new historical design was thus bound to culminate in an aesthetic perception of history, one which could only be apprehended in terms of tracing the harmony between the individual and the spiritual. History and reality were to be approached as works of art, sidelining any spontaneous individuality lacking in idealistic value. This was supremely ironic for an intellectual endeavour which had originally sought to integrate the concrete in its apprehension of reality. As Iggers does not fail to note with a touch of irony, 'In a sense, historicism ha[d] little to do with history any more … Meinecke [was] able to reach a position which he recognized as Neo-Platonic in its doctrine of eternal, but individualized ideas.'[74] History in all its spontaneity and diversity had been displaced by a 'desperate mysticism'[75] whose various entities were immune from rational investigation.

Indeed, in his attempt to hold on to his historical optimism, Meinecke reduced historicism to a vague system that smacked of arbitrariness, wishful thinking and profound irrationalism. Crucially, too, it was far removed from the investigation of concrete problems and more concerned with the consecration of an Unknowable than with that individual which had originally guided the inception of historicism. His retreat to a *Kulturgeschichte* was not without consequences. The mysticism entailed by his approach marked the surrender to the supra-rational, no longer genuinely interested in probing the depths of the individual and defeating that very empiricism which had accompanied the introduction of the concept of individuality. As Gerald Strauss has commented sarcastically:

> If rationalism analyzed too much, *Historismus* probes too little. For the 'dry light of reason' Meinecke has only substituted the humid murkiness of emotional sensation in which the spectator loses himself as in a comforting opium dream. Thus Meinecke defeats his own purpose, for while the empirical part of *Historismus* seeks to crystallize the individual out of the mass of humanity, the irrational part sub-merges him again in the name of an absolute Something.[76]

Henceforth, the historical particular no longer stood out for its own sake but only insofar it was construed as the concrete expression of an ideal, 'an eternal cultural value of truth, goodness, beauty and sanctity' in Meinecke's own words. Historicism's original vocation of consecrating all historical individualities against the perceived oppressive uniformity of Enlightenment rationalism gave way to an aesthetic approach with undeniable Hegelian undertones and which inevitably entailed a selection process, in spite of Meinecke's claims to the contrary. Indeed,

> If *Weltbuergertum und Nationaltstaat* remind us of Hegel, so does *die Enstehung des Historismus* to some extent. Both works basically violate the historicist principle that every individuality should be judged in terms of the values immanent within it. Historicism appears in both worlds less as a unique historical phenomenon than as an almost absolute norm, the highest stage reached until now in the understanding of things human; Meinecke uses this norm to judge the various thinkers whom he discusses ... The chapters on the emergence of historicism as a view of life read like those in which Meinecke, thirty years earlier, had traced the development of the German national state. They are less the biographies of actual individuals than stages in the development of spirit to self-fulfilment.[77]

Meinecke therefore offered by way of interpretation of history – if this could still even be characterized as such – its 'positivizing'[78] in the name of *Kultur*; this conveniently enabled him to uphold a permanently optimistic reading of the Prussian and, later on, German past and present, even after the Second World War. His final major work, *Die Deutsche Katastrophe* (1946), is testimony to his intent of preserving German *Kultur* intact from the taint of Nazi barbarism, blaming any corruption of or deviation from his idealized picture on the 'daemonic' forces in the world.

Meinecke's case therefore perfectly illustrates the dead end which the concept of Historicism had ultimately reached. On the one hand, the concept of individuality, divorced from any metaphysical framework, inevitably threatened to lead to excesses and misuses as Meinecke was keenly aware; on the other hand, the only way it could be salvaged was by re-spiritualizing it; this however could only be done by restricting history to the study of those individuals tending towards the 'good, beautiful or true'.[79]

Conclusion

It can be argued that historicism, understood in this manner, was doomed to fail from the moment of its inception for it was based on a premise that albeit revolutionary, was untenable on the long run: that of the various individualities – and behind them, history – as expressing a *Weltanschauung*. This premise was deeply flawed and proved far too ambitious; as innovative and laudable as was an attempt to read 'Meaning' into history, it was bound to fail, caught up on the one hand between the danger of pure relativism and on the other, an aesthetic and idealising vision.

Meinecke's ultimate conception of historism as that of the manifestation of an unfathomable higher order in the shape of ideals amply demonstrates the level of absurdity historicism was now made to aspire to. More generally, the general evolution of historicism throughout the nineteenth century – culminating with his *Historism* – and its gradual refutation as either relativism or idealizing outlook proved the untenability of this doctrine.

This largely accounts for Meinecke's rejection by post–Second World War historical scholarship, as well as the more general overthrow of German historicist thought in favour of social history. Still, even though more recent historical scholarship has demoted historism from its former pedestal and steered clear from any attempt to derive any 'meaning' from it, it has preserved the methodology inherited from it; historicism's 'idea of objectivity, its critical apparatus of historical scholarship, the concern of the historian to understand a historical situation within its own terms'[80] are alive and well. However, as Iggers reminds his readers at the end of his work *The German Conception of History*, this should not lead us to confuse historicism with a mere methodology, as is still regularly the case, and in doing so reduce it to Ranke's overused formula '*wie es eigentlich gewesen*'.⁸¹ Meinecke's historicism was first and foremost a *Weltanschauung*. Ironically, it was precisely this which consecrated it as intellectually revolutionary but also inevitably spelled its demise.

Notes

1. Ernst Troeltsch, *Der Historismus und seine Probleme* (Tübingen: J. C. B. Mohr, 1922), 102 (quoted by Frederick Beiser, *The German Historicist Tradition* (Oxford: Oxford University Press, 2011), 2).
2. Frederick Beiser, 'Historicization and Historicism: Some Nineteenth-Century Perspectives', in *Historisierung: Begriff–Geschichte–Praxisfelder*, ed. Moritz Baumstark and Robert Forkel (Stuttgart: J. B. Metzler, 2016), 42–54; Georg G. Iggers, 'Historicism: The History and Meaning of the Term', *Journal of the History of Ideas* 56, no. 1 (1995): 129–52. On the history of the term, see Dwight E. Lee and Robert N. Beck, 'The Meaning of "Historicism"', *American Historical Review* 59, no. 3 (1953–54): 568–77; Ernst Rothacker, 'Das Wort "Historismus"', *Zeitschrift fur deutsche Wortforschung* 16 (1960): 3–6; Donald R. Kelley, *Foundations of Modern Historical Scholarship: Language, Law, and History in the French Renaissance* (New York, NY: Columbia University Press, 1970), 1–15; Maurice Mandelbaum, *History, Man, and Reason: A Study in Nineteenth-Century Thought* (Baltimore, MD: John Hopkins Press, 1971), 41–140; Gunter Scholz, 'Historismus, Historizismus', in *Historisches Wörterbuch der Philosophie*, vol. 3, ed. Joachim Ritter (Basel: Schwabe, 1971–2006), cols. 1141–7; Otto Gerhard Oexle, '"Historismus": Überlegungen zur Geschichte des Phänomens und des Begriffs', *Jahrbuch 1986 der Braunschweigische wissenschaftliche Gesellschaft* (1986): 119–55.
3. Beiser, 'Historicization and Historicism', 46.
4. See Daniel Fulda, 'Historisierung und ihre Widerparte', in *Historisierung*, ed. Baumstark and Forkel, 17–35, at 18f.
5. Beiser, 'Historicization and Historicism', 52.
6. Karl Heussi, *Die Krisis des Historismus* (Tübingen: J. C. B. Mohr, 1932), 21; Jörn Rüsen, *Konfigurationen des Historismus: Studien zur deutschen Wissenschaftskultur* (Frankfurt: Suhrkamp, 1993), 331; and Georg G. Iggers, *The German Conception of History* (Middletown, CT: Wesleyan University Press, 1968), 124.
7. See Wilhelm Windelband, *Präludien: Aufsätze und Reden zur Einleitung in die Philosophie* (Freiburg i.B. and Tübingen: J. C. B. Mohr, 1884); and Ernst Troeltsch, 'Die Krisis des Historismus', *Der neue Rundschau* 33 (1922): 572–90.
8. Brent W. Sockness, 'Historicism and Its Unresolved Problems: Ernst Troeltsch's Last Word', in *Historisierung*, ed. Baumstark and Forkel, 210–30.

9   According to Friedrich Jaeger and Jörn Rüsen, Meinecke retreated from the political realm in reaction to the advent of mass democratic movements. See Friedrich Jaeger and Jorn Rüsen, *Geschichte des Historismus* (Munich: C. H. Beck, 1992), 135ff.
10 John Toews offers an unusual definition of historicism which captures Meinecke's project rather well: 'Historicism was defined most of all by the belief that reconstruction of the meaning of the past could sustain the meaning of existence in the present, and that historical understanding was a necessary condition for determining the creative possibilities of human individuals both in the present and in the future.' See John Toews, 'Historicism from Ranke to Nietzsche', in *The Cambridge History of Modern European Thought*, 2 vols., ed. Warren Breckman and Peter E. Gordon (Cambridge: Cambridge University Press, 2019), vol. 1, 301–29, at 301.
11 Friedrich Meinecke, *Historism: The Rise of a New Historical Outlook*, trans. J. E. Anderson (London: Herder and Herder, 1972), 387.
12 Ibid., 393.
13 Frederick Beiser, *The German Historicist Tradition* (Oxford: Oxford University Press, 2011), 1.
14 Ibid., 442.
15 Ibid., 390.
16 Johann Wolfgang von Goethe, *Letter to Knebel* (1784).
17 Meinecke, *Historism*, 423.
18 Johann Wolfgang von Goethe, *Aus meinem Leben. Dichtung und Wahrheit* (Tübingen: Cotta, 1811–1814), chapter 14.
19 Meinecke, *Historism*, 441.
20 Ibid.
21 Ibid., 453.
22 Ibid., 454.
23 Wilfried Nippel, *Johann Gustav Droysen: Ein Leben zwischen Wissenschaft und Politik* (Berlin: C. H. Beck, 2008), 9.
24 Friedrich Meinecke, *Erlebtes 1862–1901* (Leipzig: Koehler & Amelang, 1941), 132.
25 Ibid., 6.
26 Ibid., 379.
27 Ibid., 132.
28 Friedrich Meinecke, *Das Leben des Generalfeldmarschalls Hermann von Boyen*, vol. 1 (Stuttgart: J. G. Cotta, 1896), 82.
29 Ibid., 83.
30 Carl Hinrichs, 'Introduction', in Meinecke, *Historism*, xxviii.
31 Ibid., xxxix.
32 Meinecke, *Das Leben des Generalfeldmarschalls*, 89.

33 Friedrich Meinecke, 'Kausalitäten und Werte in der Geschichte' (1925), in *Schaffender Spiegel: Studien zur deutschen Geschichtsschreibung und Geschistsauffassung* (Stuttgart: Koehler, 1948), 82.
34 Friedrich Meinecke, *Weltbürgertum und Nationalstaat: Studien zur Genesis des deutschen Nationalstaates* (Munich and Berlin: R. Oldenbourg, 1911), 132ff.
35 Wilhelm Dilthey, *Das Leben Schleiermachers*, 2nd ed. (Leipzig: Vereinigung Wissenschaftlicher Verleger, 1922), vol. 1, 178ff.
36 Meinecke, *Weltbürgertum und Nationalstaat*, 9.
37 Ibid., 190ff.
38 Ibid., 15ff.
39 Ibid., 132ff.
40 Friedrich Meinecke, *Machiavellism: The Doctrine of Raison D'Etat and Its Place in Modern History* (London: Routledge, 1924), 378.
41 Ibid., 378.
42 Leopold von Ranke, *Sämtliche Werke*, 54 vols. (Leipzig: Duncker & Humblot, 1867–90), vol. 49, 329, 339.
43 Meinecke, *Machiavellism*, 379.
44 Ibid., 383.
45 Ibid., 383f.
46 Ibid., 381.
47 Ibid., 384.
48 Leopold von Ranke, *Ausgewählte Schriften* (Berlin: Askanischer Verlag, 1918), 266.
49 Friedrich Meinecke, *Die Idee der Staatsräsonin der neueren Geschichte* (1924), ed. Walther Hofer (Munich: Oldenbourg, 1957), 433.
50 As Georg Iggers quite accurately remarks: 'The basic weakness of German historicist doctrine was contained in its philosophy of value. This weakness was the most serious, because it involved the core of historicist theory, the ideas that objective truths and values exits, that they are manifested in certain persons and in institutions that have developed historically, and that history is the sole guide to the understanding of things human. But in the course of the nineteenth century the theological and metaphysical assumptions upon which this philosophy rested increasingly lost their credibility. Historicism thus came to be confronted by ethical nihilism as the logical consequence of its position that all values and cognitions are bound in their validity to the historical situation in which they arise.' See Georg G. Iggers, *The German Conception of History: The National Tradition of Historical Thought from Herder to the Present* (Middletown, CT: Wesleyan University Press, 1968), 270.
51 Meinecke, *Machiavellism*, 418.
52 Ibid., 412.
53 Meinecke, *Werke*, 442f.

54 Troeltsch, *Der Historismus und seine Probleme*, 211: 'Relative values are not the same as a general relativism, which ends in anarchy, mere chance and sheer caprice; they stand for the interweaving of the factual and the ideal aspiration, which is always in a state of flux and always freshly creative, and can therefore never be defined in timeless and universal terms.'
55 Meinecke, *Schaffender Spiegel*, 223f.
56 Ibid., 429.
57 Ibid., 426.
58 Ibid., 426 (my emphasis).
59 Iggers, *The German Conception of History*, 201.
60 Meinecke, *Historism*, 577.
61 Iggers, *The German Conception of History*, 215.
62 Ibid., 220.
63 See Isaiah Berlin's foreword in Meinecke, *Historism*, xxviii.
64 Iggers, *The German Conception of History*, 217.
65 Meinecke, *Werke*, 425.
66 Ibid., 426.
67 Iggers, *The German Conception of History*, 243: 'Historicism now reached the end of its road: the last eternal values and meanings had dissolved, all that was left was historical, temporal and relative. Even God had died, and history had yielded to historicity (*Geschichtlichkeit*) and temporality (*Zeitlichkeit*), the basic condition of never being able to transcend time.'
68 Friedrich Meinecke, *Vom geschichtlichen Sinn und vom Sinn der Geschichte* (Stuttgart: Koehler, 1951), 13: 'Has ... historism, and the relativism that is its special product, the power by itself to heal the wounds inflicted by it?'
69 Meinecke, *Schaffender Spiegel*, 120.
70 Meinecke, *Vom geschichtlichen Sinn und vom Sinn der Geschichte*, 21.
71 Meneicke, *Schaffender Spiegel*, 84ff.
72 Friedrich Meinecke, *Aphorismen und Skizzen zur Geschichte* (Leipzig: Koehler & Amelang, 1942), 154.
73 Philip J. Wolfson, 'Friedrich Meinecke (1862–1954)', *Journal of the History of Ideas* 17, no. 4 (1956): 525.
74 Iggers, *The German Conception of History*, 222.
75 Robert Pois, 'Two Poles within Historicism: Croce and Meinecke', *Journal of the History of Ideas* 31, no. 2 (1970): 253–72, at 271.
76 Gerald Strauss, 'Meinecke, Historismus, and the Cult of the Irrational', *The German Quarterly* 26, no. 2 (1953): 107–14, at 113.
77 Iggers, *The German Conception of History*, 218.
78 Roger Pois, 'Two Poles within Historicism: Croce and Meinecke', at 266.
79 Friedrich Meinecke, 'Kausalitäten und Werte in der Geschichte' *Historische Zeitschrift* 137, no. 1 (1928): 1–27, at 17.

80 Iggers, *The German Conception of History*, 278.
81 Ibid.

Bibliography

Beiser, Frederick. *The German Historicist Tradition*. Oxford: Oxford University Press, 2011.

Beiser, Frederick. 'Historicization and Historicism: Some Nineteenth-Century Perspectives'. In *Historisierung: Begriff – Geschichte – Praxisfelder*, edited by Moritz Baumstark and Robert Forkel, 42–54. Stuttgart: J. B. Metzler, 2016.

Dilthey, Wilhelm. *Das Leben Schleiermachers, vol. 1*. 2nd ed. Leipzig: Vereinigung Wissenschaftlicher Verleger, 1922.

Fulda, Daniel. 'Historisierung und ihre Widerparte'. In *Historisierung: Begriff – Geschichte – Praxisfelder*, edited by Moritz Baumstark and Robert Forkel, 17–35. Stuttgart: J. B. Metzler, 2016.

Goethe, Johann Wolfgang von. *Letter to Knebel* (1784).

Goethe, Johann Wolfgang von. *Dichtung und Wahrheit*. Tübingen: Cotta, 1811–1814.

Heussi, Karl. *Die Krisis des Historismus*. Tübingen: J. C. B. Mohr, 1932.

Iggers, Georg G. *The German Conception of History: The National Tradition of Historical Thought from Herder to the Present*. Middletown, CT: Wesleyan University Press, 1968.

Iggers, Georg G. 'Historicism: The History and Meaning of the Term'. *Journal of the History of Ideas* 56, no. 1 (1995): 129–52.

Jaeger, Friedrich and Jörn Rüsen. *Geschichte des Historismus: Eine Einführung*. Munich: C. H. Beck, 1992.

Kelley, Donald R. *Foundations of Modern Historical Scholarship: Language, Law, and History in the French Renaissance*. New York, NY: Columbia University Press, 1970.

Lee, Dwight E. and Robert N. Beck. 'The Meaning of "Historicism"'. *American Historical Review* 59 (1953–54): 568–77.

Mandelbaum, Maurice. *History, Man, and Reason: A Study in Nineteenth-Century Thought*. Baltimore, MD: John Hopkins Press, 1971.

Meinecke, Friedrich. *Das Leben des Generalfeldmarschalls Hermann von Boyen*, vol. 1. Stuttgart: J. G. Cotta, 1896.

Meinecke, Friedrich. *Weltbürgertum und Nationalstaat: Studien zur Genesis des deutschen Nationalstaates*. Munich and Berlin: R. Oldenbourg, 1911.

Meinecke, Friedrich. *Machiavellism: The Doctrine of Raison D'Etat and Its Place in Modern History*. London: Routledge, 1924.

Meinecke, Friedrich. 'Kausalitäten und Werte in der Geschichte'. *Historische Zeitschrift* 137 (1928): 1–27.

Meinecke, Friedrich. *Erlebtes 1862–1901*. Leipzig: Koehler & Amelang, 1941.

Meinecke, Friedrich. *Aphorismen und Skizzen zur Geschichte*. Leipzig: Koehler & Amelang, 1942.
Meinecke, Friedrich. *Schaffender Spiegel: Studien zur deutschen Geschichtsschreibung und Geschistsauffassung*. Stuttgart: Koehler, 1948.
Meinecke, Friedrich. *Vom geschichtlichen Sinn und vom Sinn der Geschichte*. Stuttgart: Koehler, 1951.
Meinecke, Friedrich. *Die Idee der Staatsräsonin der neueren Geschichte* (1924), edited by Walther Hofer. Munich: Oldenbourg, 1957.
Meinecke, Friedrich. *Historism: The Rise of a New Historical Outlook*. Translated by J. E. Anderson. London: Herder and Herder, 1972.
Nippel, Wilfried. *Johann Gustav Droysen: Ein Leben zwischen Wissenschaft und Politik*. Berlin: C. H. Beck, 2008.
Oexle, Otto Gerhard. '"Historismus": Überlegungen zur Geschichte des Phänomens und des Begriffs'. *Jahrbuch 1986 der Braunschweigische wissenschaftliche Gesellschaft* (1986): 119–55.
Pois, Robert. 'Two Poles within Historicism: Croce and Meinecke'. *Journal of the History of Ideas* 31, no. 2 (1970): 253–72.
Ranke, Leopold von. *Sämtliche Werke*, vol. 49. Leipzig: Duncker & Humblot, 1867–90.
Ranke, Leopold von. *Ausgewählte Schriften*. Berlin: Askanischer Verlag, 1918.
Rothacker, Ernst. 'Das Wort "Historismus"'. *Zeitschrift fur deutsche Wortforschung* 16 (1960): 3–6.
Rüsen, Jörn. *Konfigurationen des Historismus: Studien zur deutschen Wissenschaftskultur*. Frankfurt: Suhrkamp, 1993.
Scholz, Gunter. 'Historismus, Historizismus'. In *Historisches Wörterbuch der Philosophie*, edited by Joachim Ritter, vol. 3, cols. 1141–7. Basel: Schwabe, 1971–2006.
Sockness, Brent W. 'Historicism and Its Unresolved Problems: Ernst Troeltsch's Last Word'. In *Historisierung: Begriff – Geschichte – Praxisfelder*, edited by Moritz Baumstark and Robert Forkel, 210–30. Stuttgart: J. B. Metzler, 2016.
Strauss, Gerald. 'Meinecke, Historismus, and the Cult of the Irrational'. *The German Quarterly* 26, no. 2 (1953): 107–14.
Toews, John. 'Historicism from Ranke to Nietzsche'. In *The Cambridge History of Modern European Thought*, edited by Warren Breckman and Peter E. Gordon, vol. 1, 301–29. Cambridge: Cambridge University Press, 2019.
Troeltsch, Ernst. *Der Historismus und seine Probleme*. Tübingen: J. C. B. Mohr, 1922.
Troeltsch, Ernst. 'Die Krisis des Historismus'. *Die neue Rundschau* 33, no. 1 (1922): 572–90.
Windelband, Wilhelm. *Präludien: Aufsätze und Reden zur Einleitung in die Philosophie*. Freiburg i.B. and Tübingen: J. C. B. Mohr, 1884.
Wolfson, Philip J. 'Friedrich Meinecke (1862–1954)'. *Journal of the History of Ideas* 17, no. 4 (1956): 511–25.

8

Karl Löwith's historicization of historicism

Bruno Godefroy

Abstract

The aim of this chapter is to highlight both the ambivalence and the radicalism of Löwith's position. The first part of this chapter focuses on the historicization of historicism itself, that is, on what Löwith means by historicization and on the main steps of this process. The second part shows some of the reasons that can explain this project, more precisely why Löwith does not think that historicism can be answered by recurring to a normative foundation, but has to be the starting point of any attempt to overcome it. In other words, I attempt to explain why the given existential and historical situations are, for Löwith, unavoidable. Finally, the third part highlights the theoretical rationale for the historicization of historicism, that is, the role of this project in Löwith's philosophy, whose attempts to deconstruct the modern historical consciousness ground on an opposition between the historical and the natural world.

Introduction

Karl Löwith's own life embodied the historical situation that he continuously analysed in his works: the transition from the bourgeois nineteenth century and its privileged elites to the twentieth century, its revolutions and the apparition of mass democracy. Born in Munich in 1897, Löwith volunteered during the First World War, was critically injured in 1915 on the Italian front and imprisoned in Italy until 1917. After the war, Löwith enrolled at the university of Munich before switching to Freiburg, where he became a student of Husserl and Heidegger, who had the most lasting impact on his thought, even if Löwith took a critical position early on. His promising career as a scholar in Germany came to an end in 1935 – Löwith lost his position because of his Jewish origins, emigrated to Italy, then to Japan before arriving in the United States in 1941. In 1952, he accepted a position in Heidelberg, where he stayed until his death in 1973. This first-hand experience of the instability of the historical world became a fundamental element of his thought. Considering the intellectual context of Löwith's works, the importance of his critique of historicism comes as no surprise. His first important works were published in the 1930s, precisely at the time of a lively discussion on the 'crisis of historicism'.[1] Husserl and Heidegger, who had a great and lasting influence on his thought, were also directly involved in this discussion.[2] His first book on Nietzsche, published in 1935, his book on Jacob Burckhardt published in 1936 as well as his classic *From Hegel to Nietzsche*, which was published in 1941 and focused on the 'revolutionary break' in nineteenth-century thought, can all be considered as interventions in this debate. However, Löwith also extended the critique of historicism beyond its original context, especially in the 1950s. *Meaning in History*, published in 1949, became a well-known reference for the critique of any attempt to give history a meaning and, more generally, of the excessive importance of history in modern thought. Even if the background of the Cold War plays an important role in the reactivation of this critique, the continuity with his writings from the 1930s is obvious.

The adaptability of his critique of historicism to different contexts goes together with a broad definition of the concept. Löwith's use of the concept in his works is not entirely consistent, since 'historicism' is for him both a technical term and a polemical label. He uses this concept to refer both to the historiographical school in nineteenth-century Germany and to a more general 'historical consciousness'. The historiographical school, represented by historians such as Georg Niebuhr, Leopold von Ranke or Johann Gustav Droysen, focused on establishing history as an independent science. According to historicist principles, the historian should only focus on historical facts; history can only be explained out of itself, and it does not follow any transcendent or transhistorical principle. Löwith, however, does not limit the problem of historicism to the historiographical school, as others did.[3] He does not make a difference between historicism in a narrow sense and historicism in a broad sense precisely because his critique aims at what he sees as the common ground of all modern historical thought. The influence of Nietzsche's broadside against historical thinking is explicit in his writings. In his general use of the concept, Löwith is also close to Max Weber, who associates historicism with value relativism, or even to Ernst Troeltsch, who considers the crisis of historicism not as a crisis of historiography, but of historical thought in general. Troeltsch's definition of historicism as a 'fundamental historicization of all our way of thinking about man, his culture and his values'[4] comes very near to Löwith's criticism of a modern 'historical consciousness'.

However, despite this influence, Löwith advocates a different solution. He does not side with Nietzsche's emphasis on 'life' (*Leben*) against history, nor does he accept, as Weber did, that science cannot overcome value relativism. While some of his contemporaries like Leo Strauss and Eric Voegelin advocated a strong normative foundation against relativism – such as natural right or theology – there is no such transcendent principle in Löwith's thought. However, even if he does not attempt to overcome historicism by transcending history, he does not agree with Troeltsch, who argued that it is possible to find an answer to historicism in history itself, by using historical science in order to discover objective cultural values. Löwith's solution is at the same time ambivalent in its method and radical in its outcome. Instead of trying to overcome historicism by recurring to a strong normative foundation, Löwith's critique of historicism relies on historicism itself. Overcoming historicism requires, according to him, to historicize it, that is, to turn its own method against itself in order to uncover the historical genesis of the historical consciousness, thereby showing its roots and its contingent development. Although the methodological guideline of his project is obviously ambivalent, as it explicitly remains within the historicist framework, its aim could not be more radical, as the outcome of this last use of a historical method is expected to be a position that is entirely beyond the historical consciousness.

Löwith's project has been widely commented, but only few critiques focus on the role of historicism in his thought. However, three of his most well-known contemporaries, Leo Strauss, Hans-Georg Gadamer and Jürgen Habermas, did address this topic. Their positions regarding Löwith's project give a good overview on the different criticisms that he has faced. Strauss and Löwith had a long correspondence in which their differences clearly come to light. Strauss understands the problem of historicism in similar terms but considers that Löwith's position remains within historicism since he refuses, as Strauss advocates, returning to the non-historicist tradition of Ancient philosophy. On the contrary, Löwith's philosophy remains, according to Strauss, grounded on historicist principles, since Löwith accepts the idea of a historical development of philosophy, of philosophy as relative to the historical situation of man. Habermas's criticism is different. On the one hand, he points out a methodological issue, as Löwith's attempt to overcome historicism relies itself on a historical method. It remains unclear, according to Habermas, how a historical genealogy can manage to call its own principles into question. On the other hand, Habermas is also sceptical when it comes to the main outcome of Löwith's philosophical project, which emphasizes the predominance of the natural world against history, but without making clear whether this can be a normative foundation for the human world, especially for its political dimension. For Habermas, this lack in Löwith's philosophy – despite the importance of the political situation in his writings – indicates a 'private renunciation to the political world' pervading his thought.[5] In other words, Löwith's philosophy might be able to overcome historicism, but this comes at a high price, since his emphasis on the natural world tends to exclude the human world. Gadamer's criticism is much less developed than Strauss and Habermas's, but it is representative of a slightly different reading of Löwith's works. According to Gadamer, Löwith insists on the natural world not only for philosophical reasons, but mostly to compensate for an existential situation. 'Fatalism', a despair of any meaning in human existence, motivates his rejection of history and his return to the natural world.[6]

All of these positions are true to some extent, but they do not entirely do justice to Löwith and, by doing so, they avoid a main difficulty. First, most of these criticisms focus on what they present as deficits in Löwith's philosophy and give the impression that some of these issues might be mistakes that could be corrected. As I would like to show, these problems, which do indeed weaken Löwith's position, are nonetheless coherent with his attempt to overcome historicism. This is the reason why, by considering these issues as mere mistakes, critiques avoid addressing the main difficulty. If these problems, as I shall show, are inherent parts of Löwith's attempt to overcome historicism, then this attempt itself should be the centre of attention. In other words, critiques should ask whether historical thought can be overcome altogether while at the same time preserving the possibility to find meaning in the human world and to address political questions. Habermas's critique is particularly insightful as it stresses the political dimension of this problem. Strauss, because he conceives the problem of historicism in similar terms, defends an answer to the political dimension of the problem – a return to natural right – which could be compatible with Löwith's position, but is not entirely convincing either. Once again, I would like to show that this particular side of the problem is coherent with Löwith's attempt to overcome historicism, precisely because this attempt is especially radical. Only by showing the inner logic of his position is it possible to show the tension between how he attempts to overcome historicism and the reasons behind this project.

The aim of this chapter is to highlight both the ambivalence and the radicalism of Löwith's position. The first part of this chapter will focus on the historicization of historicism itself, that is, on what Löwith means by historicization and on the main steps of this process. The second part will show some of the reasons that can explain this project, more precisely why Löwith does not think that historicism can be answered by recurring to a normative foundation, but has to be the starting point of any attempt to overcome it. In other words, I will attempt to explain why the given existential and historical situations are, for Löwith, unavoidable. Finally, the third part will highlight the theoretical rationale for the historicization of historicism, that is, the role of this project in Löwith's philosophy, whose attempts to deconstruct the modern historical consciousness ground on an opposition between the historical and the natural world.

The historicization of historicism

'Historicization' means, for Löwith, more than the history of ideas as the method that he used in most of his works. Under the influence of Nietzsche, who has a central importance in his thought, he understands 'historicization' as a genealogical critique or, in Heidegger's terminology, as a 'destruction' of the tradition.[7] 'Historicizing' historicism is a process that, by using historical methods – such as contextualization or the reconstruction of the evolution of ideas – aims at 'destructing' historicism itself. In other words, historicism is used one last time – against itself, to uncover it as a product of history. This method, genealogy as destruction, is particularly clear in *Meaning in History*, which uses a backward narrative, starting from the present before going back to previous steps.

There are three main layers in Löwith's genealogy of historicism, three historical periods that are associated to major thematic breaks and form the backbone of his destruction of historicism. The first layer is the development of historical thought after Hegel in the nineteenth century, which Löwith summarizes as an evolution 'from Hegel to Nietzsche'. As Leo Strauss writes in his review of the book, 'Löwith, having from his youth followed the postwar development with passionate attention and critical sympathy, and having arrived at a point almost beyond his reach, sums it up and takes leave of it by presenting a lucid and sober account of this development.'[8] Starting with the contrast between Goethe's classical humanism, for whom nature was still more important than history, and Hegel's metaphysics of history, that linked history to the suprahistorical development of the spirit, Löwith shows how, after Hegel, an absolute 'historicism' came to being and abandoned any suprahistorical claim and any value judgement in favour of the facticity of the historical events themselves. 'Hegel's true students transformed his *metaphysics* of the history of the spirit into an *absolute historicism*, that is, they conserved from the absoluteness of the spirit that develops itself in history only the historical part and placed the events in time [or the *Zeitgeist*] as the highest force, also upon philosophy and upon the spirit.'[9] The same idea can be found in the historical school and in Leopold von Ranke's defence of the 'positive', of what achieves success in history. No suprahistorical point of view can perceive the worth of historical events. Their legitimacy manifests itself only in their success in history.

Hegel's attempt to reconcile reason with history, to perceive in the historical reality a rational development, ended with his followers, who place history above the spirit. With regard to the political context, the end of this compromise also marks for Löwith the failure of bourgeois society and of its attempt, since Rousseau, to unify the individual and the citizen, the society and the state, and to neutralize conflicts. By presenting the modern state as the result of the rational development of history, Hegel could legitimize it as the successful *Aufhebung* of the contradictions of bourgeois society. However, Hegel's reconciliation ends with Marx and Kierkegaard. While Marx emphasizes the conflicts in bourgeois society and the predominance of the immanent historical development, Kierkegaard turns to the individual existence and opens the way for the philosophy of existence, which gives up the cohesion of bourgeois society in favour of the tension between the individual and the masses. This disintegration is followed by several attempts to force a reunification of the society and the state, such as in Ernst Jünger's *Arbeiter*, in which the soldier-worker becomes the figure of the renewal at the core of the totalitarian state.[10]

This is the first thread in the historicization of historicism. It shows how, for Löwith, the historical thought became prevalent as a result of a transformation of Hegel's thought during the nineteenth century. While Hegel's conception of history still relied on a suprahistorical foundation, the spirit, and by doing so preserved a theological structure in his philosophy of history, his followers broke with this foundation and attempted to think history out of history itself. By emphasizing the rationality of the historical development, Hegel could also legitimize bourgeois society as the result of the development of a suprahistorical principle. Historicism, however, stands according to Löwith for the breakdown of this model of society. The first step of the historicization has therefore two aims: It retraces the last step of the historical development and emphasizes the parallel between historicism and its political context.

The second layer uncovered by Löwith is the role that Christianity plays in the development of historical thought in general. As it is here not limited to the nineteenth century, 'historicism' has to be understood in the second sense – the broader sense of 'modern historical consciousness'. Why is Christianity at the origin of this historical consciousness? Löwith underlines the difference between the classical notion of history, *Historie* in German, and the modern notion of *Geschichte*.[11] *Historie* finds its origin in the Ancient Greek verb *historein*, the activity of exploring, knowing and recalling past events, historical, political, but also natural events. Therefore, history as a practice only deals with what can be known, what is constant, and remains subordinated to the non-changing human nature and the *physis*, the perpetual cycle of growth and decay. There is no history as a single, independent and coherent process, but only various histories. The modern historical consciousness, on the contrary, cannot emerge without history in singular – as 'Geschichte', the concept of history as a coherent meaningful process oriented towards an end. Such a concept of history has nothing to do with the classical concept of history as *Historie*, nor is it simply evident. The modern historical existence has itself a historical origin. According to Löwith, this 'perversion' of the original sense of history is the product of Jewish-Christian faith:

> The 'discovery' of the historical world and of the historical existence, whose meaning lies in the future, is not the result of a philosophical analysis but of a hopeful expectation that was originally directed towards the kingdom of God and then towards the kingdom of man, who since F. Bacon is a creator of himself. Indeed, modern historiography lost the Christian trust in a coming fulfillment, but the vision of the future as such remained dominant. This vision permeates all post-Christian European thought and all preoccupation with history, with its direction and its aim.[12]

Although Löwith acknowledges the importance of Bacon and, in other texts, of other thinkers of the Enlightenment, another moment is more important for explaining the end of the classical conception of history and the appearance of the modern historical consciousness.

The break that comes with Christianity is on a particular level: It is the separation of the historical from the natural world, that is, the breakdown of the conception of a unique world in favour of history, reflected in the modern distinction between natural sciences and human sciences. This tension between natural world and historical world is the third layer of Löwith's historicization, which also shows the main ambiguity of this process. Since the historicization of historicism aims ultimately at escaping the historical consciousness, Löwith emphasizes the alternative between natural world and historical world as a systematic distinction. But at the same time, he acknowledges that we are 'so accustomed to historical thinking' that we need to associate this option with a historical period, namely with Ancient Greek philosophy. For this reason, the last step of the historicization process only stays on the verge of the historical consciousness that it wants to deconstruct.

The classical notion of the world in Ancient philosophy is not compatible with the modern interest in history. It is an order, complete and beautiful, whose parts can change, but not the world as such. Consequently, the world cannot be a process oriented towards an aim, since it is changing but also complete at each moment. The modern conception of history, which puts the historical process above the stability of the natural world, presupposes a break with the ancient model:

> If the physical cosmos is not recognized as highest and best order, but only as the biggest among the *visible* things, if what is highest and best, the *summum bonum*, is an invisible God, creator of the world and object of faith, and if the whole world is a personal, passing creation, then emerges, through the biblical God, an anthropological notion of the world that is also the base of our notion of the historical world.[13]

For Löwith, the first step of the break with the ancient notion of the cosmos comes with idea of a creation of the world by a personal God, which leads to a devaluation of the world as a supreme good. There is an apparently counterintuitive continuity between the anthropological notion of the world that comes from the Christian tradition and the modern notion of the historical world. The idea of a creation of the world by an almighty God changes the relation not only between God and the world, but also between man and the world. Man is not only, like the natural world, part of the creation, he is also its most important element. As the *Genesis* makes clear, the world is not an encompassing whole anymore, but has a purpose insofar as it provides for man, the 'crown of the creation'. It is in this sense that Löwith's paradoxical claim has to be understood and, in this sense, that the conception of a revealed creator god led to a notion of the world subordinated to man.

The world becomes 'saeculum', a finite world of finite duration, judged by God at the end of times. Augustine confirms this destruction of the ancient cosmos: The world is not self-sufficient but, like the entire creation, subjected to sin and waiting for its redemption. It even loses its unity and becomes a 'city of God' and 'city of man'. Here lies the main consequence of Christianity, according to Löwith: It leads to a 'deworldized' (*entweltlicht*) world. The natural world is lost and replaced by an anthropological and historical notion of the world, created by God and subjected to the needs of man. The modern 'worldization' (*Verweltlichung*) of the 'deworldized' Christian world – or, in other words, its 'secularization' – that leads to the complete disappearance of the world in favour of history is a turning point, but only a further development of the original break that came with Christianity and with the destruction of the ancient notion of cosmos. This modern transformation affects a world that is already devalued. By cutting it from God, it then becomes a mere spatial extension, an empty place that cannot have any meaning. Without a substantial world, without a cosmos, the only remaining anchor is history. Hence, for Löwith, man does not 'live' in the world anymore, but 'exists' in the 'horizon of history'.[14] The modern 'historical existence' could only prevail after the overcoming of the two obstacles that ordered and limited the experience of history: the 'cosmological' limit in Ancient philosophy and the 'theological' limit in Christian thought that still subjected history to God, even if it was the decisive break that ultimately made the historical consciousness possible.

The inescapability of the 'situation'

This brief summary, even if it of course simplifies Löwith's philosophical project, is necessary to understand what is at stake in his critique of historicism and, consequently, to reconstruct Löwith's motivations behind his project. By doing so, it is possible to tackle the main issue in this project, namely why a critique of historicism should rely on historicism itself. The answer to this question is partly philosophical, since Löwith attempts to justify his position as a *philosophical* position, but also involves his historical and existential situation. Löwith – despite his critique of the philosophy of existence – argues that the 'situation', which includes the predominance of historical thought, is inescapable. However, this claim can be better understood by focusing on the parallel between Löwith's argument and how he himself deals with his own historical and existential situation.

Starting from the given situation is a characteristic of the philosophy of existence, which Löwith criticized in the 1930s: Heidegger, Jaspers, but also Carl

Schmitt were the main targets of this critique.[15] However, even if Löwith has an obvious sympathy for philosophy as contemplation *sub specie aeternitatis*, there is also an existentialist element in his thought. First, with regard to the historical situation as such, his critique of historicism – and of the modern historical consciousness – takes itself a historical form precisely because historicism and its consequences, such as relativism, belong to the present situation, which he takes as a starting point. He develops this position in a letter to Leo Strauss from August 1946: 'I think in a more *historical* manner than you do, because the historicity of reason has become an evidence to me and, therefore, I also think in a more *a*historical manner because I always see the absolute historical right in the present, with view to the future.'[16]

He continues by explaining why Strauss's solution is more determined by the historical consciousness both want to overcome, since Strauss absolutizes a historical moment – Ancient Greek philosophy – and tries to return to it. For Löwith on the contrary, no return is possible. As he puts it, he starts from the present situation – 'so *are* we now' – to ask 'what man can still become' beyond this situation. In his own words, 'I think *as a result of an extremely historical consciousness* already completely *ahistorically*.'[17] By so doing, Löwith attempts to overcome the historical consciousness from the inside. Moreover, if this historical situation can be the starting point to overcome the modern historical consciousness from the inside and to create something new, it is precisely thanks to historicism. This is the reason why Löwith is so ambiguous about it.

What is this historical situation? I have already mentioned the breakdown of bourgeois society as it develops during the nineteenth-century philosophy. This is one aspect of the historical situation, together with the modernization process that took place in Western societies and led ultimately to the 'disenchantment of the world'. Löwith recognizes early the importance of Max Weber and endorses his views on the historical situation. Like Weber, he sees no point in going against the rationalization and modernization process. On the contrary, only this process makes freedom within the 'iron cage' possible, just like historicism does, by destroying all traditions and suprahistorical principles and by making therefore a new beginning possible. Accepting the historical situation as it is also means that there is nothing to expect from a meaningful evolution of history, such as a progress, but that history remains an 'open field of possibilities' that can be explored. For Löwith, the disenchantment of the world is a 'positive chance' to turn to a 'sober acceptance of everyday life and its "demands"', as Weber declared at the end of *Science as a Vocation*.[18]

Unlike similar projects, such as in Strauss and Voegelin, this critique of historicism does therefore not presuppose a 'crisis of modernity' but it accepts, on the contrary, the modern situation as a starting point. Löwith's acceptance of this historical situation is one of the main characteristics of his project. In order to get rid of the remnants of the tradition, it is necessary from his perspective to use historicism one last time against itself, that is to historicize it, and then to understand the possibilities that lie in the present. Accepting the historical situation is therefore part of his own philosophical project. However, such a systematic explanation may be incomplete, as it does not take less rational elements into account. The 'situation' that Löwith is accepting is not only a historical, but also an existential situation.

Löwith's acceptance of the 'situation' as such is obviously related to an *existential* situation and to the way he reacts to it. To use another concept of the philosophy of existence, 'limit situations' made him clear how much the historical world is contingent and unreliable. After two world wars, after 1933 and his exile around the world, it becomes clear that, in his own words, 'wanting to orientate oneself in the middle of history by using it as a point a reference would be the same as, during a shipwreck, wanting to hold on to the waves'.[19] Since history showed that it has no meaning, it cannot provide any anchor to overcome this meaninglessness. But two topics explicitly discussed in his works – suicide and hope – give a more precise view on Löwith's understanding of the existential situation and show how this relates directly to his acceptance of the 'situation' as such.

Already before the First World War and at its beginning, suicidal thoughts played an important role in Löwith's life. In an autobiography that he wrote in 1926, he describes his first encounters with this 'tentation' as a student before the war and also during it, as a soldier, as he was considering, while being on guard, how to use his weapon to put an end to his life.[20] He even considered his participation to the war as an attempt to die without having to kill himself. There is no clear explanation for this. As he puts it, it belongs to what a melancholic adolescent has typically to go through. However, in his case, this interest for suicide cannot be reduced to a temporary romanticized feeling, since it is also grounded on philosophical questions.

Suicide comes back as a philosophical topic in his later works, first in the context of his critique of the Christian remnants in the philosophical tradition, a critique that was already present in his historicization of historicism. Löwith wrote several texts on this topic, tying the rejection of suicide in different philosophies – especially in the philosophy of existence, which became prominent at his time – to a hidden Christian heritage.[21] But this rejection is not only a problem because it hides this heritage, it is also a philosophical problem as such since suicide is, according to Löwith, of central importance to understand the specificity of human nature, which is characterized precisely by the possibility to radically call its nature into question and, by doing so, to affirm freedom. This becomes especially important in the anthropology of his late works, where he turns to the relation between man and the natural world, after living behind the historical world.

What do we learn from his views on suicide? They show that his 'resignation' when it comes to the acceptance of the historical situation is also rooted in his acceptance of an existential situation. They confirm his views on the meaninglessness of historical existence at a deeper level, but they also indicate how he deals with this situation. On the one hand, he chooses to live but on the other, he keeps the question alive and only suspends its resolution by defending the possibility of suicide. This stalemate situation is coherent with his attitude towards a historical situation that is equally unsatisfying: an attitude of conscious and resolute resignation.

A second element adds a further depth to this position, namely his radical rejection of hope as such. This rejection comes in a particular context: After the Second World War, European countries experienced a rapid economic growth fuelled by the reconstruction. Moreover, in the context of the Cold War, utopian discourses reappeared, such as Ernst Bloch's *Prinzip Hoffnung* – The Principle of Hope – published in 1954. Karl Löwith's views on hope clearly stand out in this context. All of his writings have a somehow pessimistic, resigned undertone, but he also directly addresses the problem of hope in a letter to Eric Voegelin, in 1950, in which he mentions an epilogue in *Meaning in History* that 'calls hope as such into question'.[22] *Meaning in History* is part of the project aiming at the historicization of the modern historical consciousness and focusses especially on its Christian origins, as it tries to link the modern fascination with history as a meaningful process heading towards an aim to Christian eschatology. Behind this genealogy is a more fundamental question: Do we live for the future, with hope and expectations?

Löwith's own view on this question, even if it is not explicitly mentioned, is quite clear as he refers in this context to the myth of Pandora.[23] Hope, which remains in the box after Pandora opened it, is also an evil, since men's hopes are blind and foolish. However, even if this Ancient view is, according to Löwith, equally 'sober' and 'wise', hope's value has completely changed since the Christian turning point. The last things are seen as the first in importance and the meaning of life and history lay in the future. According to Löwith, this view has a lasting influence, despite the prevalence of a scientific worldview in modern times. Even if the belief in the end of times and in the Last judgement has died out, there still remains a hopeful belief in a meaning of history, as well as the idea of a continuity of the 'historical progress'. While he rejects the first as a remnant of Christian eschatology, Löwith sees some truth, albeit a 'cynical' one, in the latter: Mass destructions are followed by reconstruction, mass murders by higher birth rates.[24] However, this continuity does not make sense in the linear structure of history inherited from the Christian tradition, but only if the structure of history is cyclical. Therefore, modern times are characterized on the one hand by a hope in the future, a remnant of a tradition that has actually disappeared, but on the other by a 'continuity' that only makes sense in a pre- or post-Christian context. This is why, according to Löwith, overcoming this ambiguity requires a radical critique of hope as such in order to reach a position free from any tradition.

Beyond historicism: The natural world

The aim of Löwith's historicization of historicism is precisely to reach such a position. The historical and existential situations may explain why he chooses to *historicize* historicism, but this particular attempt to overcome historicism as such only makes sense as an attempt to reach a new position. We encounter here one of the main issues of his philosophical project as a whole and it would be impossible to present all its different aspects. But it is still important to understand this project as the horizon of Löwith's critique and how, in the end, it is possible to escape the historical consciousness.

First, which conception of history remains after such a radical critique? Löwith's aim is to reintegrate the historical events as parts of 'the nature of all beings', to recover the 'naturalness of history'.[25] In order to do so, he aims at a conception of history as a 'dialectic of happening and acting' (*Dialektik von Geschehen und Handlung*). On the one hand, history 'happens'. It can be influenced by human action but, as he puts it, 'what happens in history is always both more and less than what acting humans wanted and intended. We "make" history and are overwhelmed by it.'[26] The dimension of 'happening' is especially important, since it means that history has no purpose, no meaning nor a subject. The 'agent of history', if it is still possible to use such a term, is only *dynamis*, a pure movement without direction. With this conception, Löwith achieves at least two important aims. First, history in the classical sense – related to human actions – is still possible but the attempt to grasp 'History' as a whole is meaningless, since it is always 'happening', and therefore never complete. Second, by linking history to *dynamis*, Löwith brings it close to *physis*, to nature, thus achieving the most important task in his philosophical project. By bringing history into nature, he can subordinate the historical 'second' world to the all-encompassing world of nature, and thus he is able to overcome the Christian 'deworldization' (*Entweltlichung*) at the origin of the historical consciousness.

There is only one problem with this project, which Löwith discusses on different occasions. As it bears similarities with Nietzsche's attempt to overcome the Christian tradition, it has to avoid the difficulties that, according to Löwith, led to Nietzsche's failure. The core of Nietzsche's thought, according to Löwith, is the doctrine of the eternal recurrence of the same, which enables him to revive a cyclical conception of time and thus to erase Christian eschatology as well as any attempt to find a meaning in history.[27] However, Löwith considers this project as a failure because of his multiple contradictions. Since, for Nietzsche, the eternal recurrence is an act of the will, of an individual will to overcome the present state and to create a new future, Löwith sees it as an incomplete break, as it keeps an eschatological direction and remains within an anthropological conception of the world. Similarly, it remains to be seen how Löwith, from his own perspective, can achieve the transition from his historicist historicization of historicism to a completely *a*historical thought.

This is precisely what he attempts in his later works, and this is the key for understanding his whole philosophical project in general and the aim of his critique of historicism in particular. In order to avoid all the difficulties that have been mentioned earlier – the Christian tradition, Nietzsche's will, the historical consciousness – he adopts a phenomenological approach that aims at making present, without mediation – actually without a subject – the natural world in everyday sensual experiences, especially in experiences that show that the world is independent but that man is also always related to it – such as the experience of the regular alternation of day and night, of the birth and death of natural beings, of the weather, or the experience of the alternation of sleeping and waking.[28] By doing so, the naturalness of the world – which is much more fundamental than the historical world – should come to light, as well as its encompassing and overwhelming character. As a natural being, man is part of the world that it experiences, but the world overwhelms him and does not need a human subject to be. The natural world is therefore, after the loss of all meaning in the historical world and in existence, the last possible foundation, but a foundation without any agency or any meaning.

Conclusion

Löwith's ambiguity when it comes to the definition of historicism, which refers in his works both to the historiographical school and to a more general historical consciousness, is a consequence of how radical his critique is. It is radical in at least two ways: first, as it dives deep into the history of ideas, focusing not only on nineteenth-century historical thought, but also on Christianity and its break with Ancient philosophy. Secondly, this critique is particularly radical since it does not aim at overcoming historicism in a narrow sense, but the historical consciousness as such. However, this critique remains at the same time ambiguous as it attempts to overcome the historical consciousness by historical means. Some of the motivations behind this ambiguity can be understood if we take into account Löwith's attitude towards the historical situation and his own existential situation. When doing so, the coherence of his position becomes apparent, which also makes finding an answer to its inherent problems difficult. Indeed, his solution is itself as radical as his critique, but such a naturalization of history may lead to new problems. If the natural world overwhelms so completely the historical world, is there still any place for human agency, especially for politics? Is it possible to conceive the human world – and politics – completely ahistorically? This question is crucial, since Löwith's critique of historicism is not least motivated by a reaction against its ideological consequences. However, it seems that the naturalization of the historical world, although it might prevent any politicization of history, could exceed its aim and lead to a complete depoliticization, to the suppression of any meaningful political action. If this is really a consequence of his thought, the outcome of Löwith's critique of historicism may even be too radical for the aims of his own project.

Notes

1   Ernst Troeltsch, *Gesammelte Schriften 3: Der Historismus und seine Probleme; Das logische Problem der Geschichtsphilosophie* (Tübingen: Mohr, 1961); Friedrich Meinecke, *Die Entstehung des Historismus* (Munich: Leibniz-Verlag, 1946).

2   Charles R. Bambach, *Heidegger, Dilthey, and the Crisis of Historicism* (Ithaca, NY: Cornell University Press, 1995).
3   Karl Heussi, *Die Krisis des Historismus* (Tübingen: Mohr, 1932).
4   Troeltsch, *Historismus und seine Probleme*, 102.
5   Jürgen Habermas, 'Karl Löwiths stoischer Rückzug vom historischen Bewußtsein', *Merkur* 17, no. 184 (1963): 589.
6   Hans-Georg Gadamer, *Hermeneutik II: Wahrheit und Methode; Ergänzungen* (Tübingen: Mohr, 1986), 414.
7   Martin Heidegger, *Sein und Zeit* (Tübingen: Niemeyer, 1967), §6.
8   Leo Strauss, 'Review of *Von Hegel zu Nietzsche*', *Social Research* 8, no. 4 (1941): 513.
9   Karl Löwith, *Sämtliche Schriften 4: Von Hegel zu Nietzsche* (Stuttgart: Metzler, 1981), 274.
10 Ibid., 547–55.
11 Karl Löwith, *Sämtliche Schriften 2: Weltgeschichte und Heilsgeschehen* (Stuttgart: Metzler, 1983), 296–8.
12 Ibid., 352.
13 Karl Löwith, *Sämtliche Schriften 1: Mensch und Menschenwelt* (Stuttgart: Metzler, 1981), 298.
14 Löwith, *Sämtliche Schriften 2*, 353.
15 Karl Löwith, *Sämtliche Schriften 8: Heidegger; Denker in dürftiger Zeit* (Stuttgart: Metzler, 1984).
16 Leo Strauss, *Gesammelte Schriften 3: Hobbes politische Wissenschaft und zugehörige Schriften; Briefe* (Stuttgart: Metzler, 2008), 617.
17 Ibid.
18 Karl Löwith, *Sämtliche Schriften 5. Hegel und die Aufhebung der Philosophie; Max Weber* (Stuttgart: Metzler, 1988), 364.
19 Löwith, *Sämtliche Schriften 2*, 360.
20 Karl Löwith, 'Fiala, Die Geschichte einer Versuchung', *Internationale Zeitschrift für Philosophie* 1 (1997): 136–67.
21 Löwith, *Sämtliche Schriften 1*.
22 Karl Löwith and Eric Voegelin, 'Briefwechsel', *Sinn und Form* 59, no. 6 (2007): 789.
23 Löwith, *Sämtliche Schriften 2*, 218.
24 Ibid., 221.
25 Ibid., 324.
26 Ibid.
27 Karl Löwith, *Sämtliche Schriften 6: Nietzsche* (Stuttgart: Metzler, 1987).
28 Löwith, *Sämtliche Schriften 1*, 381.

Bibliography

Bambach, Charles R. *Heidegger, Dilthey, and the Crisis of Historicism*. Ithaca, NY: Cornell University Press, 1995.

Gadamer, Hans-Georg. *Hermeneutik II: Wahrheit und Methode; Ergänzungen*. Tübingen: Mohr, 1986.

Habermas, Jürgen. 'Karl Löwiths stoischer Rückzug vom historischen Bewußtsein'. *Merkur* 17, no. 184 (1963): 576–90.

Heidegger, Martin. *Sein und Zeit*. Tübingen: Niemeyer, 1967.

Heussi, Karl. *Die Krisis des Historismus*. Tübingen: Mohr, 1932.

Löwith, Karl. *Sämtliche Schriften 1: Mensch und Menschenwelt*. Stuttgart: Metzler, 1981.

Löwith, Karl. *Sämtliche Schriften 2: Weltgeschichte und Heilsgeschehen*. Stuttgart: Metzler, 1983.

Löwith, Karl. *Sämtliche Schriften 4: Von Hegel zu Nietzsche*. Stuttgart: Metzler, 1981.

Löwith, Karl. *Sämtliche Schriften 5: Hegel und die Aufhebung der Philosophie; Max Weber*. Stuttgart: Metzler, 1988.

Löwith, Karl. *Sämtliche Schriften 6: Nietzsche*. Stuttgart: Metzler, 1987.

Löwith, Karl. *Sämtliche Schriften 8: Heidegger; Denker in dürftiger Zeit*. Stuttgart: Metzler, 1984.

Löwith, Karl. 'Fiala, Die Geschichte einer Versuchung'. *Internationale Zeitschrift für Philosophie* 1 (1997): 136–67.

Löwith, Karl and Eric Voegelin. 'Briefwechsel'. *Sinn und Form* 59, no. 6 (2007): 764–94.

Meinecke, Friedrich. *Die Entstehung des Historismus*. Munich: Leibniz-Verlag, 1946.

Strauss, Leo. 'Review of *Von Hegel bis Nietzsche*'. *Social Research* 8, no. 4 (1941): 512–15.

Strauss, Leo. *Gesammelte Schriften 3: Hobbes politische Wissenschaft und zugehörige Schriften; Briefe*. Stuttgart: Metzler, 2008.

Troeltsch, Ernst. *Gesammelte Schriften 3: Der Historismus und seine Probleme; Das logische Problem der Geschichtsphilosophie*. Tübingen: Mohr, 1961.

Index

Aalders, Willem Jan 126
Adler, Max 73
Adorno, Theodor 76
Albert, Hans 76
Ankersmit, Frank 63
Antoni, Carlo 65
Aquinas, Thomas 131
Arendt, Hannah 142
Aron, Raymond 8, 70, 141–55
Assmann, Aleida 28
Assmann, Jan 28
Augustine 194

Bachelard, Gaston 71
Bacon, Francis 193
Bal, Mieke 5–6
Banning, Willem 126
Barth, Karl 23, 35–6, 43, 47–8, 126, 131
Baur, Ferdinand Christian 40, 44–5
Beard, Charles 97–103, 107–8, 111
Beck, Robert 100
Becker, Carl 3, 97–100, 103, 108, 111
Beiser, Frederick C. 4, 18, 123
Bellon, Karel 132
Bergson, Henri 71, 104
Berkhof, Henk 122–3, 125, 127–8, 133
Bernstein, Richard J. 129
Bevir, Mark 5
Bloch, Ernst 198
Blumenberg, Hans 76
Boaz, Franz 98
Bod, Rens 6
Bohr, Niels 99
Borowski, Audrey 8
Bourdieu, Pierre 58
Breysig, Kurt 109–11
Brom, Gerard 129
Brom-Struick, Willemien 129
Bruins Slot, Sieuwert 130
Brunschwicg, Léon 148

Bultmann, Rudolf 23
Burckhardt, Jacob 188

Canguilhem, George 148, 152
Chaldenius, Johann Martin 166
Chamberlain, Arthur Neville 141
Chantepie de la Saussaye, Pierre Daniel 129
Cohen, Hermann 7, 15, 17, 19–24, 26
Comte, Auguste 59, 64, 73
Copjec, Joan 1–2
Croce, Benedetto 98–9, 103, 106–7

Darwin, Charles 73
Dewey, John 98
Dilthey, Wilhelm 18, 21, 64, 103, 106–7, 144, 147–8, 151, 153, 155, 166–7, 169–70, 173
Dooyeweerd, Herman 122–3, 125, 127, 131–3
Dorrien, Gary 7, 64
Droysen, Johann Gustav 67, 109, 166–7, 169, 188
Dühring, Eugen 3

Ehrenberg, Hans 23
Eichhorn, Johann 38
Einstein, Albert 70–1, 99
Elias, Norbert 66
Eppstein, Paul 76
Ermarth, Michael 98

Faber, Heije 126
Fauconnet, Paul 149
Felman, Shoshana 28
Fessard, Gaston 151
Feuerbach, Ludwig 165
Feuerhahn, Wolf 6
Feyerabend, Paul 2
Fichte, Johann Gottlieb 100
Fleck, Ludwik 71

Foucault, Michel 1–2
Franklin, Benjamin 36
Freud, Sigmund 104
Freyer, Hans 64, 67–8, 70, 74–5
Friedlander, Saul 28
Fromm, Erich 2

Gadamer, Hans-Georg 189, 190
Godefroy, Bruno 8
Goethe, Johann Wolfgang von 8, 165, 167–71, 175–6, 191
Gogarten, Friedrich 23
Graetz, Heinrich 15, 17, 19–22, 26
Griesbach, Johann 38
Grünfeld, Ernst 76

Habermas, Jürgen 189–90
Haitjema, Theo 126–7
Hamann, Johann Georg 109
Harnack, Adolf von 35, 41–5, 47–9
Hartman, Geoffrey 28
Hartog, Arnold de 127, 132
Hayek, Friedrich A. von 74
Haym, Rudolf 3
Hegel, G. W. F. 3, 23, 35, 37–40, 45, 47, 65, 73, 75, 100, 109, 148, 154, 172, 178, 191–2
Heidegger, Martin 144, 153, 187–8, 191, 195
Herder, Johann Gottfried 58, 64, 109, 166, 170
Herrmann, Wilhelm 43, 47–8
Hessen, Boris 71
Heussi, Karl 101–2, 111
Hintze, Otto 110
Hitler, Adolf 76, 145, 147, 150
Holborn, Hajo 110
Hook, Sidney 100
Horkheimer, Max 98
Howard, Thomas A. 4, 16
Hözel, Emil 68
Huizinga, Johan 128
Humboldt, Wilhelm von 58
Husserl, Edmund 64, 144, 187–8

Iggers, Georg G. 123, 177, 179

Jaeger, Friedrich 123
Jaffé, Edgar 61, 73
Jaspers, Karl 195

Jefferson, Thomas 36
Jünger, Ernst 192

Kant, Immanuel 35–41, 43, 47, 69, 74, 104, 169
Kierkegaard, Søren 192
Kohnstamm, Philip A. 132
Kojève, Alexandre 148
König, René 67–8
Kuhn, Helmut 109–11
Kuhn, Thomas S. 2
Kuyper, Abraham 122

Lacan, Jacques 2, 148
Lagarde, Paul de 40, 44
Lamprecht, Karl 109
Langer, Lawrence 28
Lask, Emil 65
Lebovic, Nitzan 123
Lederer, Emil 61
Lee, Dwight 100
Leeuw, Gerardus van der 129
Lewin, Kurt 66
Litt, Theodor 75, 109
Löwith, Karl 8, 141–2, 187–201
Lukács, Georg 67
Luther, Martin 40, 43
Lyotard, Jean-François 27–8

Machiavelli, Niccolò 171–2
Mandelbaum, Maurice 66, 97–8, 102–11
Manent, Pierre 145
Mann, Golo 145
Mann, Thomas 145
Mannheim, Karl 62, 64–8, 70, 75–7, 103, 106–7, 109, 142, 144, 148
Marcotte-Chenard, Sophie 8
Marr, Wilhelm 18, 20
Marx, Karl 100, 104, 109, 153, 192
Megill, Allan 4
Meinecke, Friedrich 8, 16, 23, 26, 65, 67, 102, 110, 131, 142, 144, 148, 165–80
Mendes-Flohr, Paul 17
Menger, Carl 58
Merleau-Ponty, Maurice 148
Mesure, Sylvie 155
Milton, John 36
Moerkerken, Pieter Hendrik van 131
Möser, Justus 58, 166

Mozart, Wolfgang Amadeus 3
Mussolini, Benito 98
Myers, David N. 7

Niebuhr, Georg 188
Niebuhr, Reinhold 47
Nietzsche, Friedrich 18–19, 21, 28–9, 64–5, 68–9, 71, 104, 166, 188–9, 191, 200
Nipperdey, Thomas 67
Nora, Pierre 28
Nore, Ellen 102
Novick, Peter 97, 108

Oexle, Otto Gerhard 4–5, 123
Ozouf, Mona 28

Palti, Elías 133
Pareto, Vilfredo 104
Paul, Herman 8
Paulus, Heinrich 38
Pit, Adriaan 131
Plenge, Johann 75
Pocock, J. G. A. 133
Popper, Karl R. 16, 58–9, 71, 167

Queneau, Raymond 148

Ranke, Leopold von 4, 8, 23, 59, 74, 99, 101, 105, 107, 109, 111, 165–7, 171–3, 175–7, 180, 188, 192
Rauschning, Hermann 76
Reddy, William 125
Rickert, Heinrich 23, 45, 61, 65, 68, 71–2, 74, 77, 104, 109, 144, 147, 151, 166
Riedel, Manfred 59
Ritschl, Albrecht 35, 37, 40–1, 43–4, 47
Ritter, Carl 68
Roberts, David 98
Roessingh, Karel 126, 128
Rosenzweig, Franz 7, 15, 22–6, 28
Rothacker, Erich 58, 74–5, 103, 108
Rousseau, Jean-Jacques 192
Rueschemeyer, Dietrich 76
Rüsen, Jörn 4–5, 123

Savigny, Friedrich Karl von 58, 109, 166
Scheler, Max 75, 104
Schelling, Friedrich von 100

Schlegel, Friedrich 58, 142
Schleiermacher, Friedrich 7, 35–40, 43, 47
Schmitt, Carl 67, 69, 196
Schmoller, Gustav 58, 61, 67, 72
Schopenhauer, Arthur 69, 104
Schorske, Carl E. 21
Schumpeter, Joseph 61
Schweitzer, Albert 16
Semler, Johann 38
Sidgwick, Alfred 127
Simkhovitch, Vladimir 100
Simmel, Georg 71, 74, 104, 144, 147–8, 151
Skinner, Quentin 133
Smith, Theodore Clarke 99–100
Snethlage, Jacob Leonard 127, 131
Socrates 76
Sombart, Werner 61, 67, 73
Sorensen, Lloyd 102
Spann, Othmar 67, 75
Spengler, Oswald 64
Spinoza, Baruch 22
Spranger, Eduard 75
Steinmetz, George 7
Strauss, David Friedrich 4, 16
Strauss, Gerald 178
Strauss, Leo 8, 141–2, 146, 167, 189–91, 196–7

Tessitore, Fulvio 65
Tillich, Paul 47
Toews, John Edward 5
Treitschke, Heinrich von 19–20, 109
Troeltsch, Ernst 5, 16–17, 35–7, 43–7, 58, 60, 62, 64, 66–71, 73, 75, 77, 103–4, 109, 111, 125–8, 131, 142, 144, 148, 153, 165–7, 173, 188–9
Turner, Kathleen 125

Urban, Wilbur Marshall 102, 109

Vagts, Alfred 101–2, 107, 111
Veldhuizen, Adriaan van 7
Vermeil, Edmond 152
Verstegen, Ian 98
Vico, Giambattista 109
Vierkandt, Alfred 75
Voegelin, Eric 8, 189, 197–8

Walsum, Gerard van 130
Weber, Alfred 61, 64–7, 70, 75
Weber, Max 44, 61–2, 66–7, 69, 72–4, 77, 144–5, 147–9, 151, 153, 155, 188–9, 196
Wette, Wilhelm de 38
Wiese, Leopold von 62, 74–5
Wieviorka, Annette 28
Williams, Raymond 57

Windelband, Wilhelm 18, 65, 68–9, 72, 166
Wittkau, Annette 3, 64
Wolfson, Philip 177

Yerushalmi, Yosef Hayim 7, 15, 26–9
Young, James 28

Zuidema, Sytse Ulbe 122–3, 125, 128, 132–3

www.ingramcontent.com/pod-product-compliance
Lightning Source LLC
Chambersburg PA
CBHW072236290426
44111CB00012B/2112